WILDERNESS
A NEW MEXICO LEGACY

WILDERNESS
A NEW MEXICO LEGACY

Corry McDonald

*Photographs
by
Charles H. Karnes*

Sunstone Press
Santa Fe, New Mexico

"This book is dedicated to all of the people listed in the index. Their various parts in the actions are described in the book."

Copyright © 1985 by Corry McDonald
All Rights Reserved.
No part of this book may be reproduced in any form or by any electronic or mechanical means including information storage and retrieval systems without permission in writing from the publisher, except by a reviewer who may quote brief passages in a review.

FIRST EDITION

Printed in the United States of America

Library of Congress Cataloging in Publication Data

McDonald, Corry, 1914-
    Wilderness: a New Mexico legacy.

    Bibliography, p.
    Includes index.
    1. Wilderness areas--New Mexico.   I. Title.
QH76.5.N6M28   1985   333.78'2'09789   84-26691
ISBN: 0-86534-056-0

Published in 1985 by SUNSTONE PRESS
Post Office Box 2321 / Santa Fe, New Mexico 87504-2321 / USA

CONTENTS

INTRODUCTION		6
CHAPTER 1	Sandia Mountain National Wilderness	9
CHAPTER 2	Manzano Mountain National Wilderness	19
CHAPTER 3	Bandelier National Wilderness	26
CHAPTER 4	Aldo Leopold National Wilderness	35
CHAPTER 5	Banco Breaks Defacto Wilderness	44
CHAPTER 6	Wheeler Peak National Wilderness	49
CHAPTER 7	Latir Peak National Wilderness	61
CHAPTER 8	Apache Kid National Wilderness	69
CHAPTER 9	Mount Withington National Wilderness	78
CHAPTER 10	Sierra Ladrones Defacto Wilderness	83
CHAPTER 11	Guadalupe Escarpment National Wilderness	90
CHAPTER 12	Capitán Mountain National Wilderness	106
CHAPTER 13	Polvadera Peak Defacto Wilderness	117
CHAPTER 14	The Legal Process	126
BIBLIOGRAPHY		129
INDEX		133

INTRODUCTION

Wilderness areas in New Mexico may be a surprise to many people. And some newcomers find our mountains a threat after being engulfed by them for the first time. That New Mexico has been the site of Spanish settlements and colonies for four hundred years makes wilderness seem improbable. But our desert "badlands" wilderness areas and our lush forest areas point up a special characteristic of these roadless wonders: diversification. No two are alike.

The wilderness concept was conceived and born in New Mexico in the post-World War I era. Aldo Leopold, a Forest Ranger in the southwestern part of New Mexico in the early 1920's, was a pioneer. The Gila Wilderness, largely through Leopold's intense campaign, was designated on June 3, 1924, as the first area in the country to carry the Wilderness classification with a capital "W." Forest Service regulations pertaining to the problems of controlling grazing, timbering, mining, forest fires, insect infestation, road and fence construction, wood hauling, hunting, fishing, wildlife propagation, and even cabin building were part of the Wilderness Act of 1964. These did not bloom at first issuance but evolved over many tribulations throughout the nation.[1] *(NB: Footnotes refer to numbered references at the end of the book.)*

But the wilderness concept was not an exclusive New Mexico creation. Many people elsewhere had ideas prior to and after Leopold. Thoreau in his *Walden Pond* expressed an appreciation of wilderness that was startling for its time. And John Muir almost single-handedly moved Congress to make a National Park of Yosemite in 1890. John Wesley Powell bridled at the public land vandalism of his age and lead the fight in Washington, D.C. to preserve areas in their natural state. Bob Marshall in 1933 used words to more precisely define wilderness in his book *The People's Forests*. His words were closely followed in the Wilderness Act nearly three decades later.

New Mexico's U.S. Senator Clinton P. Anderson was chairman of the Senate committee which wrote and obtained the enactment of the Wilderness Act of 1964. The Senator rode and hiked with Aldo Leopold through most of the Gila and he and his committee drew in the dedicated experts from the Wilderness Society and the land agencies.[2] Representative Wayne Aspinall of Colorado managed to bottle up the bill for years as a strong proponent of mining and timber interests but he lost the combination in 1964.[1]

The key concept of the Act is expressed in its opening sentence:

In order to assure that an increasing population, accompanied by expanding settlement and growing mechanization, does not occupy and modify all areas within the United States and its possessions, leaving no lands designated for preservation and protection in their natural condition, it is hereby declared to be the policy of the Congress to secure for the American people of present and future generations the benefits of an enduring resource of wilderness."

Old wildernesses in New Mexico by my definition are those first enacted. The Gila, Pecos, Wheeler Peak, White Mountain, San Pedro Parks, Salt Creek, and the Bosque del Apache National Wildernesses were all enacted by 1974. Some people think of the Gila and Pecos Wilderness areas as the only real wildernesses in the state because they have been only to those two. And more has been written about them than our newer wilderness areas. A partial bibliography on those areas is contained at the end of this book to get you started if you are interested.

Our newer National Wilderness areas, 14 of them, have been enacted since and these are the focus of this book. Those of us who have worked to get them enacted think of them as our new wildernesses. There are some other areas not yet enacted which are considered by those of us who know them well as defacto wilderness areas.

Each of these areas is so different and unique that it is difficult to follow an identical pattern in telling about them. Each has its own folk-lore and has had different threats to its wilderness status. Each has responded differently to the threats and events swirling around and over these areas. Many of the events have been documented in various ways, some of them unwittingly or peripherally about the areas. Despite all of those differences, each chapter is an attempt to describe the location of the named area and its unique physical characteristics. Some clues have led to attempts to look into the prehistorical involvement of men and wildlife in the area; each chapter makes note of the events which took place during the early Indian and Spanish periods, and describes some of the threatening flurries of mining activity in the vicinities. And some recent events impacting on each area are described.

The whole is not a guidebook although it has some of the features of one. It does, if somewhat begrudgingly, tempt you to generate a deep personal interst in one or more of these areas; and to become possessive to the point of loving an area or at least respecting it.

Hopefully, you will learn that you are its owner, protector, and custodian or steward and act accordingly. The Wilderness Study Committee can help you make such a connection. The U.S. Forest Service can also make maps and facts available.

There are unique facets in some of the proposed wilderness areas that bear upon elements of the Wilderness Act. The management problems pertaining to the feral burro in Bandelier as an exotic outcompeting the native species is typical. Many of the features of the Act are examined through the lens of specific events in many of the areas.

Finally, backpacking on the trails of each area is described, both as to how to locate the roadheads and what to expect on the particular trails. Occasionally, when drinking water is a problem, the location of springs or seeps is mentioned. The methodology of wilderness travel is woven into the warp of the story, as is bow hunting and wildlife observations.

Each chapter stands on its own. They are arranged in the approximate order of my chronological acquaintance with the areas. Wilderness legislative involvement would have provided another order and the emergence of the New Mexico Wilderness Study Committee could have been given more emphasis. Yet another regimen could have been followed if the dates of wilderness enactment had been selected as the criterion. Over the years priorities of concern have come and gone as various threats menaced each area. Like other troubles, the threats came in bunches but had to be faced separately. Consequently, the degree or sequence of the threatened areas provided no crisp order. You are invited to peruse the chapters in any manner that your fancy beckons.

Wilderness is defined as a tract or region uncultivated and uninhabited by human beings; and area essentially undisturbed by human activity together with its naturally developed life community. A wilderness area is defined as an often large tract of public land maintained essentially in its natural state and protected against introduction of intrusive artifacts (as roads and buildings).

The Wilderness Act of 1964 states in Section 2(c):

A wilderness, in contrast with those areas where man and his own works dominate the landscape, is hereby recognized as an area where the earth and it community of life are untrammeled by man, where man himself is a visitor who does not remain. An area of wildeness is further defined to mean in this Act an area of undeveloped Federal land retaining its primeval character and influence, without permanent improvements of human habitation, which is protected and managed so as to preserve its natural conditions and which (1) generally appears to have been affected primarily by the forces of nature, with the imprint of man's work substantially unnoticeable; (2) has outstanding opportunities for solitude or a primitive and unconfined type of recreation; (3) has at least five thousand acres of land or is of sufficient size as to make practicable its preservation and use in an unimpaired condition; and (4) may also contain ecological, geological, or other features of scientific, educational, scenic, or historical value.

Once enacted, an area is thereafter properly called The (Gila) National Wilderness, for example, and is administered by either the United States Department of Agriculture through its Forest Service, or the United States Department of Interior through its National Park Service, or the Bureau of Land Management, or the Fish and Wildlife Service.

Biblical references to wilderness as the "abomination of desolation" seemed to be the name for any place out of town. It was inhabited (in our ancestors' minds) by wild beasts and bandits lying in wait for the intruders. Those who could afford it had an armed escort. And such were the first white men who appeared in our New Mexico centuries ago.

We no longer fear such obstacles, although there has been some small amount of vandalism of cars parked at trailheads. But a certain amount of caution makes good sense. Nature in the raw must be met on its terms, not yours. One of the less innocuous threats is hypothermia. It is briefly covered in the Wheeler Peak Wilderness chapter. I would be remiss if my stories led you into trouble for lack of warning. The Wheeler Peak Wilderness chapter also describes backpacking gear adequate for high-country use. Technical rock climbing is not treated in this book because none of the routes referred to require it. Timber skiing is dangerous and exhilarating and should not be attempted without adequate preconditioning and skiing skill. Snowshoeing can be a source of fatal mistakes if you are alone and your equipment fails. Snakebite and broken legs can also be fatal if you hike alone in some of your less frequented areas. Dehydration and sunstroke can also be fatal, particularly in some of our lower-altitude areas. Because of its nearness to a large city, The Sandia Mountain Wilderness appears to cause an inordinate number fatal accidents annually to unprepared persons.

You are urged to develop your wilderness skills and equipment slowly while gaining familiarity and confidence in each piece while you have a safe alternative to fall back on in emergency. You won't get many invitations if you are constantly having to rely on your companions to remember the essentials.

Some caution, then, and numerous trips of various kinds with experienced friends can help you benefit from the wilderness's outstanding opportunities for solitude or a primitive and unconfined type of recreation.

You can find all of the caveats in other books on back country safety.[3] If you do get in trouble, New Mexico is fortunate to have a mountain rescue organization loosely federated under an Emergency Services Council. The Albuquerque Mountain Rescue

Council is generally called upon when an accident is in technical (climbing) terrain. The Sandia Search Team is generally involved in broader searches. The St. John's Search and Rescue Team is Santa Fe based and the Los Alamos Mountain Rescue ranges widely when trouble calls.

The way you contact these fast-moving organizations is to call the State Police. Each State Police District has well equipped Mission Coordinators and Search and Rescue Groups. These are all volunteer organizations and should not be called without adequate reasons.

One last note is about the plague. Fleas from rodents can get on you and your dog. There have been reports of cases generated in the Sandias and Manzanos. Get information from your doctor, from your outdoor organization, or from the Veterinary Services at Kirtland Air Force Base if you want to decrease your chances of contact with the fleas.

So now that you are thoroughly warned, on to happier things. Although the events described have had considerable impact upon the wilderness areas involved, no conscious attempt is made to assess the degree of benefit or insult.

The circumstances surrounding the legislative status are different for each area proposed for Wilderness Enactment. Those different circumstances are treated in some detail in each chapter as they apply to each area. An oversimplified version of the process follows. The several federal agencies which are charged with administration of certain public lands interpret their responsibilities under the Wilderness Act differently, both in initial selection and in subsequent management.

The U.S. Forest Service has historically followed a purist line, possibly on the basis that they would rather be criticized for being too strict than too lax. Consequently, the citizen groups attempting to induce legislative action on a given Wilderness generally propose an area considerably larger than the Forest Service wants to consider. After enactment, the same citizen groups are inclined to criticize the Forest Service for too strict a management policy. Michael Frome[1] describes these viewpoints most succinctly.

The Forest Service's Roadless Areas Review and Evaluation process (RARE) has been carried out in two different political environments. RARE I was done during the Ford administration, and the criterion for selection and classification of the areas reflected the purist attitude of the Forest Service at that time. RARE II was done during the Carter administration and gives evidence of including a wider spectrum of choices than the earlier efforts. For one example, the earlier emphasis on disqualifying roads seemed to be less slavish during RARE II. Roads which can revert to wilderness condition if unused may be less of an issue than they formerly were.

The U.S. National Park Service appears to follow a protective line of administration which is biased by their basic charter. They do not allow hunting in National Parks; yet, they allowed and encouraged live capture of feral burros in the Bandelier Wilderness. The Fish and Wildlife Service selected land in its Bosque del Apache National Wildlife Refuge which is transected by railroads, freeways, pipelines, powerlines, and a secondary highway. The Bureau of Land Management has had no opportunities for enactment until the recent passage of the Federal Land Policy and Management Act of 1976 (BLM Organic Act) (P.L. 94-579). Its Section 603 pertains to a fifteen-year wilderness review.

The formation of the State Wilderness Commission under New Mexico Governor Jerry Apodoca gave support to the citizen groups striving for completion of the public land planning processes which are expected to result in eventual wilderness classification of the remaining de facto wilderness areas. The New Mexico Wilderness Study Committee is a citizen group made up of a coalition of outdoor organizations and individuals who believe that they have some responsibility for public lands in the United States and particularly in New Mexico. Most of the recent enactments were initiated by that citizen group and their efforts persist. Consequently, the activities of the Wilderness Study Committee are described in each chapter. Comments on the RARE II process are made in the various chapters as appropriate. It is unlikely that the RARE II process will be completed for several years.

CHAPTER 1:
Sandia Mountain National Wilderness

The Sandia Mountain looms up on the eastern outskirts of Albuquerque, New Mexico and overlooks the city. The crest elevation is almost 11,000 feet, approximately 5,000 to 6,000 feet higher than the elevation of the city. The mountain is north-south trending. The crest trail is approximately 26 miles in length. Get a wilderness map at the Sandia Ranger Station in Tijeras Canyon just south of I-40 on NM 14.

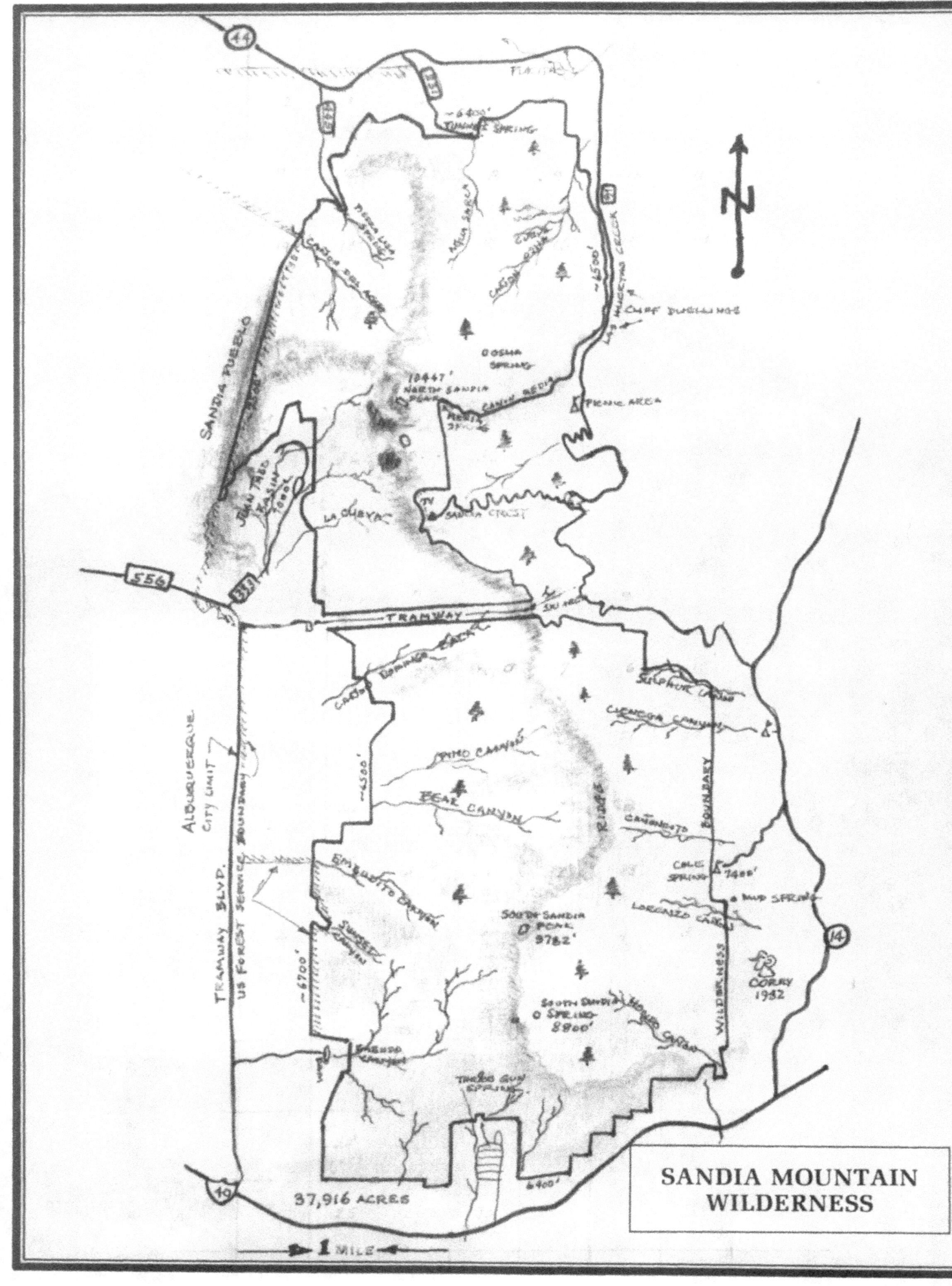

He was performing a task usually done by the women, cracking bones. Rendering marrow out of them. He had found the fresh bones of a big buck right on the ridge. The lion must have been a mature tom because the backbones had been crushed with one bite. The task was simple enough. Crack the bones at one end. Bake them in a fire and catch the drip in a pot.

The marrow was to be mixed with beans and rabbit or bird meat. Packed into a fist-sized pot and sealed with a green leaf, carried in a sling of buckskin, it provided a meal for a hunter. Today he hadn't broken the empty pot, so he could fill it with marrow. Another strange thing he had done today: he had carried a hand axe from his home all of the way up to the ridge. Whatever happened, the hand axe was left on the ridge. It is there today, in the same position. It has a mass of about one kilogram and fits nicely in one's fist.

The ridge of the Sandias just north of South Peak overlooked the broad ribbon of the big river running south. He had no way of knowing that the aquifer under that river was almost as deep as the mountain was high, but he had been down there between the big mountains and the river only once, hunting antelope. The people on that side of the mountain were better antelope hunters than he and his people.

He had to get his people a fat deer each moon. This time he was taking home only a pot full of marrow. He covered up the roasted bones and blackened rocks about two steps away from his hand axe. A man found both the fire pit and the axe, many centuries later. He also was bow hunting for deer.

The river has now shrunk until it is only a dark green stream-course. The sun has to be just right to reflect from the water which only rarely runs above ground in the Great River, the Rio Grande. And now there is enough water in that underground river for a large city between that mountain and that river.[1] It is Albuquerque and the area has almost half a million people along fifty miles or so of river.

That mountain has remained wild and untamed even if it towers a mile above and near the big city. It has resisted the massive "taming of the wilderness" that has inexorably been going on for centuries. True, there is a puny road that goes up to a forest of TV towers along the north ridge. Also true that about fifty-five percent of the mountain has been disqualified as wilderness by one means or another.

The remainder, however, the other forty-five percent, is nearly as wild as it was when the bone-cracker covered his smelly fire. The uses of the Sandia Mountains have changed very much and, unless we practice contstraint, the mountain will be lost for all time as a wilderness, as an undeveloped natural area as God first made it.

Let us recount what has been happening to our mountain since the bone-cracker. The people in the small pueblo near Mud Spring used axes with lashed-on handles instead of the hand-axe. Centuries later, the wood gatherers from Albuquerque used two-bladed axes to help feed the fireplaces of a growing population. The first automobile made it to the top of the mountain in about 1920. It was an Army truck with Signal Corps gear on it. It took a month of wood chopping to get it up there from Capulin Spring.

The old wood road going up Las Huertas Creek from Placitas, past Sandia Man Cave, was graded and regraded, rock filled and graveled periodically. The holiday traffic always raised a pall of dust that settled on the greenery and picnickers alike. The road was extended around Palomas Peak to connect with the Crest to the ski-area road from the south. So it became possible in the mid- 1940's to drive all of the way around the mountain. The Las Huertas road traversed the Ellis Ranch, some of which since has become the Sandia Conference Grounds under the jurisdiction of the Presbytery of Santa Fe.

Public concern for the Sandia Mountains began to grow in the 1950's. Houses started to show up in areas that the people thought were inside the National Forest boundaries. Some of them were. Inholdings around the edges began to be negotiable. Summer homes were being built in woods and the forest margins. A few robberies and some vandalism of these new houses in the eastern flanks of the mountain discouraged residents. And there was a period of vacant houses with broken doors and windows.

A few timber sales on the east side of the mountain above Capulin Springs generated some wood roads on the contours. Picnickers sometimes discovered large logging trucks coming downhill toward them on weekdays. Logging contractors changed their schedules at the Sandia Ranger's request to bring the loads down at night. The cuts were kept about one hundred yards back from the black-topped road to the crest so the logging process would not be seen by too many people. But most of the logging roads have since been closed, since there were only about five or six groves that yielded much good timber. The 1975 Land Use Plan indicated very little merchantable timber elsewhere on the mountain[2]. There are a few trees too big to get your arms around scattered throughout the mountain, often near the springs. The timber on the Sandia Mountain is probably a good example of the greater worth of standing timber as a part of the watershed, the natural eco-system, than it could ever be as a commercial element. Like much of our mountain desert timber throughout the state, Sandia Mountain trees are slow growing, knotty, and brittle. Most cannot withstand the impact of felling, so it is no tree farm. Standing, the trees are beautiful, and so is the mountain.

A rash of firewood cutting followed during the mid-fifties. The chain saw came onto the scene about that time. On one Sunday a fairly green tree fell across the road just in back of my moving station wagon, bending my rear bumper. Shortly thereafter, some rules were enforced, at least on weekends. Live cutting, among other things, was prohibited.

The ski area expansion took place throughout the 1950's and 1960's. The tramway was installed in the mid-sixties and the Crest parking facilities were expanded during the same period. The forest of steel, the TV antennas and the transmitters on the Crest at the electronic site, grew to more than two hundred units. Drinking water was hauled in since there is no supply available at that elevation (10,678 feet). There is no sewage facility.[3]

Snow-play areas were started at various locations along the road. The crowds at some locations were so large they blocked off some of the automobile traffic. Parking was generally inadequate at peak periods until the road was upgraded as far as the ski area. The inner-tubers no longer can slide out into the roadway.

The La Luz Trail on the west side was rerouted during the mid-sixties with many switchbacks to reduce the average grade. That process converted a four and one-half mile trail to about a seven and one-half mile tour. The old trail was steep and rocky because it washed out in many stretches. The new trail tends to make people cut across the switchbacks, causing some unnecessary erosion. The La Luz Run is an annual event and winners ascend the trail in about one hour.

In 1969, some consideration was given to including the entire 26-mile Crest or Ridge trail in the "Kit Carson Trail," a branch of the Continental Divide trail proposed in the National Trails System Act, Public Law 90-543, October 2, 1968. A New Mexico Trails Committee generated a State Trails System Act (1973), Chapter 372, House Bill No. 97. Bill No. 85 and Senate Bill No. 71 also pertained. As members of the Trails Advisory Committee, several of us worked on the enabling legislation. Little has been done at this writing on the entire plan, although some federal funds have been received by the state.

By the late 1930's, both large and small game had been "plinked" off the mountain. In 1938, the Forest Service and the State Game and Fish Department agreed upon the reintroduction of Rocky Mountain bighorn sheep into the northern Sandias. They thrived and some have been transplanted subsequently to the Pecos Wilderness Area. The Sandia game Refuge was defined at the time of the first plant. A wildlife recovery started to take place.

One or two gun-hunts for deer took place in the late 1940's, but some of the recreational users objected to the firing of guns on their populated mountain. They seemed to be less threatened by the bowhunters who were first given a hunting season in 1954. There were very few bowhunters for the first few seasons. The success of the hunters was low at the start. A government hunter lived in the Tijeras Canyon until the mid-1960's and was charged with taking problem bears and lions upon request. He reduced both to zero by 1966.

There was sufficient recovery of the lion population to open up a permit season in 1976. By that time, the mountain lion had been declared big game instead of a varmint. As a result, they could be hunted by permit in much of the state from August through mid-June. The lions had time out to have their young. However, some of them whelp as early as April and May. My guess placed about six lions on the mountain in 1976.

The winter range of the deer is on the west side of the mountain with the greatest concentrations in the old Elena Gallegos Grant, until recently in the ownership of the Albuquerque Academy Trust. Late bow hunting through January had been permitted through special licensing by the state and the Academy. The deer population on the mountain appears to be following a generally decreasing trend through the west. Although there are some areas of concentration of deer herds in the state, the deer populations of our proposed wilderness areas seem to be suffering the same decline.[4] Comprehensive studies have not pinpointed the most probable cause unless it is poaching.[5]

In 1967, a fire, starting at the western base of the mountain near or at the Juan Tabo picnic grounds, swept up the mountain to the ridge and burned for three days. We were treated to slurry tankers as well as a night and day display of flames and smoke. People who had never been on the western escarpment said: "What could burn up there? It all looks like bare rock." The swath that burned was probably one of the most sparsely covered areas on the west side. Fortunately, the fire did not break over onto the more heavily timbered east side. The oak brush patches put on a spectacular display of fireworks at night. There have been only several dozen small spot fires in the last forty years on the mountain.

Plans were formulated in the mid-sixties by the Forest Service to construct a road from the Crest to Placitas at the northern base of the mountain. The proposed routing appeared to overlay some of a proposed hiking trail route. The Albuquerque Wildlife and Conservation Association objected to the routing on the basis that it went through the lambing grounds of the Rocky Mountain bighorn sheep.

The Forest Service obliged and moved the proposed route downhill. The New Mexico Mountain Club and several other conservation organizations expressed alarm at the proposed road to Placitas from the Crest and little more was heard of the problem. In mid-1969, the Forest Service quietly let a contract to clear the right-of-way from the Crest road straight north for five miles to a point northeast of Sandia Peak. It was done quickly and it really stirred the conservationists.

The Environmental Policy Act of 1969 had some influence upon an awakening public conscience, as well as requiring the public land agencies to issue Land Use Plans for units under their jurisdiction. The

Environmental Statement for the Sandia Mountain land Use Plan, issued April 14, 1975, is one of the results.[3] Several Public Hearing inputs are distilled into the LUP. It is generally a good document, is a fair assessment, and is an interesting story. However, it is two centimeters thick, so it is more than a casual undertaking.

During the period of the data gathering and the public hearings, public concern for the mountain peaked. Some of the alternatives considered were a bit frightening to some people. One could conjure up a developed mountain scenario from it which sounds like a mountain amusement park on a massive scale. The spectres of high use-frequencies projected into the 1980's and beyond sent shivers throught the mountain users who feel propietary in their concerns. We in the Wilderness Study Committee feel that the only defenses against such pressures can be realized under the Wilderness Act.

In the spring of 1970, on Earth Day, a large number of people from the central part of the state appeared at the intersection of the brushed-out section of the then proposed "Ellis Loop Road" up near the TV towers. The previous year had seen some untidy firewood cutting on the margins of the several "brush cuts" for the future road. A small amount of burning for clean-up purposes generated a little smoke and a lot of raised eyebrows. The excessively wide swath was a tactical mistake. However, the proposed road standard required it.

The New Mexico Wildlife Federation, at the urging of its Albuquerque contingent, retained an environmental lawyer attached to the National Wildlife Federation. Negotiations were carried on at both local and national levels for almost a year. All of the conservation organizations were in the act by 1971, and the senators and representatives all made some pronouncements except Congressman Runnels (it was not in his district). In response to the public outcry, including that of the New Mexico Mountain Club, the Cibola Forest Supervisor, Wally Lloyd, decided that plans for the Crest to Placitas road would be dropped. A good cross-section of the letters is reproduced in the Land Use Plan. Shortly after the Sandia LUP was issued in final form, Wally Lloyd retired and Bill Hurst, the Regional Forester, followed suit about six months later. These were dedicated and fair men. The Sandia Land use plan is a monument to their sense of fair play.

There is usually a heavily chaperoned annual hunt for three or four of the Rocky Mountain bighorn sheep. There is a drawing for the limited number of special permits and the State Department of Game and Fish "Game Warden" carefully points out specifically which animal may be shot with a rifle. The Sandia herd of a hundred or more is kept in balance with their pasture by this process and also by using this healthy herd as planting stock for other areas in the state. For example, some of these animals were flown in by helicopter to the Pecos high country and the Gila. In passing, mountain lions appear to prefer deer meat to tough mutton. Lambs which get hurt often fall victim, however.

One of the courageous actions taken by the Sandia Ranger, Jack Miller, and backed up the whole way by his superiors, was the vehicle closure of 1971. Within about six weeks of the new model introduction of a motor bike and a 4-wheel-drive Jeep, such vehicles made it to the top of the mountain on the west side for the first time. Milo Conrad, the Mountain Club firebrand who started the concept of the New Mexico Wilderness Study Committee, gathered the photographic evidence and blew the whistle. The Cibola Forest Supervisor signed the closure and enforced it. The motor bikers were furious. The thin soil on the decomposed granite will bear their marks for fifty or more years. It takes something like five hundred years in our dry climate to generate a centimeter of soil from that granite base. Perhaps the sulfuric acid pollutants emanating from the city will speed the breakdown of the rock, much as the same chemical (sulfur dioxide) has eroded the buildings and statuary in Venice, Italy.

The growth of foot traffic on the trails has been monitored periodically by the New Mexico Mountain Club. The data gathered is among that used in the LUP in a similar study.[2,3]

In the 1930's and the 1940's, horse traffic on the trail from the Seven Springs area in the Tijeras Canyon up past Carlito Springs and on the South Peak took its normal toll. By the late 1940's, the trail northwest of Carlito Springs was nearly impassable because the soil and gravel had been washed out of thousands of rocks. These rocks were generally about the size of two fists and were treacherous to walk or ride on because they were all loose and would turn when stepped upon. That section has since been filled in and bypassed. The damage was similar to that done near Beatty's Cabin in the Pecos Wilderness by many generations of horsemen. It now has been replaced in the 1970's with trail treads worn and torn by Vibram soled boots. These lugged rubber soles appear to chop up the wet trail treads more than the smooth-soled boots. However, the lugged rubber soles make for a lot more secure footing on the decomposed granite of the Sandia's west side. Rock scrambling with Vibrams is a delight where once it was chancy with smooth-soled boots on those house-sized boulders.

Vandalism has taken some strange forms in the Sandias. One example worth recounting because of its very mindlessness had to do with the ripping up the Cienega Wheelchair Trail and the interpretive signing for the blind. The whole was beaten up and so badly mauled that the contract personnel hired to clean it up felt strongly enough to write letters to the editor of the *Albuquerque Journal*. It was again splashed with paint after it was rebuilt. All over the mountain, the fire grills have been torn out from time to time by someone with a chain or tow cable probably hooked onto a truck. Very few signs are shot at, compared to other areas, however. The Piedra Lisa Tank was shot during one cold snap in the winter of 1975. Three shots and three huge icicles were there for weeks until the weather broke. More than five hundred beer cans were dumped in Las Huertas Creek near Sandia Man Cave. It took us more than two hours and two pickup loads to clean them up one Sunday evening after we had bow hunted all weekend in the Osha Spring area.

The Game Refuge status in the Sandias is something of a problem. Guns are not allowed; control of violations is the crux of the matter. The State Department of Game and Fish is financed from proceeds collected from the hunters and fishermen. Since only a few hunters can bow hunt for deer, a few can gun hunt for lion, and about ten can hunt for sheep, there is not much tariff to support even a part-time patrolman on the mountain. So what happens when someone climbs up the hill and rips off a few clips of shells or shoots up a box of 22's? The picnickers and the hikers complain of being shot at. There may not be a patrolman available, even if the shooter stays up there all afternoon. So the Forest Service is called and everyone is out on some detail and will not be back until 5:00 p.m. Consequently, no action. Is it any wonder that some of the hunters are talking about changing from Refuge status if it cannot be enforced?

Twice since then I have seen two dogs chasing deer on the west side. The first time was in upper Juan Tabo north of the La Luz Trail. Another time was in the upper reaches of Bear Canyon. Many times we have seen tracks of dogs after deer during January and February. I have seen one kill site perhaps a week after the event. Mountain lions generally have to catch their prey within one to two hundred meters because they do not have enough stamina to run down a healthy deer. Dogs, fed on commercial dog food, however, do seem to have enough stamina to pursue even healthy and prime bucks for ten or fifteen miles or more.

The first "sighting" was at night when Phil Tollefsrud and I were sacked out north of the La Luz Trail in Chimney Canyon at about the 8,800-foot elevation level. The big doe came within twenty five meters of out camp and two dogs with collars almost passed through out camp. Our flashlight must have disconcerted them. We were listening to a Lobo (University of New Mexico) basketball game on a transistor radio, snug in our two sleeping bags. The second sighting was in mid-morning in Bear Canyon. They looked tired, buck, dogs, and all. Some of the bowhunters said they shot at the dogs, but missed.

Often we started up the mountain before daybreak and several times we saw dogs in two's and three's coming down the canyons shortly after we had left out cars. So, at least, some of the feral dogs are feral only during the night and go home during the days. Others, according to some owners living next to the mountain, are sometimes gone for three or four days running. In any event, it does not pay to take your dog to the mountain during bowhunting season. Don Schauerte lost his pet that way, unfortunately. We heard that the dog stopped and barked at a camouflaged bowhunter just when the hunter was stalking some deer. I did not insist on getting the hunter's name.

Perhaps because the Coyote Getter 1080 was not permitted on Federal Lands during 1975 and 1976, the feral dog populations near the larger cities appeared to be on the increase. The 1080 seems to have been replaced by a spring-loaded cyanide capsule device on some federal and private lands where "coyotes" have become a problem. Maybe our dogs will not be attracted to the gamey coyote baits.

There is now a mineral closure in the Sandias.[3] One of the earliest references to mining in the Sandias which I have seen is in the accounts of the stormy Coronado stay at Tiguex (near Bernalillo).[7] One of the Spaniards tried to follow an Indian across the Rio and into the Sandias, supposedly because he thought that the Indian was going to a gold mine on the mountain. This was in the spring of 1541, and the Spaniard did not return to Tiguex.[7]

Early mining for turquoise is known to have taken place in the vicinity[8] of Cerrillos and Golden, but the site was given a bad report by the Onate scouts.[8] A tunnel and shaft were driven into a lead on the west side of the mountain, not far below the Sandia Crest at the 10,000-foot level.[8] In recent years it was called the La Luz mine. Several stories in the newspapers around the turn of the century had it that the mine had been "salted" and sold a dozen times.

Tunnel Springs started out as a mine in the 1870's. There are a lot of prospect holes south and west of Placitas. The most extensive was the tunnel at about the 6,400-foot level about a mile southwest of Placitas. The "values" were not too encouraging and the prospect was abandoned.[9] Water at about seven gallons per minute flowed out the drift even after it had caved in. It became the source for the Tunnel Springs Fish Hatchery in the early 1900's. The hatchery was abandoned in the 1920's, reopened, and closed finally in the 1930's. There is now a trail-head parking lot at the bottom of the Tollefsrud Trail at that location. The water still makes great coffee without any chlorine or other impurities. There was another fish hatchery at Seven Springs in Tijeras Canyon that was operated from about 1934 until 1965. Jim Peckumn told me that it probably was lack of water that closed both.

There are two "roads" in our Wilderness that never should have happened in the first place. The oldest one goes to the spring at about the 9,000-foot level, a mile northeast of North Sandia Peak. Several fairly exciting prospect trenches are at the 8,700-foot level. The old mining road's greatest use was realized by some bootleggers who found the spring water great for booze about 1928. A few woodcutters have used it since and some of the 4-wheel-drive folks went halfway up to the spring in 1970. It now has too many deadfalls and boulders in it even to be of use for cross-country skiing. The other road goes quite vertically out of Juan Tabo. The rock climbers call it Movie Trail. It was used to haul the cameras up into the west face for Kirk Douglas in "Lonely Are the Brave," a great movie. The access permit was issued in the mid-1960's. It would not be issued today without a wild public outcry. Besides, cameras are now more portable.

In the last few days of the 94th Congress, the Endangered American Wilderness Act was introduced by Senators Church and Jackson. It contained the Sandia Mountains, all 30,700 acres of our proposal. We had added the northeast corner when the Loop Road was defeated. Our North Sandia Peak Wilderness as proposed was 14,500 acres and the South Peak Wilderness was a proposed 16,200 acres. At the last minute the Forest Service added another two hundred acres to simplify an administrative problem along their brush cut to Sandia Peak. The bill contained a number of areas in other western states, but did not make it at the last minute. The national election was catching all of the wind at that time, November 1976.

The bill was reintroduced early in the 95th Congress. It was supported by our Senators and Representatives, and was enacted on February 24, 1978, by President Jimmy Carter. The bill also contained many other areas, including the Manzano Mountain Wilderness and the Chama River Basin. Senator Lee Metcalf of Montana had been one of the early supporters of the Endangered American Wilderness Act but died in office just prior to its enactment. His constancy to the cause will be missed as we ride out the wild water of RARE II.

The Forest Service's earlier reasons for selecting the Scenic Area category for the South Sandias were based on their interpretation of the Wilderness Act pertaining to purity. They indicated that the smog and noise from the city, as well as the feral dogs, all disqualify the South Sandias and that we would pervert the intent of the Wilderness Act if we insisted on National Wilderness designation. Senator Church of Idaho, one of the draftors of the 1964 Wilderness Act, said on May 5, 1972, at a hearing of his Subcommittee on Public Lands:

Sights and sounds from outside the boundary do not invalidate a Wilderness designation or make buffer and threshold exclusions necessary, as a matter of law.

WILDLIFE DYNAMICS IN THE SANDIAS

The Rattlesnake Escalator is what it is. On the south side of the Sandias, above Tijeras Canyon, the rattlers have been observed over the years to go up and down the face of the mountain with the seasons. No doubt the availability of food has much to do with it but the temperatures seem to correspond to their active phases. In the heat of the summer, they appear to be up around South Sandia Spring and above. In the spring, they appear to stir first in the lower elevations around the lower rock formations. In the fall, they seem to successively come down the mountain as the season progresses. Snake sightings in my notes seem to conform to this escalator theory. It was first called to my attention by that "old government hunter" who lived near Fidel's Bar in Tijeras Canyon in the 1950's and 1960's.

The Raven Patrol on the Sandias is sometimes a rare sight. They are not only looking for something to eat like freshly killed deer dressings and even pretty ripe carion, but they may find an owl perched in a vulnerable spot.

Owls from the Sandias occasionally raid the raven roosts along the Rio at night whenever they need a young raven for nourishment. In turn, the ravens try to kill a roosting owl in the daytime. Such an attack is a chilling experience to observe. The owl is virtually blind in the sunlight and, if it does take off, it flies erratically, and sometimes runs into a tree or cliff while being pursued by a rush of ravens.

If you want to test the vigilance of the ravens, just sit down in the shade somewhere on the west side and be perfectly still. Better yet, lie flat on your back and only move your eyeballs. Even if you are camouflaged, a pair of ravens will show up in five or ten minutes. (I wish they could be trained to pick up trash!).

TIMBER SKIING IN THE SANDIAS

My term for it is timber skiing, one mode of wilderness travel. It is not Alpine skiing, nor is it cross-country skiing, although it has some of the elements of both. In its simplest form, it is heading downhill through the timber and glades east of the Crest parking lot with some cable bindings, Head or Hart Standards underfoot, and absolutely no pride. One does not cross his same track once if he does not want to. There are no trails, although there are some ancient woodroads down near State 44, the road just north of the La Madera Ski Area.

The pride part comes into play when there is no graceful way to stop short of charging into a tree. So you sit down. It works reliably if there is not much crust. Sometimes it helps to put both arms across your face and lay down flat on your back while slithering under a low-branched fir tree feet first. Another time in which pride takes a shock is when you cut too close to a small tree that is about tip high in the snow. The four to five foot ones are the most treacherous. You are blithely drifting along at no more than ten miles per hour and suddenly find yourself in the well around this tree. The branches somehow keep the snow from packing firmly around it, but it looks innocent enough from five or ten yards away. You stop suddenly in a grand lurching plunge unless you turn aside or manage to jump over it.

The process, however, is true free wilderness skiing. No lifts, no trails, no crowds, but a slight spirit of risk. It is essential to have a friend along, although we have had no unfortunate breaks or sprains in fifty years of it. Three years out of five there has been enough snow in the Sandias to do it. Even at the decrepit age of enforced retirement, it is still great fun.

Yes, I said no pride. There in the Sandias one simply hitchhikes up the road to the Crest. There are enough pickup trucks and vans "making the grade" that will answer to a friendly thumb. So we have had to walk all of the way up to the top a couple of times when the road conditions were bad, either to just plain get to the top or to get back to our car in the upper parking lot. Late in the day when you are too much in a hurry to get to skiing, you drive to the Crest and "plunge in." About dark, when there are no more Sunday drivers charging up the hill, you may have to walk. However, you get home deliciously tired.

Let me tell you about equipment. The poles for deep, soft, untrodden snow are "up to your armpits." They have baskets, or rings, that are at least six inches in diameter. The leather handles and straps are used underhanded to circumvent broken wrists when falling.

The gloves are mittens, well waxed or snow proofed, which go well up on the arm over the cuff of a poplin ski jacket. The pants are not stylish, but they overlay some fishnet, long-handled underwear, to the waist. The car keys are zippered in a pocket. The ski jacket has a hood. A blizzard can interrupt the fun and games. Another pocket has a whistle and a flare, with matches in case you did not miss that tree. If you need a compass, you should not be "loose in the Sandias."

As for the skis — come along with us on your trail skis. They are great on trails, on crusted snow, where there are no Sandias. They are so narrow they plunge in fresh, untrammeled snow. You might as well be skiing on the bottom, among the sprags, in our New Mexican snowflakes. Have you ever been spragged? Cross-country skis will do it to you — four miles from the car. After a hard winter, they were all right for the Finns.

Ah, yes. The skis. the kind that hold you up, that float you on the powder or whatever, are just plain, standard downhill skis. I weigh about 180 pounds and take at least 190-cm-long skis. The kind you can get in the Ski Swap (last year's skis — castoffs, for $10-$12). So you run across some boulders and "generate some grooves" in them — should you sweat? Not much with that kind of replacement cost. But how fancy should we get about waxes? Hey, chum, what is the fastest wax? Use it. You want to "ski free"? Use it. Aluminum parafin, maybe?

If you want to climb hills, put on your socks. Yes, socks. It is a canvas tube that slips over the back of your downhill skis and ties over your toe. It can be a beaver skin, sheared to erect the hair to prevent backward slipping, if you want. But you can walk straight uphill. No need for herringbone. Take off the tube socks and zip downhill on fast wax!

The boots? Old soft ski boots. You might have to walk in them. They should bend at the ball of the foot. They should have a groove in the heel for the spring at the back of the cable bindings.

The cable bindings? There is no forward or torque release on them at all. You use some cable clips that are attached to the sides of the skis to permit your heel to lift with each step. Then when you want to turn around to go downhill, pop the cables in the rear clips to snug down your heels. Have a keeper strap on each ski to keep it close by if it comes loose in a tumble and you will not have to chase it down the mountain. If you are in avalanche territory, leave these keeper straps off.

Now, about falling or stopping. In deep snow, a Christie works well unless you get one ski much above the other. It does take some width to work, however. Some old mine or woodroads are only as wide as your skis are long. So, sit down and keep the skis pointed straight. A timber fall across such a road is quite usual. I've only jumped over one of them in my life. I was going too fast. It is hard to tail-wag to hold your speed down on narrow roads in deep snow. Watch for small clearings and even pull up and stop. The breeze will taste sweet a lot longer.

Back to falling. If you always haul your knees together every time you tend to go out of control, it often saves the day. Even if you do fall, you won't break a leg. It is probably because two legs are harder to break than one. If you are going too fast and fall with your skis windmilling, even cable bindings won't stay on, particularly if you have soft old boots. I have fallen literally thousands of times (no pride) and have never even sprained an ankle on skis. I have used skis with all of the newest bindings and boots on manicured runs and have come close to sprains because they were set up too tight. The knees-together flop even worked in that situation. Old memory tracks: as a kid on the way home after dark I went over a jump and sprained an ankle with old rawhide bindings. I learned to fall right after that.

Finally, the eyes. Glasses are a nuisance and can get lost in a bad spill. I use an elastic band around the back of the head. Then I put ski goggles over them. A cap with a peak helps if it is snowing. Glasses and goggles can save your eyes if you cut too close to a tree, but the brush can carve up your cheeks unless you duck at the right time. After I started wearing bifocals, I was always seeing moguls right in front of me. So, I got a second pair of glasses with no bifocal section for skiing and hiking. Now the only problem is to keep them from steaming up. You may have to ventilate them by pulling them away from your face momentarily. Or, use a product which keeps them from steaming up for several days.

Now, put on a backpack with a 40-pound winter load. Do your skis still hold you up in the unpacked snow? Is everything on your pack lashed down so that, if you have to lie down on it to stop, you won't lose something?

Sometime you will find that when you are hauling your heavy boots and skis up somebody's trail, a speed merchant with cross-country skis and knickers will sail past you with a sneer. Invite him to detour off the trail and see how long he sails in the deep snow. You will pass him again on the way down as you coast past him.

A sometimes interesting variant of timber skiing is to climb uphill all morning on snowshoes, towing your skis on a thong. You can stack your skis, one on top of the other by removing part of the lower binding, drill holes through the tips, and drag the skis along with a nylon cord. Bearpaw snowshoes stow diagonally across your back on the way down that afternoon. When you sit down to stop, the bearpaws can tap your skull enough to tell you to be more careful. But at least you can coast downhill instead of having to push your cross-country skis downhill too. A pair of breathable gaiters will keep your socks dry and the snow out of your boot tops. A fanny pack is a lot cooler than a daypack, A two-square-foot plastic sheet on a stump will keep your seat dry. Yes, you put both poles together to help shove you back onto your feet. Even roll over to get your skis downhill and across the fall-line We yell "timber" when we have fallen. Others pull up and wait for us. (Did anybody bring an ace bandage?)

SANDIA WILDERNESS TRAILS AND ROUTES

Recent maps of the Sandia Wilderness issued by the Forest Service are a considerable improvement over previous efforts as far as showing the trails ac-

Agua Sarca area of Sandia Mountains. Southeast view.

curately. Mike Hill's Guide[12] does a good job of showing the routes ordinarily used by rock climbers. Some trails and routes you might not think of taking are included here:

One old pack trail, the one that was shown on some of the old quad maps dated in the 1940's going north from the ridge north of Carlito Springs and which cuts the 7,600-foot contour about four miles further north above Cole Springs, was opened up by the fairies or somebody with a diamond blaze. The Forest Service does no know who did it and no one seems to want to admit it. In general it is neatly and narrowly done and obviously by some horsemen because of the clearing and blaze heights. It required no theatrical head ducking to traverse it on a tall bay in 1977. Some folks call it Faulty Trail because it does follow several faults along the contour. Others call it Mystery Trail.

A trail from the TV towers on the Crest to Tunnel Springs near Placitas, about ten miles, was completed in the fall of 1976. We in the New Mexico Wilderness Study Committee and the New Mexico Wilderness commission are proposing the name "Tollefsrud Trail" as a memorial to Phil Tollefsrud, a staunch conservationist and wilderness freak. Phil hunted the mountain (deer-bowhunting) and was instrumental, with Milo Conrad, in bringing legislation to a head. Phil died suddenly from unknown causes in late 1976. (See the Wheeler Peak chapter.)

The Piedra Lisa Trail, a five-mile, low-level trail from Juan Tabo to the Piedra Lisa Spring on the Bernalillo watershed, traverses the western lobe of the Wilderness. It crosses the Cañon del Tabo, Cañon del Agua, and swings across some of the Agua Sarca drainage. We have fond hope that there will be no more trails in that sector of the mountains but rather only a route marked with ducks and connecting with the Tollefsrud Trail at Tunnel Springs.

Let me spot you onto some one-day circuits which are mostly routes and not trails. Get the quadrangle map or one which has contours shown and whose scale is about two inches per mile.

Starting at Tunnel Springs, go southwest and take the ridge to the west of Agua Sarca Canyon up to about the 9.500-foot elevation. Cut due east across the shinnery oak glade until you intersect the Tollefsrud Trail; then back down to Tunnel Springs.

Drive five miles from Placitas up Las Huertas Creek, park your car, and take the east ridge almost due south for about one mile up to Palomas Peak. Return the same way unless you have a hang glider. This is east of the Wilderness.

Park at Dry Camp turnoff of State Highway 44. Take your cross-country skis about a quarter-mile east, southeast to Tecolate (Owl) Peak. Eat sandwiches and listen to the traffic down below. This is also outside of our Wilderness.

Note on water in the Sandias: plan on carrying it with you. A safe assumption is that all of it is contaminated some of the time.

Park at Cole Spring. Go due west about two miles up hill to the Crest Trail. Turn right, walk one mile north, and come east down Cañoncito Trail past the spring about a quarter mile. Take the Faulty trail at about the 7.300-foot contour and walk south about one and one-quarter miles to the car at Cole Spring.

Park at the Forest Boundary in Pistol Canyon and walk up to Three Gun Springs. Take the trail up to the ridge overlooking Embudo Canyon. The trail intersects Embudo Trail and goes on up to Deer pass just south of South Peak. If you are still fresh, drop over to the Crest Trail and go south a mile to South Sandia Spring. If it is not snowy, you may want to rock-scramble west from the spring down to the Three Gun Springs trail you went north on about four hours earlier.

Park in Sunset Canyon. Climb up to the scree slopes just below the cliff faces. Cut off south at about the 8,200-foot level and you will run into a trail generally headed south. It comes out in Embudo Canyon. How you get back to your car in Sunset is your problem.

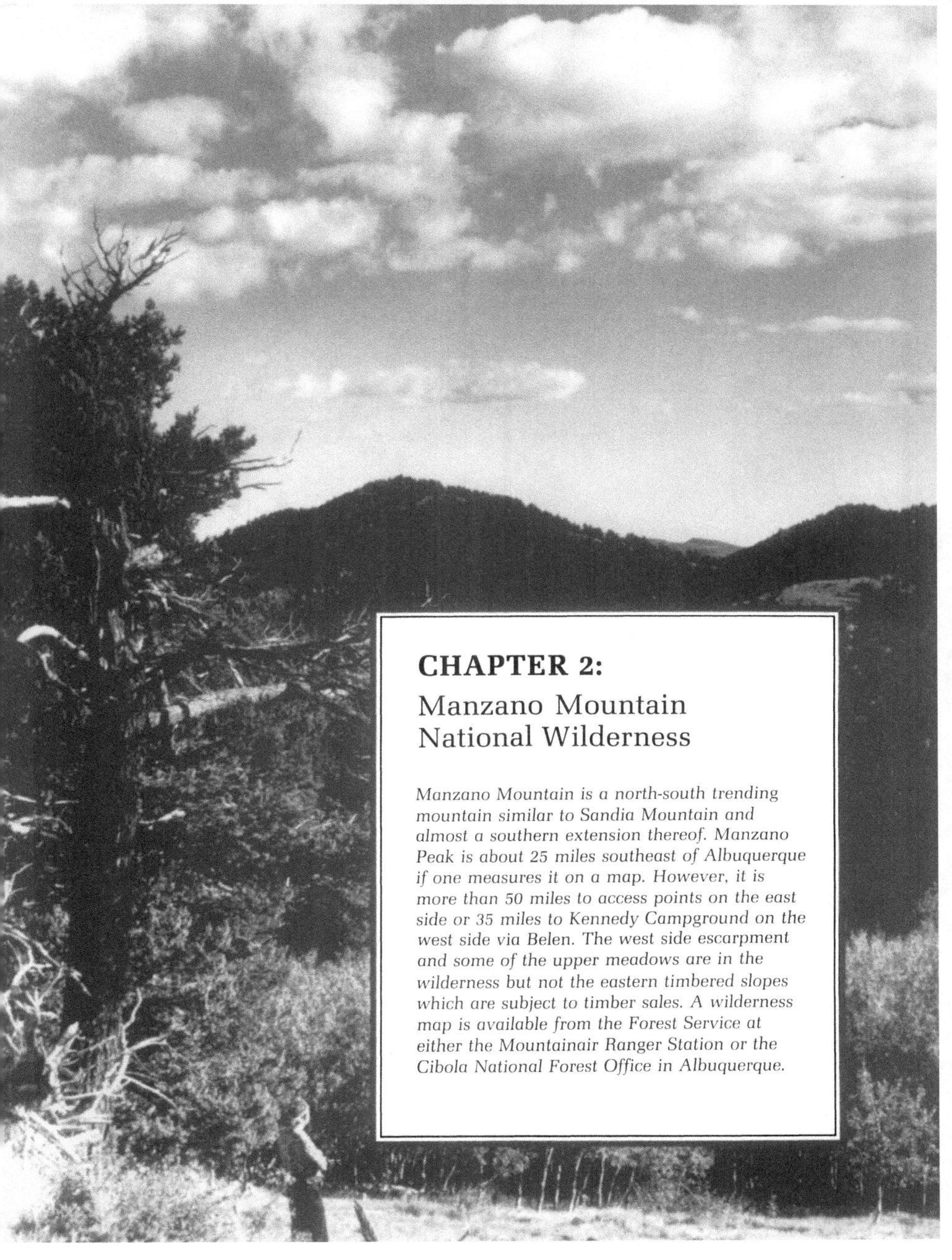

CHAPTER 2:
Manzano Mountain National Wilderness

Manzano Mountain is a north-south trending mountain similar to Sandia Mountain and almost a southern extension thereof. Manzano Peak is about 25 miles southeast of Albuquerque if one measures it on a map. However, it is more than 50 miles to access points on the east side or 35 miles to Kennedy Campground on the west side via Belen. The west side escarpment and some of the upper meadows are in the wilderness but not the eastern timbered slopes which are subject to timber sales. A wilderness map is available from the Forest Service at either the Mountainair Ranger Station or the Cibola National Forest Office in Albuquerque.

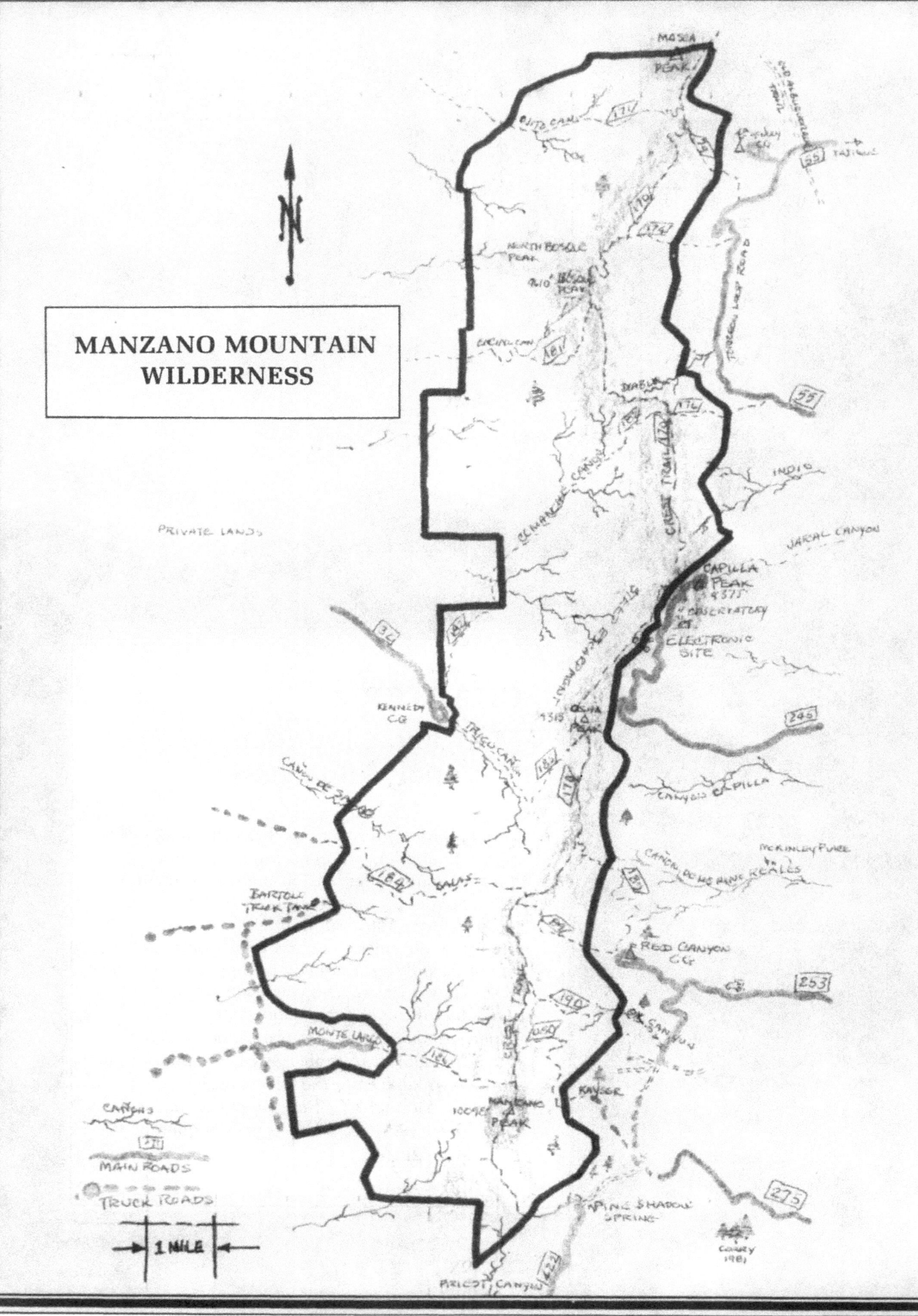

The Indians used the salt beds of Laguna del Perro and Lake Pago for centuries before the Spaniards came. The two salt lakes between Willard and Duran to the southeast made cleaner salt. The salt blocks were carried on their backs by the pueblo Indians over the Manzano Mountains and down into the valley of the Rio Grande. The most used route to the up-river pueblos was the Old Albuquerque Trail which crossed the main ridge just north of Mosca Peak.

The salt mining was usually done in late fall for several reasons. The salt beds had a chance to dry out after the summer rains and the notoriously muddy ground on the east side of the Manzanos hardened up for easier traveling with a load by October and November. The Apaches were preoccupied with hunting before the snows came and were consequently less likely to raid the salt hauls. However, the Apaches also needed salt for preserving some of the meat which they did not dry into jerky or consume immediately. The salt was also used with ashes to cure the hides for winter clothing.

I believe primitive man had to carry the salt blocks in hides for a couple of practical reasons. Rock salt irritates one's skin, so it had to be carried in some kind of container. One would surmise that baskets would break under the load. They were used to carrying half a deer carcass, generally with the meat boned out, with the aid of the hide in a back-pack mode. So, the hides were used to carry salt also. In time they observed that the hides that were used to haul salt did not smell as bad. Finally, they probably discovered that ashes repeatedly applied and scraped into the hair side finally removed the hair and left a more useful and supple buckskin.

Although the Apaches probably preferred to rob salt shipments from the Indians in the vicinity of Gran Quivira because it was closer to their redoubts in the Jicarilla Mountains just north of White Oaks, they also harassed the traffic to Quarai, Abo, and Scholle pueblos in the Manzano foothills to the southeast and south. Some have claimed to be able to read such a message in the pictographs just south of Abo Pass. I think it was a favorite ambush location where the attackers had a lot of time awaiting their prey and were inclined to "doodle" on the rocks.

There were at least two locations in Tijeras Canyon between the Sandia and Manzano Mountains that made good ambush points for men without mounts. One was about a half mile east of Carnue and the other near the old Sedillo Pass through which the original foot trail made its way. The Old Albuquerque Trail provided a more covert route up Gallina Canyon.

After the Indians managed to get Spanish horses, the salt blocks were carried on travois poles pulled by horses. The haulage method was originated by the Plains Indians, adapted from their much earlier use of dogs to pull smaller pairs of poles.[1]

Long after Quarai was abandoned, the old Mission at Manzanito Creek (at the present town of Manzano) provided a starting point for the Spanish occupation of the eastern flanks of the mountain. The records are not positive,[2] but the name appeared to be established as early as 1676 A.D. The original compounds, buildings, and apple orchard were apparently damaged during the pueblo revolt of 1680. The tree ring dating of the present orchard places its start in the early 1800's. The Spanish village in its present location dates from 1929. Several other apple orchards have since come and gone on other locations in and near the small towns in the general area. These later varieties did not adapt as well as the original plantings.

Ultimately the Albuquerque Trail turned into a road. It was still in use until the early 1920's, when traffic from Estancia, Torreon, and Tajique began to convert from wagons to automobiles and trucks. The pinto bean crops in 1921 and 1922 bought the dry land farmers and ranchers a dozen or more cars. The old Trail was subject to gully washers and was gradually abandoned for the muddy road that ran north to Moriarity and south to Mountainair. The firewood wagons generally traveled on the route that is now South Highway 14 because it was shorter and the cars could not make some of the grades.

The road through Tijeras Canyon east of Albuquerque was upgraded for the early automobile traffic following World War I. The crushed rock surface was given a thin veneer of blacktop in 1925 but was constantly churned up by the firewood wagon wheels. It was graded and paved in the mid-1930's but was still rough when I came through it in 1940. In 1979, the Freeway was completed.

So much for the perimeter of the mountain. The interior area of the mountain clump was used for game hunting, some sheep grazing, and a good amount of firewood gathering by the people of Estancia Valley. At the turn of the century, the railroad induced more settlement, and the dryland farmers with their copies of the Homestead Act tried to occupy the land. The ranchers and sheepmen begrudgingly made some adjustments for a price and pinto bean crops were planted. Small successes accompanied the wetter years but blew away by the mid 1920's and 1930's. The activities on the mountain itself started to pick up at about the same time as the railroad ties were cut in Escabosa Cañon for the spurline up from Willard.

Archibald Rhea, Fred Rhea's father, had located, during the 1890's, a big spring up on the east edge of the section of the mountain which we now know as Bosque Peak. He homesteaded the top of that mountain because of that spring. It is an incongruous place. The high aspen meadow sits upon the mountain ridge as if it were leveled off by a giant cleaver. Those meadows received about twenty-five inches of moisture per year and they fattened up not only his bony cattle, but his sheep. Fred had built a three-room cabin and some corrals in 1906, using some of the timbers from his father's old house. The flat meadow on top of the mountain was a mystic place from late April through November. Deer and grouse, rabbits and turkeys, doves and eagles abounded and were hardly disturbed by the cattle and sheep. His wife often played a treadle pump organ. Happy days.

Mrs. Cora McKinley had been visiting and helping Mrs. Lily Rhea that week up at the Bosque cabin. Little Archy Rhea had been born a couple of weeks before. His father, Fred, came in for dinner and mentioned seeing smoke down by the Rio. He recalled being told by an Indian that the trees along the south ridge of Mosca Peak had burned when he was a boy. The Rheas were uneasy about the fire because the grass was dry all around the house and Mrs. Rhea could not travel yet. Mr. Rhea decided to have his sheep graze off the tall grass in the fenced yard, just for safety's sake.

The smoke Fred Rhea had seen came from a big brush fire started by embers from the afternoon Santa Fe train.

A.D. liked what he saw in the "Pinos" canyon; soon he had his sawmill going and built a frame shack there in about 1910. During the war years, a tree-farmer named Kelly set out a fifteen-hundred-tree apple orchard in some of the area that A.D. had cleared. A.D. bought the orchard in 1921 and had some good crops. By that time, Cañon de los Piños Reales was called Spruce Canyon. The King's trees were gone. In the early 1960's, A.D.'s son Marvin built a new house on their property.

Going back a few years, the Indians at Abo on the south end of the mountains knew a few secrets.[3] They had a gold and silver mine up the hill in what is now Priest Canyon. It didn't attract attention because their resulting ornaments had too much lead in them to catch the sun right. The Apaches ran them out every good year to take what part of the harvests they could find. The Spaniards did better. They cleaned out the mine and took the ore down to Zacatecas in Mexico for proper smelting. The Indians caved in the mine during the Pueblo Revolt. It was supposedly worked out, anyway.

The screaming of the two big saws in the Kayser Mill on the southeast side of the mountain in 1924 went on night and day. There were some pretty good groves of Douglas fir and some ponderosa on that lower part of the mountain. Residents of Mountainair were alarmed at the constant reports of smoke near the mill. The sawdust and slabbing piles burned frequently. The workmen came home to town infrequently because the road to the mill was washed out so badly that it smashed the timber wagon wheels on the boulders.

The Forest Service "fixed" the road into the Kayser Mill Canyon mill site in the late 1930's when they acquired it. Although they removed or blasted the biggest rocks and filled the worst parts with gravel, gully washers since have scoured it out again and again each time it has been repaired. The road leads to one of the more beautiful parts of the mountain. (See Trails and Routes at the chapter's end.)

One cold night during a howling snowstorm in the winter of 1943, an Army Air Corps pilot thought he had a landing field on Bosque Peak. He plowed down an aspen or two, separated his two engines before he stopped, and killed his navigator. The pilot survived for about two or three days. The Air Corps hauled the engines out on mules and dropped a few pieces along the way. The airframe was still there in 1978.

The deer hunting season of 1947 must have been a memorable one for some — on the Bosque. The locals reported that more than 150 deer were hauled out of there past the Fourth of July Canyon Forest Service Cabin where the Check Station was that year. In 1948, there were few deer remaining and there were hundreds of BAR (Browning Automatic Rifle) empty shells and clips all over the mountain top. That was an illegal process — and an illegal hunting weapon. I know of no one being fined or sentenced. But hunting has not been good on the mountain since.

My first Manzano deer hunting trip was in 1948. I had broken my hunting bow about two weeks before opening day, and I was still making another the night before we took off for the hunt. So, I did not get much sleep. The season started at noon and the shooting began. The others in my party all had guns and looked on my bow with disdain. A buck came running in the crunchy snow from the wrong direction on a trail in back of me — and woke me up. My first thought was that it was a hunter making too much noise and I was afraid to move for fear of getting shot. When I saw the buck, the critical instant had passed.

The next weekend I enjoyed watching a lion below me in Cañon de la Mina (a branch of Comanche Canyon). It was watching the big canyon below as half a dozen hunters bustled up and down the game trails. I backed out quietly and let it be.

The last time I bow hunted for deer in a gun-hunting area was in 1950 in Kayser Mill Canyon. Since I had gotten my first deer in New Mexico there the year previous, I was back and alone. A big camp full of gun hunters was set up just above the old mill site. While I was standing among some rocks in a natural blind, a gun hunter stopped not 25 yards away and blasted at the hillside above. He "jumped out of his skin" when I asked if he hit the buck. He said, "Naw. Just sound shootin'. Tryin' to spook somethin' up." So I campaigned two years for a bow-hunting season.

Foolish, it was. A friend named Mauldin was a part-time car dealer in Albuquerque during the 1950's. Sports cars, mostly. The rest of the time he had a ranch, he said, east of Priest Canyon and "south of

Thunderbird." Raised quarterhorses, said he. "Cummon down an' see me." "Bring your (MG) TC." So, I drove down that Saturday, alone, the back way, through Tomé, and to Scholle. A mile past Scholle, turn off, go north. Horrid road, for a sports car. Could not find Mauldin. Finally found a trailer, a house trailer, and a dozen horses that came to look at me in the sunset. Were they expecting oats? Maybe Mauldin, the sport, was in that Dripping Springs Bar back there on the highway? I never found out.

However, he seemed to be able to grow horses at his 7,500-foot elevation that could beat horses from Texas at Ruidoso for six seeks or so until they acclimated. Maybe Mauldin's mustangs should have been raised on the Bosque (Peak) at more than 8,500 feet elevation.

One of the few horsemen I have ever seen on the mountain was near the top of Monte Largo Canyon. It was Dick Ray from Belen. He was probably playing hookey from high school, because it was a week day. Dick is a small man but solid and lithe. Maybe he is the handsomest cowboy I have ever seen. Horses really perform for him, perhaps because he is light and knows what he wants the horse to do. He has since become one of us wilder-freaks. The last I heard of him, he and his beautiful wife Vimmy were running the Lobo Lodge up near Cumbres Pass. But that is another story.

As youngsters, Jesus (Chewy) Baca and his brother used to herd his father's sheep on the Manzano Mountain. The Forest Service decided that the sheep were getting to be too hard on the mountain flora. The grazing permit was changed to cattle. The hillside pasturage improved. The cattle were ranged on the west side during the winter months and transferred to the east side in the summer.

The Bacas built a trick tank at the mouth of Bartolo Canyon of the west side. It is a large galvanized rain catchment area supported by a wooden framework which drains into a metal storage tank that feeds a drinking trough for the cattle and wildlife.

They previously had tapped a water seep in Monte Largo Canyon and brought the water down hill in various pipes partially buried. Next, it was neoprene hose, and currently it is polyethylene tubing. The seep has retreated up the canyon over the years, and they have had to go progressively higher. The Forest Service has bridled at their latest proposal. I have asked that their old materials, long abandoned, be cleaned out and removed from the National Forest.

Every fall, gun hunters leave piles of trash and some mindless vandalism in their wake. Chewy cleans up what he can and pleads with the Forest Service for some help. Consequently, he looks upon some of his old tanks and pipe as not very important. This whole process is repeated by grazing permittees in much of the National Forest margins.

The use of temporary water catchments and plastic tubing above ground around the perimeters of Wilderness Areas does not seem to be sufficient reason for disqualifying an area. Permanent dams, perhaps, could be serious enough.

Tom Green did a lot of the boundary work on our Manzano Mountain Wilderness Proposal. Phil Tollefsrud knew the mountain well; he refined a number of corridor boundaries for some of the intrusions like piplines, old roads, water tanks, cattle-loading chutes, and other nonconforming features. Phil participated as a member of the Forest Service's Study Group for consideration and development of the Manzano Land Use Plan (LUP) in late 1975 and early 1976. All of the matters raised in the LUP process were not resolved by the time Phil died in November of 1976.

Our proposed Wilderness Area included 37,000 acres (14,970 hectares). From the map you can see that the area includes the roadless area and those territories on the east side above the highest timber sales. The western escarpment contains wild canyons which provide winter harbor for a wide variety of wildlife. The northern slopes, even on the west side, catch and store snow to recharge the aquifiers and watershed for the alluvial fans below.

The Endangered American Wilderness Act, introduced by U.S. Senator Church, late in the 94th Congress (1976), included the Manzano Mountain Wilderness in its original draft. The intermediate mark-up draft did not contain it, perhaps because of some delicate bookkeeping on areas in various states. The 95th Congress reintroduced the bill with our Manzano Mountain Wilderness Area contained in it and it was signed on February 24, 1978, by President Jimmy Carter.

You should become familiar with the old Apple Mountains. Drive to the Saddle just south of the Capilla Peak Lookout, take the Crest Trail south of "Electronic Shack" for a mile or so. Love our mountain, but leave it — unmolested and serene. (Lightning will strike you if you leave any mark of your passing!)

MANZANO WILDERNESS TRAILS AND ROUTES

There wasn't much snow in that Bosque winter of 1911. What little there was seemed to be in a long cornice just below the drop-off on the east side of the Bosque Meadow. The big spring on the Bosque and the stream in Gallina Canyon were but a trickle that summer. The Rheas moved down to the new town of Tajique — cattle, sheep, and all. Lightning started a fire on the south ridge of Mosca Peak again where the Indian had remembered one in his youth. That is probably the only reason you can climb Mosca today. The scrub oak thicket can be penetrated easiest along that ridge north of the saddle at the head of the trail from Fourth of July Canyon.

Tom Green climbed up from the north side to the Peak in 1976. A couple of us did it in 1962 or 1963, but found it brutal. Our 1975 hike up the south ridge was

Trigo Canyon — typical of rugged westside Manzano Mountain Canyons.

far easier. The new trail just to the east of Mosca starts up by the Old Albuquerque Trail and meets the Gallina Canyon trail in the saddle south of Mosca about a mile. Mosca (fly) Summit has various hatches of flies the year around. One day in May we must have stirred up the flies uncommonly well, because a veritable flying circus of swallows followed us up the mountain. One winter day in 1970 we found a football shaped mass of ladybugs while we were hunting for the cairn on the peak. They surely looked dead but were only torpid.

You can walk from however far above the Thunderbird spread you can drive on the Kayser Mill road. The trail is beautiful going up the Kayser Mill Canyon to the Crest Trail. Then it is only a half-mile or so south to Manzano Peak. Or, it is a mile north to the Ox Canyon Trail on the same Crest Trail. The mile and a half back to your car from the Ox Canyon picnic ground is a long haul, especially if it is muddy.

The hike from the Cerro Blanco Trail along the Crest Trail south to Bosque Peak is a bit hard to follow because it is not much traveled. The trail down to the Torreon Loop Road past the Cave is good.

The trail from the Bosque south to Capilla Peak gets a bit indefinite in spots. (I keep trail notes.) It seems to go down hill more than it should and the edge of the mountain is a little ragged. But it is nice to have your final destination in sight most of the time. Otherwise you might just wander down an old wood road into Indio Canyon. We knew we had better look at the compass when we found the road (trail) blocked by a four-wheel drive of sorts — it was a Scout with all wheels removed — and probably bogged down until spring.

Go back to zero. Climb back where this "road" diverted us from the trail. An old sign at the "intersection" said "Canyon del Ojo .5 mile." the "point" of point 5 seemed lost in time. The sleet splashed on the map. I hoped these keys we traded with "the others" (coming in the opposite direction) fit the car at Capilla Peak. They did. Along about dark.

Wintertime. We had climbed up the road to Capilla from the New Canyon Camp Ground (at the bottom of the hill). On skis, with skins. The road, which is at least twisty in summer, was blown pretty solid, contoured, 45 degrees by snow when we went up it. Up near the "saddle" where the road crosses over from the east to the west side just south of the Capilla Campground, we found a cornice. The cornice was packed by the wind and snow blowing off the west side to make a bank eight or ten feet high. It was like home. A snow cave came easy and the night in it passed in a wink. More snow during the night. A magic morning! On top of the world.

Shortly after lunch we found a strange track. We thought we had heard a motor, and assumed it was an airplane. After all, it was 1965. We had seen our first snowmobile (track). Skiing down that same winding road was misery. The snowmobile tracks and our skis didn't fit. I must have had snow packed in my watch pocket by the time we got down to the car.

The next winter there wasn't much snow. The deer stayed on top. At least some did. Three of us found the tracks of a couple of snowmobiles and the guts of a deer on the ridge south of the Saddle. Poachers seem to come in all walks of life. The walk down was not very cheerful even though we found the snowmobile crossing muddy stretches leaving a fleck of blood here and there (they dragged the dead deer downhill).

The trip from Capilla Saddle south to Osha Peak is nothing but a delight along the Crest Trail. Except — unless — you miss that infamous left turn. In that case, all ten of you discover you are at Upper Jaramillo Spring. Ah si! Esta too bad. No sign say Jaramillo. Starting to rain. Head uphill — we are on the west side somehow. The Crest Trail has to be up there. Somehow we top out, and find it. Turn to the right, a la derecha. Tired, all of us. Find a flat spot, enough for ten sleeping bags. Wind and rain.

All night long, rain sleeting down. Fog streaming through the trees, condensing on them. The wind, after you go to sleep in your tube tent, fitfully strips that fog-moisture off the trees and blasts it onto your flimsy tent, intermittently, interminably.

The next day, on south past Gallo Peak, on the Crest Trail. The torrential rain and the galactic winds of night (before last?) flooded out the forest duff off the trail and blew it bare. A foot wide and like a path made by machine. Chewy Baca's cattle did it. Not enough people up here to impact a trail like that. but look! A fresh buck track? Is it a big doe? In that one bare ribbon of a path. No, there are the dew claw marks. It was a buck.

A few of us swing down the mountain, a quarter mile to the east and check out the contour level at the top of the contract timber cuts. That is the boundary of our proposed Wilderness Area. Finally, Manzano Peak. Several reluctant bulls on that ridge nibbling on the tenderest grass. If such a mountain were in Ireland, it would be as green as that.

Another trip. Up Kayser Mill Canyon on the east side. Into Monte Largo and over north into Bartolo Cañon and up the (game) trail to Gallo Peak, socked in by clouds on the whole west side. Chewy Baca has a neoprene hose out of a Monte Largo spring to something, someplace down below. He is a guard at Sandia. I'll have to ask him: "Esta fountain de Baca?"

Another time. This time it was with the Mountain Club. Into John F. Kennedy Camp Grounds. Up Trigo Canyon. A lion track and a scuff spot. Pungent! To the Crest Trail and then boon-docked it down Cañon de Los Pinos Reales. There are still some big trees up near the ridge because it was too steep to get them out without smashing them up. So what is left untouched is in our wilderness area.

Again park at John F. Kennedy Camp Grounds. Go up Trigo Canyon trail to the Ridge Trail. Turn left or to the north along the ridge until you intersect the Comanche Trail. Go down Comanche to the Forest Boundary and walk south about a mile back to your car. A good day's hike.

Drive into Bartolo Canyon and park near the big trick tank. Climb up the cañon trail to the ridge, take the Ridge Trail north to the intersection of Salas Canyon Trail. Descend that old trail to the cañon mouth and walk back south to your car in Bartolo. Close all gates so marked.

The peak to the northwest of Mosca is Guadalupe Peak and is on Isleta Indian land. If you want to hike on the reservation, it is best to get a permit from the Governor at Isleta. I have been talking to him about the possibility of adding their roadless area north of Mosca Peak as an Indian Wilderness Area — perhaps it will be the first in the nation.

An interesting one-day trip anytime that the snow is not more than half a meter deep is up Trail 89, west from Red Canyon Campground (6 miles southwest of the town of Manzano). It is at the end of an all-weather road. The mud can get horrendous if you pick the wrong place to park in the campground or off-road.

It takes an hour-and-a-half to reach the Crest Trail. Turn south for two or three hours on the trail to Manzano Peak. Then backtrack to the Kayser Mill Trail (#80), descend it to the road head. A short distance from the mouth of the Canyon, the road (422) intersects the Kayser Mill Road. Take Forest Road 422 north about four and a half miles (7 km) back to your car. The trip is about sixteen kilometers, total.

A variant of the above is to leave the Red Canyon Campground by way of Trail 189 which goes up the mountain northwest of the campground and intersects the Crest Trail just north of Gallo Peak. Turn south on the Crest Trail, and descend the Ox Canyon Trail to the 422 road. The round trip is about seventeen kilometers if you do not boondock from Ox Canyon Campground over to Red Canyon. The Crest Trail signs are often torn down by vandals or bears. You can generally find the bare poles still planted and possibly the smashed sign pieces in the adjacent brush. Remember to take your trash bag along and be careful that it does not get snagged in the process. It is beautiful country, well worth keeping it clean.

Yet another variant is to descend on the new trail from Manzano Peak to Pine Shadow Spring. It is about three miles and the views are interesting. It is probably best to have a car there because it is now like eleven kilometers back to Red Canyon. The road is rough even on foot, let alone a jeep. Passenger cars get discouraged by a few bad pitches on the connecting road.

CHAPTER 3:
Bandelier National Wilderness

Bandelier National Monument and Wilderness is about 20 miles due west of Santa Fe and about 6 miles south of Los Alamos. Access by State Road 4 is about 40 miles from Santa Fe or about 4 miles from White Rock. State Road 4 traverses west and roughly parallel to the northern wilderness boundary and provides access to several trailheads. Get a map and permit at Monument Headquarters.

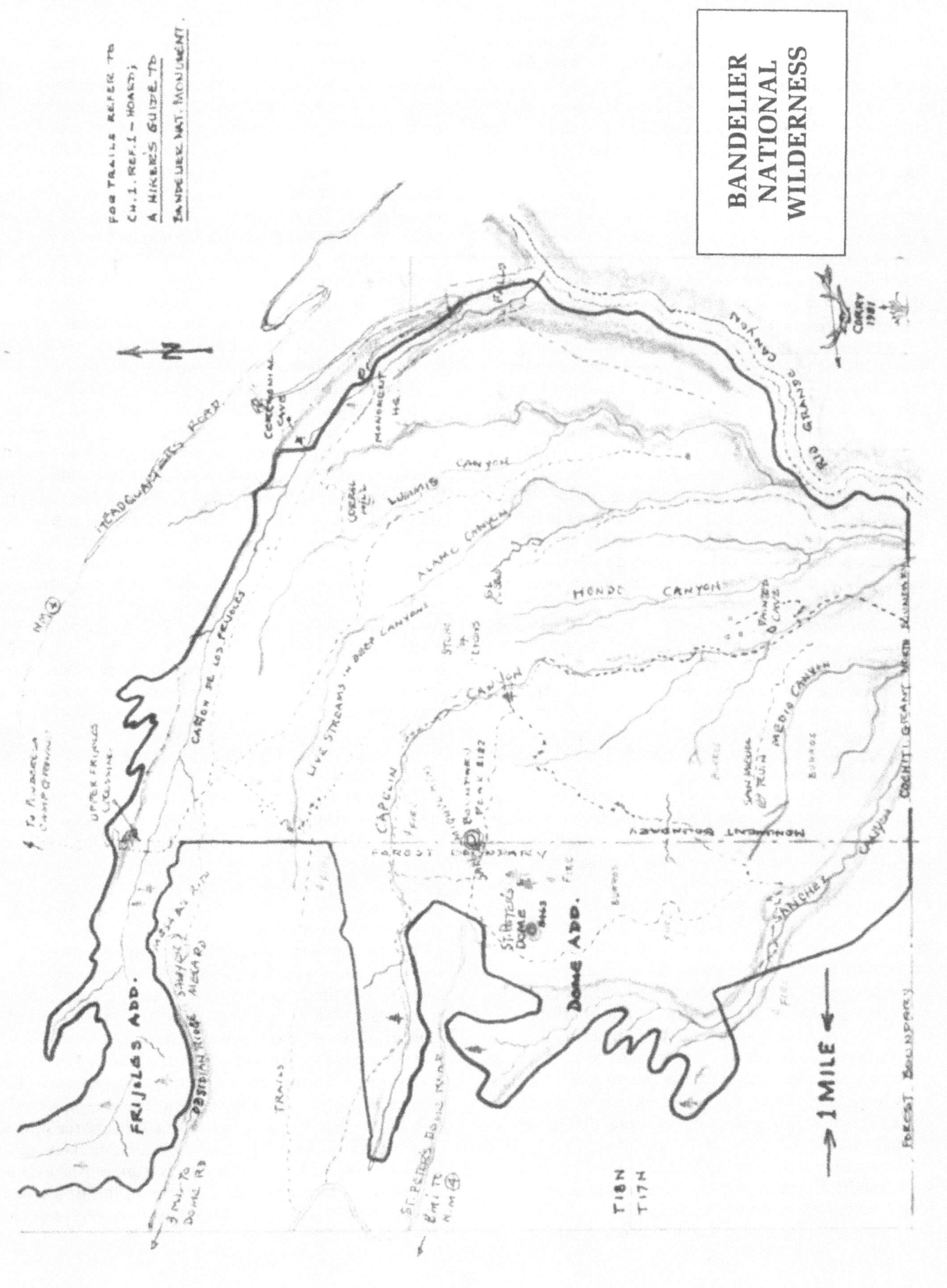

The south wind had been blasting all night long but other than its noise causing a minor restiveness, it had little effect on the people sleeping in the three dwellings. What did awaken them was a very red sun just peeking around both sides of a rocky spire on the mountain range on the other side of the valley. The sun shone wanly through their front doors which had been open all night.

That early spring was the same one during which Charlemagne's armored foot-soldiers were slogging their way southward through the mud of Central Europe. The old Roman Road had been badly vandalized by some earlier retreats. That spring was wet and cold in Europe. But those were civilized men with modern weapons and lofty intentions.

The sun, made red by its shining through curtains of dust being blown up-river, warmed the bones of those primitive small people in the rock and earthen houses. The dust had all but blotted out the big mountain range to the east since the day before. The snows had melted early that year and there would be only an occasional muddy rain or two until mid-summer.[1] The maize and wild barley stores had been eaten during the winter and the last bits of the wild oats had been used to bait the scattered flocks of hungry birds. Nets, carefully made of yucca fibers, were dropped on birds that came to eat the grain. The bird meat, stretched out by that of an occasional rabbit, was enough to get these people through the spring. They killed every coyote they could ambush, mainly by squealing like a trapped or injured rabbit. Only once each spring could the best hunter get a deer. The does were particularly wary because they had just dropped their fawns and the mountain lions were playing cat-and-mouse with fawns that they couldn't see or smell when mother told them to be still.

The mesas slanted downward toward the great river from the mountain range to the west. Some streams trickled down erosion canyons eastward to the river gorge. Two of the larger streams plunged over the mesa's edge in white, vaporous attempts to reach the red-brown river far below in the gorge. Green watercress grew in these secret places and the women knew how to mix this delicacy with their sparse meat provender. Coarse salt from the lakes a hundred miles to the southeast, mixed with a few ground chili seeds, made the pot-full of food worth the day's effort. The bird meat had been cooked over a chamisa bush-wood fire so that a slight taste of sage remained.

The houses were only holes in the ground.[2] Floors were two feet below ground level, generally round and as much as ten to twelve feet inside diameter. An earthen bench surrounded a central floor pit. The walls were rock and earth about three feet high; roofs were made of poles, woven with green brush, and plastered outside with adobe earth. Some of the roofs had rocks and grass. There was only one opening, the door, facing directly east. These small people could stand up straight and also could curl up to sleep comfortably on the bench. On cold nights, some preheated rocks were brought into the house and dumped on the floor. A skin covered the doorway.

Each house was tailored by the inhabitants to their own needs. In the summer, thick earthen roofs kept interiors cool during the heat of the day, and let some heat soak through in the early morning hours when the night cooled off. The diurnal range of temperature was about 30 °F. A summer day of 90 °F would plunge to 60 °F at night unless it was adjusted by a wind.

The winter sun would warm a scraped off roof (with less mass than in summer). The better homes had boughs and hides thrown over the hogan roofs just before the sun went down to retain some of the heat. Usually this was all of the heat required unless winter storms lasted several days.

This was passive solar heating in an active way. Although there were advantages to single dwellings, there were many disadvantages. As the family expanded, additional rooms were needed. As the round houses were joined, rooms became rectangular.

The larger and most recent ruins at Bandelier are arranged in an open U-shape with the opening to the southeast. One large ruin (Tyuonyi) is almost a closed circle about an open central plaza. It contained as many as four rooms on each side radially, and straight radial walls divided the rooms. Very few of those rooms had interconnecting doors through the radial walls. They were lighted and accessed through a hole in the roof. Open fires produced the heat required in winter. The beamed roofs were earth covered to help carry the sun's heat overnight but were not as asjustable as the single room hogan. The pueblo rooms must have been suffocating in the summer nights after long hot spells.

These people had no armor, no swords. But they did have solar-heated homes while Europeans were hunkering down in cold stone houses with thatched roofs and smoky fires. The prehistoric Indians had bows, arrows, and lances, primarily for hunting. And so they remained until the Spanish came up the river seven hundred years later.

Changes came to these Indians, these pre-pueblo beings, however. The first, involved hunting (my own guess — perhaps because I have slept where they slept centuries ago, and because I, too, am a bow-hunter). The primitive weapons were impotent at best. Thus, after trying for weeks on end to get a fatal arrow into a deer, coupled by the vital drive of hunger, what would happen if you should suddenly see a lion with a fresh kill? My theory is: go home and get mother and the kids and all of the aunts and uncles, come back, and drive the lion off his kill and steal it from him. Perhaps you had put an arrow into the deer in the first place and the lion beat you to the kill. (Lions very seldom bring down a healthy deer.)

After a few centuries of such training, the lion learned to get his mate to stand guard against such intrusions and then stand guard while she ate, or vice versa. The behavior may have become symbolic to the hunters. Today, the Cochiti Indians claim that the two "lions" are the vestige of a religious process. I think that it became part of a hunting ritual that said let us sculpture these two chunks of sandstone into lions protecting their kill. We will practice at driving them off, and we will eat more regularly. Consequently, I would guess that a symbiotic relationship existed in Bandelier between lions and man. Man winged the deer with an inadequate weapon, lion killed the crippled deer, and man and lion ate. The Stone Lions Shrine is a vestige of that symbiosis.

Another gradual change that took place was in the weather. Over the centuries, from about A.D. 600 until A.D. 1200 or 1300, the precipitation annually received by most of New Mexico and the Southwest dwindled from 25 inches per year to no more than some three to five inches.[1] One of the few streams that kept flowing was that which still comes down Frijoles Canyon. At first, these people living in the extensive areas south of the Canyon carried their water home. Some big pots have been discovered that might have served such purposes.

Some of the people, perhaps from Chaco Canyon, dropped in and saw all of the good pit-house sites taken and decided to enlarge some of the overhangs in the sandstone or tufa cliffs along the north side of the canyon. Possibly one enterprising team of diggers contracted a cave for four deer. How many deer would pay for the Ceremonial Cave? Or Painted Cave? If all of this feels remote from your own frame of reference, you can go to Bandelier and sit outside the last cave upstream. (Calvin[3] got bad vibrations and thinks it was a fortified town. Tyuonyi was a pile of rubble when first photographed.[4]) The Spanish settlers of that era referred to the stone lions on the "Potrero de las Vacas."

Such was the scene, without people, that greeted Adolph Bandelier in 1881. He had been told by a mule driver in one of the Santa Fe hostelries that there were some bones up there in the caves near Bean Creek. When he finally saw the area, he could scarcely believe it. Reports indicate that he was pretty much of a stuffed shirt, but an over-cautious one. He related much of what he saw to the beautiful mountains in Switzerland. His early reports indicated that he looked down on the benighted Indian.[4] Some of this attitude steals through in his "The Delight Makers" (1890).

The second time he covered the area and did his digging away from the Frijoles Canyon vicinity, he became excited about the apparent antiquity of the sites.[6] He also became more precise in his language and reporting; his first visit to the large Yapashi pueblo site succeeded in breaking through his then almost glacial style of reporting. Withal, without his careful reporting, and some popularizing by the public press, the Congress might not have enacted the basement legislation in 1916 for designating Bandelier as a National Monument.

A number of things happened in the vicinity which influenced the subsequent events in Bandelier. We will brush over them quickly — only because they are such a fleeting instant in the total time man has basked in the vari-colored dusks of the gentle piñon-juniper breaks above the great river.

Cochiti Indians congregated in the late 1800's on the west side of the river below Bandelier and added to a few old houses several newer ones. (It was in 1882 that the Cochitis kicked Bandelier out of their pueblo for being too inquisitive.[6]) The Spanish occupied the Cochiti de Cañada Grant in the 1700's and conscripted the ancestors of some of these Indians to work the lands. The land at the mouth of the Cochiti Canyon box proved to be an excellent place for an apple orchard, which it is to this day.

In the 1880's, in the vicinity of Bland about twelve miles south of Frijoles Canyon, a silver strike was made on the north slopes of Bland Canyon.[7] Over the hill to the south a gold and silver vein was located in Colla Canyon, a branch of Peralta Canyon. A small town called Albemarle evolved, only to be followed by a fairly advanced stamp mill in 1898.[8]

In the 1930's, somebody went up the road with a bull dozer and ripped out the high center. The Iron King mine and other lesser ones operated briefly in that decade.[10] Soon the machinery at the Albemarle Mill started disappearing. Not long thereafter, the beautiful old grey and brown weathered boards on most of the falling-apart miners' shacks, bunkhouses, cook shacks, surveyor's office, and mill disappeared into Albuquerque and Santa Fe apartments as complete walls and other decor. Bland was fenced and closed to offset vandalism by a sensitive private owner.

During the mid 1940's, an apricot tree below the old site of Albemarle grew to full fruiting maturity. Some mine cook tossed quantities of apricot seeds into the creek sometime in the past. One seed-pit caught in the crevice above a choke-stone waterfall and took hold. It was still blooming and bearing in 1974. The old tree seemed to miss a heyday every third or fourth year, but the other years it attracted bears, birds, and bees most regularly. The scent was heady downwind.

In the late 1940's and early 1950's, a family of black bears took up residence on the ridge between Albemarle (Colla) and Peralta canyons. Frank Hibben, even then a big-game hunter, took after them with horses and dogs over hill and arroyo, during the appropriate hunting season.[12] I don't think he came back with any bear meat, but he did gin up a great story about seeing "large landlocked pools" in Peralta Creek with trout "that long" in them and herons standing around getting fat on the trapped fish. Jim

Hinsdale and I went in there, found the pools and fish all right. In the telling and listening, the pools and fish had grown three hundred percent. The herons had left a lot of tracks and a few fish, some of which Jim and I caught. After a dinner of natives (cutthroat) and a few rainbows, we sacked out under a full moon, tired. Along about 1:00 a.m. we were awakened by a strong odor. During the night, the cool air from the peaks above (Aspen Peak) started to come down the canyons. By the smell, something was dead up above.

We stirred out of our sleeping bags and climbed the side walls of the canyon and found a less pungent place to finish our sleep. The next morning we followed our noses upwind to find a steer dead and damming up part of the creek a half mile above our camp. Canteens were emptied and filled upstream and breakfast was forgotten.

The Cochiti's increased in number in their pueblo; a small diversion dam on the Rio Grande was built, and the Spanish land grant was acquired at the sheriff's sale (for default of taxes) for the University of New Mexico by Tom Popejoy, then president of the university. Several thousand tons of pumice were removed from part of the grant during the 1940's and 1950's. (Your house or wall might contain such pumice blocks, all made in Albuquerque.)

The Tent Rock Ranch became famous during the early touring car days after World War I. The Bandelier-Cochiti Canyon deer herd was hunted out by 1930. A couple of boot-leggers used the beautiful water of Cochiti Creek during prohibition.

The Forest Service did a road improvement into and through the box in Cochiti Canyon in the mid-1940's. The deer herd came back in good numbers by 1946. They had disappeared again by 1949. Hunters started calling them the Poachiti Indians. There was no doubt poaching was going on but some of us bowhunters found spent shells from at least one BAR (Browning Automatic Rifle). Indians? Hardly. One can imagine that a herd could be cut down with one long burst from a BAR, like an infantry platoon caught in the open.

The Los Alamos School for boys was located on the mesa a few miles north of Frijoles Canyon in the 1930's. It was selected by the U.S. Geological Survey by Lou Mackel, an uncle of mine, now long gone, for the site of the secret Los Alamos Scientific Laboratory in the early 1940's.

The deer in the Bandelier area, including the Cochiti de Cañada Grant, the Dome area (Forest Service) to the west of the west boundary, and to a lesser degree in the upper Frijoles Canyon and some of the Baca Location west of Los Alamos, were believed to be put on the run by saturation hunting and an increased population of burros. The general wildlife protective policy of the National Park Service provided a safe harbor for feral burros with the Monument. Even today they range widely in the vicinity and get back into the refuge at night. They know how to go under the fence in remote areas in many of the canyons and draws.

A few burros got away from prospectors during the mining phase and wandered and adapted upon locating safe harbors. Some romantic souls upon coming to the Los Alamos lab acquired a cute little burro "for the children" and then turned it loose when they left five or more years later. Some burros became feral during the war years in the 1940's when the men folk from the ranches, the grants, and the pueblos went away to war. A few surveys and studies have been made sporadically by the Public Land agencies.

The National Park Service (NPS) in late 1976 decided something had to be done about the winsome little animals (a mature jenny can weigh 750 pounds). They had fairly (or foally) outcompeted all of the big game and many of the smaller animals in the Monument and had reached a population of approximately 140 inside the fence.[11] The overgrazing is excessive and is beginning to be embarassing for the Park Service, since the area is now also National Wilderness. The general policy leans toward no exotic animals in NPS Wilderness, not even cattle. Horses can be visitors, and even mules, but not wild burros, if the Service can help it. The few springs in the Monument are generally fouled by the burros beyond human use except in dire emergencies; so take your water in with you, and treat any you take out of streams. By spring of 1977, the conclusion of the Public meeting in Santa Fe on December 15, 1976 was released:

March 28, 1977: to prevent further wildlife competition and habitat and cultural resource destruction and deterioration by these animals, and to provide the opportunity for the natural systems to restore themselves. These goals will be achieved by (1) a live capture and removal effort, (2) an annual program of direct control by shooting, and (3) exclusion by fencing.[11]

It is notable that there is an area to the southwest that is exempt from these activities "because of research activities." The map was marked USFS Study Area (meaning Forest Service?); but on a National Park Area? This area is generally west of Capulin Canyon. There are a half dozen well-worn tracks across Capulin which the burros use frequently.

The Bandelier National Wilderness Area sequence from a conservationist's viewpoint is narrated here for those find the legal process confusing, boring, or impossibly long. It is a story of dedicated people in private life, in the National Park Service, and in the U.S. Senate and House of Representatives. It is the first Wilderness enactment perpetrated and consummated by the New Mexico Wilderness Study Committee.

Milo Conrad, an electronic technician at Sandia Laboratories in Albuquerque, had been an avid member of the New Mexico Mountain Club for many years. He had observed some of the news reports on the enactment of the Wilderness Act of 1964. During

1965 and 1966 his growing awareness, coupled with his persistence, kindled some interest in the new process of citizen involvement in public land decisions. He insisted upon the establishment of a Wilderness Committee in the Mountain Club.

A number of people from many of the conservation organizations in Albuquerque, New Mexico, and Arizona had been joined in a loose coalition of organizations (both local and national) in a "Save Grand Canyon Committee" during the period of the major threats to the canyon. We were able to bring to bear, along with the dynamic actions of the Sierra Club, a concentrated public awareness and reaction toward a conclusion in which the dams in Marble Canyon and Hualapi Site downstream were defeated. The National Wilderness proposals had been made and the public hearings progressed through many iterations. Jeff Ingram, then the Southwest District Representative of the Sierra Club, stationed in Albuquerque, was the original coordinator pro-tem. I was elected coordinator when Jeff moved to Maine in 1967 and continued in that capacity until the Committee's eventual dissolution in 1971.

Dr. Bob Watt, a Los Alamos Scientific Laboratory physicist, was a river-runner and also was interested in the Canyon's preservation. He joined our efforts as a Sierra Club representative during the peak effort. I was representing the Albuquerque and New Mexico Game Preservation Associations which were renamed the Albuquerque and New Mexico Wildlife and Preservation Associations. In the early 1970's, the name again changed to Albuquerque Wildlife Federation. Jack Kutz was our Save the Grand Canyon Committee treasurer (he being from the Mountain Club). That whole Grand Canyon sequence is described elsewhere in one of the references being generated even now by Kathryn Finch at Resources for the Future, an endowed study.

As our efforts on Grand Canyon started winding down, Milo showed up during the wilderness proposal stages. He had been to a Wilderness Society workshop in Virginia, I believe, and was able to reset our sights on New Mexico wilderness problems. Bob Watt became the chairman of the New Mexico Wilderness Study committee, I the co-chairman. Milo became vice-chairman, and we were off and running in 1968. Our coalition of outdoor organizations and individuals grew through the years. You will hear about its various phases in this book. The first consolidated trip by committee members made into Bandelier in July 1971 included Milo, Heister Drum, Gerry Goodman, Bill Grocke, Bart Barton, Lou Hernandez, and myself. Many of us had been going into the Monument for years. We often touched base with the Park supervisor or one of the Monument rangers, so they knew what we had in mind.

The Park Service had been busy conducting a study during late 1970 and much of 1971. They called a Public Hearing at Los Alamos Inn on December 18, 1971, a Saturday, to make it possible for the public to attend.

Transcription of some parts of our Public Hearing Alert helps set the scene:

Joint Announcement of Wilderness Hearing
1.00 P.M., Saturday, December 18, 197/
Los Alamos, New Mexico

The Park Service study defines Bandelier as 'essentially a concentrated area of ruins and relics of aboriginal man' and goes on to say, 'Its purpose, use, and management concepts are basically different from the wilderness concept. Therefore, it is concluded that none of the lands in the roadless area studied are suitable for wilderness designation. However, large portions of the Monument shall continue to be managed with the least intrusion of contemporary works of man, consistent with the basic purpose of its establishment.

Environmental organizations in New Mexico and throughout the nation share a firm conviction that the lands in the roadless area of Bandelier National Monument qualify as wilderness and should be given the protection of the 1964 Wilderness Act. They believe that a wilderness classification is consistent with the archaeological purpose for which the Monument was established.

There is no incompatibility between the wilderness concept and the preservation of the prehistoric ruins, since the Wilderness Act, other acts of Congress and National Park Service regulations make provision for the flexibility of management of wilderness areas. Therefore, in conferring wilderness status upon Bandelier, Congress could provide for any of the management measures reasonably deemed necessary by the Park Service for executing its archaeological studies and programs and stabilizing and protecting excavated areas, such as the 'mechanical equipment, complex land-management measures in sections of the roadless area, and extension of management roads' mentioned in its wilderness study. Wilderness classification will not change the basic policies of the Monument, result in any adverse impact, or in any manner lower the standards evolved for its use and preservation.

The roadless area has been a de facto wilderness and has been managed as such for over half a century without prejudice to the historic-archaeological concept for which the Monument was established.

1. Propose that a Bandelier National Monument Wilderness of approximately 22,133 acres be established.

2. Support additions to the Monument, as proposed in the Park Service master plan, and recommend that suitable parts of these be given wilderness protection.

Seventeen New Mexico and national outdoor organizations joined in endorsing the Alert and distributing it.

Following the public hearing, the National Park Service acceded to the public's recommendation and suggested an area of about two-thirds might be wilderness. Congressman Lujan introduced a Bill in 1973 (his H.R. 3453). He negotiated an east boundary that made more sense. The matter of the enclave "to protect the Stone Lion Shrine" came up.

This one-page précis of the New Mexico Wilderness Study Committee contained the following text which accompanied the bill:

Bandelier Wilderness H.R. 3453

Bandelier National Monument presently contains 29,661 acres situated on a seven to eight thousand foot plateau in northcentral New Mexico about 45 road miles northwest of Santa Fe. This high plateau, formed of compressed volcanic ash, is cut by a number of canyons, some up to 800 feet deep. The eastern boundary of the Monument is the Rio Grande, entrenched in spectacular White Rock Canyon, 1200 feet deep and the most popular white-water boating run in New Mexico. Along the Rio Grande the lowest elevations of Bandelier occur, averaging 5250 feet above sea level. Piñon-juniper and sagebrush cover the lower mesas and hillsides while forests of Ponderosa pine, spruce, fir and aspen cloak the higher elevations along the northern and western boundaries. In addition to the Rio Grande, several streams run year around and others have water during wetter times.

By Presidential proclamation Bandelier was designated a National Monument in 1916 in order to protect the circa 1200-1600 AD archaeological sites. Fortunately since designation, traffic in the Monument backcountry has been restricted to foot and horseback travel thereby preserving a small oasis of wilderness in the once totally wild Jemez Mountains.

The trails in and out of the canyons and connecting the backcountry ruins with the Shrine of the Stone Lions may be the same ones used by the original inhabitants. Except for the pueblo ruins, several Adirondack-type shelters, and a few primitive foot bridges in Frijoles Canyon, there is no evidence of man's presence in the 22,133 acres conservationists propose for Wilderness designation.

Visitation in the developed portion of Bandelier increased from 47,059 in 1950 to 201,213 in 1970. Backcountry use has also increased from 899 in 1969 to 1375 in the first nine months of 1971. These figures, however, reflect only part of the growing use of Bandelier since they come from registrations at Park Headquarters in Frijoles Canyon. Hikers from nearby Los Alamos to the north and Albuquerque, 50 miles to the south, usually use closer entrances and are not recorded.

But use of Bandelier and human pressures on its delicate wilderness and archaeological resources will undergo even more rapid increase in the near future. Cochiti Dam, scheduled for completion in early 1975, will flood the lower part of White Rock Canyon and provide motorboat access to the Monument's now remote southeastern corner. Not only is Cochiti Lake envisioned to become New Mexico's major recreation area with an annual use by 1,600,000 people, but a major recreation subdivision of 50,000 people is being developed on the lake shore.

The Park Service's Master Plan states that '(P)rotection and interpretation of the ruins and preservation of the natural setting have been and will continue to be the purpose of the Service's management of Bandelier National Monument.' In consideration of the rapidly growing use of Bandelier, protection can be best achieved by placing the backcountry area in the National Wilderness Preservation System.

Approximately forty people testified at the December 18, 1971, public hearing at Los Alamos, New Mexico, and all testified in favor of the conservationists' proposal to include the Monument in the Wilderness Preservation System. Many of those testifying were Los Alamos high school students, and the long-term value of the Bandelier Wilderness to them is a fact deserving serious consideration.

Frank Diluzio tells this story from his old Los Alamos days: In 1952 a House Committee was investigating mismanagement of funds at Los Alamos Scientific Laboratory. It had to do with supposed misuse of gasoline for entertainment. Carol Tyler was Atomic Energy Commission Manager, and Congressman Snyder of West Virginia appeared. In the process the AEC officials took the Committee to Frijoles Canyon where Congressman Snyder saw a burro and was enamored by the eyes with the long lashes.

Later, Manager Tyler put out an order for a burro and one was captured and shipped to West Virginia. Three weeks went by, but no response from Snyder. A tracer was put on from both ends. The agent in West Virginia said that "we had been looking all over hell for a chest of drawers, but couldn't concentrate on it because we had a jackass that nobody would claim, kicking hell out of my station." Now, if you will carefully misspell burro until it resembles bureau, you will get it. The Committee never could find that extra ten gallons of gas.

As late as April, 1977, the Park Service put out an invitation for people who wanted a burro to make application, to describe how they proposed to catch it, and how they proposed subsequently to care for the burro. Following the announcement the threat was made of having to shoot the animals if enough were not taken by proposed live capture methods. I think that there is some complication which related to not being able to sell government property. Does one have to return the corpus if the burro dies? Can you sell the live one to your brother-in-law? Can you raffle one off at a baseball game? I recall a mean shetland pony which changed hands via raffles at least ten times. It had long eye lashes, too, and a cute little saddle.

All wild game is the property of the State of New Mexico. The wild horses and burros belong to the federal government and are not to be considered wild game. But now, fair game?

Following Congressman Lujan's introduction of the

Bandelier Wilderness — Boundary Peak.

Bandelier Bill in 1973, the Park Service generated a proposal to have an enclave encompassing the Stone Lion Shrine and the Stone Lion Pueblo site. It was intended that a shelter be erected to shield the Stone Lions from further weathering. They already have practically melted and somebody tried to use a prospecting pick or chisel to sharpen up the features unsuccessfully. Then somebody used what may have been charcoal to darken the eyes. It all added up to vandalism, no matter how well meant. History says that "Mexicans first knocked off one lion's head."[6]

The enclave was intended to contain a cabin to house a ranger to control the visitations to the shrine and the pueblo. There were some proposed concessions wherein the river boundary and the enclave were conjecturally traded off against each other. No action culminated during 1973. No shelter existed as late as 1979.

On March 22, 1974, the Subcommittee of National Parks and Recreation of the House Interior and Insular Affairs Committee held a meeting in Washington. Dorothy Hoard and I attended and testified. The final bill stipulated 22,030 acres and an enclave area of 500 acres.

Senator Domenici had already introduced the Agency's Bill (February 7, 1974) of 21,110 acres. Then Carl Bowman showed up at the Senator's office. Carl is the son of a Los Alamos scientist and had spent many trips in the back country of the monument without any knowledge of us, or we of him. Heister Drum, an Albuquerque attorney, had been our Bandelier honcho for several years. Neither he, nor the Park Service, was aware of Carl's interest. Milo was still vitally interested in maintaining the pressure on the legislative process in mid-1975 according to his letters to all of us. George Grossman of Santa Fe (State Highway Department engineer) meticulously did the boundaries on our final maps time and time again.

Senator Montoya supported a bill in November 1975 similar to Lujan's and Domenici's 1974 bills. The Senate bill was then numbered S-731 (Sen. Domenici). That bill had quite a bit more area than any previous ones of ours. Carl Bowman used some different criteria from ours. Different studies of the high water mark of the proposed Cochiti Dam downstream were partial reasons. The Jemez addition and the Frijolito addition added 637 and 60 acres to S-731. The final water level of the spillway of the dam was 5460.5 feet and the proposed eastern boundary was 5,475 feet to allow motor boat beaching below the boundary.

Our man in back of the scenes, our chief honcho of Bandelier, kept putting together the final proposal. The House and Senate committees finally passed it, under public law Law 94-567, a Bandelier National Wilderness of 23,267 acres. The law was signed by President Gerald Ford on October 20, 1976. Don Campbell was sent to the Washington hearings by the New Mexico Wilderness Commission. His testimony for Governor Jerry Apodaca was dated February 1976. Victory was almost an anti-climax.

The adjoining Forest Service land to the west of the Monument-Wilderness is what we call the proposed St. Peter's Dome Wilderness addition. The roadless area within the Cañada de Cochiti Grant presently owned by the University of New Mexico contains about 2,900 acres. All these areas could make a composite National Wilderness of 36,667 acres if the jurisdictional problems can be negotiated.

Dorothy Hoard has done such a delightful "Hiker's Guide to Bandelier National Monument" that the usual trails and routes have been omitted from this chapter.[13] You might consider going into the Wilderness Area from the south even though the trail access is best from the north and west sides of the area. Andy Metal now lives in the Cochiti Lake townsite and can advise you on the best jump-off points he has discovered on the south side.

Annex to
BANDELIER NATIONAL WILDERNESS

The Dome Area along the west boundary of the Bandelier Wilderness was hot and pungent on June 15, 1977. Little rain had fallen since one sluicing early cloudburst in late May. The light wind shook wraiths of pollen out of the mixture of trees along the Eagle Canyon road going to the pumice mines on the southwest corner of the Wilderness.

The Forest Service report said that the big fire was started by a motorcycle on that afternoon. It was not lightning, at least. It has been the habit of the bikers to drive up to the road closure cables and lift them over their heads as they passed underneath. The roads to the various pumice scrapes must make a wild ride. We had heard the engines several times and thought that they might be chain saws.

Some of the cables were often open during the week where they were hauling out of the mining area, but they seemed to be closed on weekends and when some of the scraping areas were shut down. To the best of our knowledge, no damage was done by the bikers and they had little reason to go off the roads.

The fire spread quickly and by the morning of June 16 it was well on its way toward Saint Peter's Dome road and making a highly visible smoke pall. Alarm ran through Los Alamos and White Rock when they got a whiff of the smoke.

As I go through my notes, they say:

"It was on Sunday, June 19, that the fire jumped State Road 4 and got into one of the Los Alamos sites where it was put out quickly. The fire had grown to 8,500 acres by then. The news reports carried statistics of one thousand firefighters being used. Some ashes have been noted on the Los Alamos cars periodically since Saturday. It is now Tuesday and the fire is almost a week old.

The Santa Fe New Mexican reported that a Bandelier Ranger was killed. Word of mouth has it that some Forest Service man was also fatally smoked. A 51-year-old fire stomper had a heart attack. The flames could be seen from Los Alamos at night. The 'slurry planes look awfully small in the clouds of smoke,' according to Mel Price. The road around to White Rock from LASL was closed. Some of the home owners in White Rock watered their roofs during the hot part of the day. The winds were 30-40 mph on Saturday and Sunday. Dorothy Hoard was home — probably keeping the home fires from burning.

The Forest Service closed all of the National Forests in New Mexico as of Saturday morning, June 19. Scott Simmons and I were in the Polvadera Peak area eighteen or so miles north of the fire on Saturday and Sunday. It was windy (30 mph or so) in that area, particularly on Sunday. Jay Sorenson and his family were rafting in the Chama River Box at the same time and were bothered by crosswinds.

Scott and I had a grandstand seat of the fire scene as we were coming out the Clara road into Espanola on Sunday afternoon. The whole Chama Valley looked as if it had a temperature inversion, even though the temperature was over 90 °F and the humidity was an unmeasurable 5% RH. The sweet aromatic smell of the pine olefines made a cup of coffee taste good to me.

We heard about the National Forest closure on the way out on the car radio not long before we ran into a fire roadblock about five miles west of Espanola. The block was on the (Clara) road along the elbow that turns northeast just before it starts to climb to the scarf on the mountain. Several hundred people were also there attending a "Summer Solstice International Brother and Sisterhood" meeting. Hopefully they were able to directly observe their sun tomorrow on the 22 of June. Much of the cloud from the fire was passing directly over their camp and making a peculiar purple-green hue in the atmosphere. Were they having some kind of an experience or getting a sign of some kind?

"A light smattering or rain washed ashes across the windshield of the dead Bandelier Ranger." (Radio news). Remember that red sunrise which greeted the prehistoric Indian at the beginning of this chapter?

The Forest Service has already called Dave Foreman (our current Study Committee Chairman) to tell him that they want to go in with a burned timber salvage operation, reforest planting, and then heal the perimeter roads. The Forest Service has been unable to get any contractor in to do the salvage timbering at the Jemez fire site and may have the same problem on this fire. We will have to get in after the fire and see how much of our 10,500 acre Dome Roadless Area is forever disqualified. How far into the Bandelier Wilderness the fire will progress waits to be seen. The latest report tonight is that the fire has consumed 11,000 acres and is not yet contained.

The final statistics are apparently 15,270 acres burned; 1,500 fire fighters were used; and it burned a week. The cost is estimated at $13 million plus $1 million to fight the fire, and $220,000 is revegetation costs.[14]

The National Park Service, on June 28, 1977, talked to Laine Heiser, the administrative aide to the New Mexico Wilderness Study Commission, and said that there were 150 to 200 deer and elk moving into the browse area of the Bandelier burros as a direct result of the fire. They plan to quickly eliminate the burros, since they cannot condone the use of a hay-drop. They would like us to send wires or letters to Secretary Andrus to the effect that we agree. I suggested to Laine that the Commission should also send an 'unfortunately agreeable' statement and she said she would get it started. I plan to call our honchos (Heister Drum and Dorothy Hoard) to see if they agree with the text of the message. I have some reservations about the capacity of the range to sustain the ungulates even with the month of rain which we are anticipating. The new grass could possibly sustain the small number of elk but the deer need forbs and brush-browse which the burros have long since removed. Consequently, I am not sure that burro removal will solve the problem.

The notes contain an Albuquerque Journal clipping dated July 6, 1977, to the effect that a two-hour thunderstorm caused a flash flood. The flood was attributed to excessive run-off as a result of defoliation from the fire twenty days earlier. The reseeding program was also disrupted. (In 1979 the [wheat] grass was waist high and the Grand Canyon canaries were still in fine voice near the southern boundary.)

CHAPTER 4:
Aldo Leopold National Wilderness

The southern tip of the Aldo Leopold National Wilderness area is about 32 miles airline east of Silver City in the southwestern part of New Mexico. State Highway 90 strikes out westward from I-25 at Caballo Reservoir south of Truth or Consequences about 15 miles. Highway 90 climbs to Emory Pass, the south trailhead into the wilderness. The road (90) thence drops downward to Silver City. The wilderness encompasses most of the Black Range as it extends north from Emory Pass. Get an Aldo Wilderness map from the ranger stations at Truth or Consequences, Silver City, on Mimbres Road, or Beaverhead when they are open.

Aldo Leopold was a Forest Ranger in the southwestern part of new Mexico in the early 1920's. He had a strange attitude for a man steeped in the "agricultural crop oriented" tree-farmer trained Forest Service of that day. He was given many different titles by his supervision over the years, some perhaps out of embarrassment at his persistent ideas and his probing for facts beyond the numbers of MBF (thousand board feet) of timber. His story is heavily documented and his attitudes now well known through his own publications.[1]

The Gila Wilderness, largely through Leopold's intense campaign, was designated on June 3, 1924, as the first area in the country to carry the Wilderness classification with a capital W. The Black Range was included in the original area. In 1931-32, the "administrative road" was driven up North Star canyon from North Star Mesa. The Forest Service Regulations about roads in wilderness were not very clear at that time. By 1933, under their Regulation L-20, the lands east of the North Star Mesa Road became the Black Range Primitive Area, and no longer considered a part of the Gila National Wilderness.

Grazing permittees put in several tanks for watering their cattle where they were successful in getting usable wells. These tanks had primitive roads leading to them so ranchers could take in salt cake and otherwise administer to their cattle. Hunters used these roads and so did the propectors. Weekend Jeep riders also found most of those old side roads in the succeeding years.

The Forest Service made an "Aldo Leopold Wilderness" Proposal in 1970. The New Mexico Wilderness Study Committee made a Wilderness Proposal of 231,737 acres, considerably larger than the Forest Service's 150,731 acres. We had worked for more than two years by the time of the December 1970 meetings in Truth or Consequences and Silver City.

That was a thumbnail, bare-bones account of a critical fifty years in the eons-long formulation of the Black Range. Let's look at it in several other contexts.

The upthrust of the main mass of the Black Range had its start around 25 million years ago based upon the finding of trilobites common in the Paleozoic geologic era. These fossils were contained in coastal sea beds which were carried upwards by massive lava upthrusts from a restless magma underlying the whole region. Down through the millenia, successive intrusions of complex combinations of hot and cold igneous and sedimentary rock masses built the mountain.[6]

The ground was still rocking aperiodically when some bedraggled Cochise Indians in Moccasin John Canyon four miles east of Diamond Peak, found a hot spring and a large fumerole in the middle of a late fall snowstorm. How long they were snowed in is unknown and how many stayed in the warm fumerole is indeterminate. They did leave some sketches on the walls and I think the little den started to cave in while they were still in it. Two of us latter-day bow hunters spent the night in that lava-lined overhang on a blustery trip toward Diamond Peak in the fall of 1969. The fumerole had cooled down in the ensuing 10,000 years. I still have a piece of realgar, a rock containing arsenic sulfide which was deposited by the prehistoric hot spring near the fumerole. The Indians probably ate snow instead of drinking the smelly water from the hot spring.

Al Price, a herder living in Truth or Consequences in the 1955-56 years, showed me some bird-points (obsidian arrowheads), some chert arrowheads for larger game, and an couple of broken lance points. The hide scrapers and a hand axe all were reported to have been found near Monument Park in the Lookout Mountain vicinity. He knew of no potsherds in the same locale so we could not approximate the time frame of the find.

Although I have talked to some of the Mescaleros at the Agency Office east of Tularosa and to the White Mountain Apaches on the San Carlos Indian Reservation in Arizona, I could not discover any other specific prehistoric information about the Black Range. There were some generalities one can derive from some of the references but even the early Spanish tended to avoid the area in favor of the more gentle and accessible Gila Wilderness to the west.[2,3,4]

Ancient Mimbreño traffic generally swung around the area to the north when they wanted to transit east-west or the reverse. There is some evidence in the Taylor Creek and Beaverhead areas of the old Indian encampments and some hogans which must have been occupied during the wetter years. They seemed to spend the winters in the Reserve, Luna, and Apache Creek area. (Perhaps they liked to harass the Mogollon Rim peoples from that base.)

There is a lot of history about the Mimbreños, particulary about their advanced technology in ceramics. They occupied the Mimbres River bottoms and the adjacent canyons for centuries and withstood frequent raids by the Mescalero Apaches who made an end run around the southern end of the Mimbres Mountains in the vicinity of Cook's Peak.[4]

The Apaches from the Arizona bases west of the Blue Range generally avoided confrontations with the raiding parties of the Mescalero Apaches, although they were related. The Silver City-Deming territory during the AD 900-1100 period was an overlapping of the raiding territories of both groups. The peaceful Mimbreños caught it from both vectors. Some of them hid in caves in the Black Canyon area and left some of their more valuable pots. A drought in the early 1300's probably drove them out.[2]

The Spanish appeared to be preoccupied with staying on a route far to the east along the Rio Grande.[5] Spanish prospectors from El Paso del Norte went into the Gila in the mid-1600's and saw some of the abandoned cultivated areas of the Mimbreños. These prospectors did not stay long because any isolated small groups of Spaniards not accompanied by soldiers were attacked by Apaches. They brought back stories of abandoned cliff dwellings but little news of gold or silver. One mention of badly worn boots and lava mountainsides was reported by Fray Antonio de San Buenaventura Olivares.[6] His geography was notably vague.

During much of the 1600's and 1700's, the whole Gila-Black Range area was a relatively exclusive hunting preserve for the Indians and these hunters were dominantly Apaches. A few sporadic attempts to prospect were made by small Spanish groups that did not bother to record their failures. There were very few remains of arrastras in the whole area and practically no prospect holes or cuts when the miners in the early 1800's first roamed the hills.

The plains Indians set up what was known as the "Comanche Curtain" to the east of the Rocky Mountains. That curtain of hostility extended from the Dakotas well down into Texas. The mountain men knew how to circumvent it by going up the Platte River and a few other routes during the seasons when they knew some of the tribes would be hunting elsewhere. Consequently, the few mountain men that came into the state during the 1600-1700 period came from the north and the Spanish gave them a cool welcome. Very few of them made it into the southwestern part of the state. A couple of Indian-French Canadians may have been killed by the Hot Springs Apaches in the eary 1700's.[6]

There is a record of a couple of Frenchmen, the brothers Mallet, who showed up in Pecos and Santa Fe in 1739. They had bought their way through the Comanche Curtain with guns which they gave to the Indians.[7] They were later ejected from the territory for using strongarm tactics. Later in 1752, another couple of French traders showed up in Santa Fe with four thousand pounds of trade goods which they had brought down from Canada via the Great Lakes. These traders brought stories of how this entire area belonged to the French and that the governor lived in New Orleans and had the Louisiana Territory in his purview. The Spanish were very cautious and stalled for time to see if any troops were standing in the vanguard somewhere. They accused the Françoises of having stolen the trade goods. The Spanish governor had meticulous records made of the transactions but these records did not get to Spain until 1754. The Françoises were escorted eastward toward the Llano Estacado, the Staked Plains, and pointed toward Louisiana with something of a sigh of relief by their hosts.[7]

The Indians in the towns along the Camino Real in the vicinities of present day Truth of Consequences, Hatch, and Las Cruces told their Spanish padres how they had seen a couple of black-bearded white men with red and purple shirts in the eastern foothills of the Black Range. These men were taking turns riding one horse and leading two Indian women who were tied to each other and the horse. They were last seen going north, in the vicinity of present day Chloride.[6] The Mallet brothers had been earlier described as having colored caps and coats in a land of homespun clothing.

The Black Range is the archetype of a wilderness defending itself. People have been involved throughout the years with its periphery but have had little involvement with its central features. It has only been in recent years that there has been enough traffic to keep some of the trails visible during midsummer. One is constantly having to do a detective job to find the trail emerging from many of the clearings. Not only is the tread overgrown in the clearings, but the understory frequently masks the blazes where the trail again enters the timber. In some locations, horsemen have lopped off the high branches possibly for more adequate pack-clearance. That has left scars more dominant than the old blazes. Withal, the mark of man has restored quickly with few exceptions.

"West of the Jornada del Muerto," says the Forest Service (1970) Proposed Aldo Leopold Wilderness pamphlet, "early settlers along the Rio Grande del Norte in south-central New Mexico looked upon the dark, forbidding appearance of the Sierra Diablo, or Devil Mountains, with fear and distrust. There in the deep canyons and along the high ridges, wily and well-armed Apaches led by Mangas Coloradas, Cochise, Nana, Victorio, and Geronimo lived and controlled all entry into their country."

The pamphlet continued: "In 1846, Lt. Emory led a small band of U.S. Cavalry across the mountains by a route which now bears his name. His trip preceded by some thirty years the coming of settlers who were hearty enough to challenge not only the Apaches but the inhospitable ruggedness of the mountains that the whites called the Black Range. Few settlers lasted long enough to make a home. Between 1872 and 1900 small mining towns sprang up in the eastern foothills of the Black Range at Chloride, Hermosa, Hillsboro, and Kingston. During the mining boom between 1882 and 1896, millions of dollars worth of gold and silver were recovered from mines and placers. Within the area proposed for Wilderness, however, few ventured and fewer left a sign of their passing. A few scattered rotting cabin logs, old mining claim corners, or an occasional cablin clearing are all that are left of the attempts to tame this wild country. If Lt. Emory, Victorio, Geronimo, or any other of those of the shadowed past could visit the area today, they would find it much as they last saw it."

You will find at the end of the chapter that there are many pleasant trails and routes which you can take through this mountain stronghold. It is much easier to make the transit without being sniped at from the rimrocks. Some of the routes are too tight or too steep for the horseman, but the backpacker should have little trouble if he keeps his head and carries enough water.

Those mining years were too exciting to brush past so lightly. Let us look at some of the events in their own time frame.

The Santa Rita copper mine was purported to have been originally located by an Indian in the late 1700's. The Spanish and Mexican miners operated the mines until about 1860 with the brief exception of ownership by the (French) Pattie brothers. The mining property was quite typically surrounded by turreted walls made of waste (stone), much as the mines of Mexico had been fortified for a hundred and fifty years. This kind of a fortification, manned by armed men, provided a virtual fiefdom, a feudal estate in which various means of indentured labor could be practiced. Many of the Indians caught in the web were never heard of again.

There was much activity in other copper mining in that vicinity, which was far removed from the Black Range. Fort Bayard was established by the U.S. Army and imposed a growing law and order in the district at mid-century. The newly declared Territory of New Mexico (in 1850) imposed no government presence in the area. Those copper mining activities had some by-product influence on the Black Range, far to the northeast. In 1860, for example, gold was discovered in Pinos Altos, about six miles north of Silver City by some drifting California miners. Then the Georgetown discoveries in 1866 flashed on the scene with the rich silver leads.[8] Georgetown is only about thirty miles west of Emory Pass, but it might as well have been a hundred miles from the yet undiscovered mines on the east side of the Black Range.

During the winter and spring of 1861, the Apaches constantly menaced the life and property of the miners. In September of that year, Mangas Coloradas and Cochise attacked the miners at the site of the Pacific mine with a force of approximately five hundred Indians. The miners won, but several thousands of them left that part of the Territory for fear of reprisals. Many new discoveries continued to be made in that southern part of the Gila Mountains for the next fifteen years.

It was much later, in the spring of 1877, that gold was discovered near the present town of Hillsboro on the eastern slopes of the Black Range. Kingston, some nine miles west up near the ridge, jumped to life in 1880. By that time the Atchison, Topeka, and the Santa Fe Railroad had come down the Rio Grande Valley. In 1881, the Apaches were still irate and constantly plagued the intruders at every opportunity. They had been uprooted from the Cooke's Peak area in the late 1870's and were madder than ever.

The Las Vegas (N.M. Territory) Mining World, April 20, 1882, announced: "This present spring it is safer than it was last year on the eastern slope of the Black Range, for the reason that Gen. MacKenzie runs that part of the Territory....There are four forts in a radius of forty miles. At Silver Camp they have organized a good company among themselves, and have on hand one hundred stands of arms, and also have a good temporary stone fort for their own protection in case of attack by the Apaches."

The new railroad unloaded not only the supplies needed for mining the Black Range at Caballo Station, but it brought in a lot of starry-eyed people with new picks and shovels and inadequate shoes. Many did not have the money to pay the stagecoach fare to Hillsboro so they walked the 17 miles. There was little water until they got close to town and it was badly polluted by the mining and sewage from the town. The stagecoach was actually an old freight wagon that followed the tracks of the pack horses and mules. The skinners would often boost the fare out of sight because they had been given a premium price to carry dynamite to the mines. The Apaches learned to start fires in the freight yard while the train was pulling out. This seems to have been a tactical invention of the Mescalero Apaches, according to F.M. Endlich's article "The Mining Regions of Southern New Mexico" (1883).

The first vehicle of any kind to get up to Kingston was an ambulance drawn by eight horses. It was driven by Col. John Logan and Col. A.W. Harris in the spring of 1881. Reports tell of endless brushcutting to make way for the rig.[8]

Very few individuals are uniquely identified with specific Wilderness areas in New Mexico. Ben Lilly is an exception to most rules. The Gila Wilderness was his stamping grounds and the Black Range was part of it. Although I do not plan to do a chapter on the Gila (it is so well documented already), I have to tell you about him. Ben would do a rapid rotation in his grave if I left him out because he had some wild old times in the Devil Mountains. So let's get him out of the way before he puts a hex on us from wherever he is.

Ben Lilly was a bear and lion hunter from Louisiana who moved into the southwestern part of the state some time in 1914.[9] He was probably 57 years old at that time. He worked on and off as a government hunter for 10 years or so. During that time he coursed over most of the Gila, Blue, and Black Ranges — night and day.

The first record of his hunting the Black Range was in 1918 with Dr. A.K. Fisher of the U.S. Biological Survey. Dr. Fisher's report was only casually about Ben but mostly on insect infestation of Diamond Creek Canyon. Ben was next heard of when he made a large blaze on a tree and wrote why he killed a steer that had caught its foot in a rock crevice near the Diamond Creek Trail. I saw a flat boulder on top of Spring Mountain with the notation "TIP (1926) LILLY" where he buried his favorite dog which had been killed by a grizzly. In another spot near the site of the old James Brothers Cabin, I saw a carefully incised lion track and two lion scrapes (including claw marks) in a limestone slab. Although somebody had been pounding on it recently, one could still make out the picture of a bee followed by a V. LILLY. It had no date. It is known that he spent some of the winter of 1930 snowed in at James Ranch near Chloride.

Ben seemed to like to leave his own petroglyphs. He left a chiseled foot print in Hot Springs Canyon on a cliff face about twice life sized. The heel had a burro shoe imprint upon it. (He was known to use such shoes.)

This chapter is not intended to include a complete chronological record of the area. I have taken the liberty of deciding which events had some impact on the Black Range. Ben Lilly pretty well cleaned out the bear and lions, particulary the grizzly.

The old Mimbres Mill, although west of the Black Range, caused considerable traffic in burro, mule, and horse-packed ores to generate a half-dozen trails from as far north as Chloride and Hermosa on the east side of the range. There were a few deposits of odd minerals in small quantities which were hauled by wagons down some of the canyons on the west side of the Range. In some cases these old roads started bad erosion gullys. The east side traffic after 1883 went east to the railroad and the upper parts of the mountain lapsed into somnolence. The Apaches still attempted to drive out "Los Godammies" as late as 1904.[8,10] As far as the records show, Ben Lilly was never harassed by Indians unless he played some practical joke on them. He went into a camp of sleeping White Mountain Apaches in Arizona one night with a bear skin over him. By the time the Indians scattered and came back, a grinning Ben was standing by their campfire.

Most of the edible game (with the exceptions of bear and lion) was cleaned out of the areas within 20 to 30 miles of the operating mines by 1900. The beaver started to come back by 1890 and the fishing improved. Some mining continued to cause stream siltation. It was not until the 1930's that the State Department of Game and Fish had replanted many of the native species. The Gila trout in Diamond Creek had somehow survived so that stream was not planted with competing species.

Let's get back to Aldo Leopold and his monumental task of getting the Gila-Black Range Wilderness Area enacted as the first National Wilderness in 1924 and thence march forward to the present. Why is it necessary to generate legislation to give legal protection to an area which has so successfully defended itself for eons?

Leopold appeared to have an uncanny ability to foresee coming events as they would affect the vast sweep of public lands. He had studied the events associated with the expanding population and had witnessed a spectrum of the inroads into the National Forests to which he was assigned.

He was not completely alone but he was lonesome in his beliefs. The Forest Service developed regulations applying to various of the uses of the National Forest.[11] These regulations did not arrive in full bloom at first issuance but evolved over many tribulations throughout the country. There was some opinion among the younger foresters that the regulations were too lax and some of the forest supervisors thought they were too strict. The supervisors, being generally good, dedicated men, felt that they could administer their forests better if they had more liberty than the "Regs" implied. Leopold went through both cycles. In any event, the Forest Service Regulations were instrumental as one of the backgrounds of the Wilderness Act of 1964.

Many of the facets of these Forest Service Regulations pertaining to National Wilderness were developed out of the problems of managing the Gila National Wilderness, the first one enacted in 1924. Immediately and full-fledged were the problems of controlling grazing, timbering, mining, forest fires, insect infestation, road and fence construction, wood hauling, hunting, fishing, wildlife propagation, and even cabin building.

Our own U.S. Senator Clinton P. Anderson was chairman of the Senate committee which wrote and obtained the enactment of the Wilderness Act of 1964. He and his committee drew in the dedicated experts from the Wilderness Society and the land agencies.[12]

Recall that the Black Range was withdrawn from the Gila National Wilderness in 1932. The Forest Service has vacillated in its wilderness management attitudes to both extremes. In some early years there was a great preoccupation with purity. Then the next thing that happened was Forest Service bulldozers grinding away at the North Star Road through the Wilderness to connect the Mimbres and Beaverhead Ranger Stations. The Black Range became a Primitive Area instead of a Wilderness.

Another round was fired on August 7, 1952. The Forest Sevice proposed to reduce the Gila Primitive Area by almost forty percent for lumbering operations. The public strenuously objected and furthermore instructed the Forest Service to enforce the wheeled vehicle restrictions against jeep invasions of the Gila and Black Range Primitive Areas on both sides of the North Star Road. A Primitive Area is an administratively controlled roadless area under U.S. Forest Service jurisdiction. Such areas are managed by selection of appropriate regulations by the Forest Supervisor and not by provisions of the Wilderness Act. A lax supervisor could allow abusive multiple uses and sometimes was forced to disregard such situations. Aldo Leopold was well aware of these threats.

A series of cloud seeding attempts at weather modification occurred in the 1950's. Silver iodide was used in the summer and carbon dioxide in the winter. Seeding was done without notice in California, Arizona, Utah, and New Mexico. Sometimes the storm fronts moved into adjacent states before much had happened locally. Ranchers were known to have rented silver iodide generators and operated them for weeks at a time. The weathermen in the region suspected that some of the major gully washers, floods, and extremely heavy snowfalls in the Black Range during these years could be blamed on the cloud seeding. Nobody proved anything, however. But the Forest Service (the Gila National Forest Supervisor) said that "weather modification projects would be foregone if the Black Range (again) becomes Wilderness." The Wilderness Act is not as specific.

Other threats soon reared their heads. In about 1950 the Forest Service went into its famous Smokey Bear syndrome. "Stamp out all fires and right now." Some very heroic episodes followed. The results were far-reaching. Extensive fuel piles accumulated. The Black Range and the Gila became one vast tinder-box and we could expect a cataclysmic holocaust at any moment. Normally, cleanup fires are started by lightning and gradually remove the understory during the rainy seasons without killing the timber.

The interference with that normal process of forest accession thus permitted the insect infestations to run unchecked by the naturally occurring fires. The forest was therefore driven closer to the climax condition than most natural unmanipulated forests ever get. The forest floor produced very few forbs and wildlife foods without the perennial fires. It was only in 1975 that the Forest Service recognized the necessity to start some prescribed burning on a limited scale. So far we have not had the holocaust which is so feared. Some lightning fires are permitted to burn, but under strict observance. Others are started when the conditions are right. (Man seems to have learned after all.) A retired forester, C.K. Collins, may have been partially instrumental in bringing a new awareness on the role of fire in the woodlands.

The U.S. Geological Survey and the U.S. Bureau of Mines are required to make mineral surveys of wilderness and primitive areas in accordance with the provisions of the Wilderness Act. Such a study was made on the Black Range from 1967 to 1969, and Geological Survey Bulletin 1319-E was issued in 1970. The Summary contains the following:

> No commercial or potentially commercial mineral deposits were found in the primitive area, but the area is near the well-known Silver City-Santa Rita mining district, and a possibility for existence of buried ore deposits cannot be eliminated. Many small ore deposits occur along the eastern and southern sides of the area studied, within a few miles of the Primitive Area boundary.

In another part it says:

> The volcanic rocks of Tertiary age, which cover most of the study area, have an aggregate maximum thickness of nearly 17,000 feet. However, none of the units is continuous over the entire area and the maximum thickness of the volcanic sequence at any one place in the area is probably less than 7,000 feet.

U.S. Senator Pete Domenici testified on May 20, 1975, to the Interior Committee on the proposed Aldo Leopold Wilderness and introduced "a letter which was given to me by Mr. Corry McDonald, Chairman, New Mexico Wilderness Committee and that I would ask that it be included in the hearing record." He had introduced our proposed bill which was numbered S.226, January 17, 1975, in the 1st Session of the 94th Congress.

During the same hearings, Woodville J. Walker for Phelps-Dodge, and Fred E. Ferguson, Jr. for the American Mining Congress, presented testimony that there might be copper under the volcanic overlay and that they cannot anticipate being technologically capable of exploiting the resource for at least thirty years. These organizations are consistent in that they made virtually the same statement in the 1972 hearings. This tactic has been in effect a stalling tactic, and the Congress has demurred passage.

Our position has been one of "put up or shut up." If no one wants to try to put a drill down through 7,000 feet of volcanic rock, then why not go at it with a shaft and tunnel from the east side of the Range? We have offered to introduce them to Robert O. Anderson (Atlantic Richfield Company Chairman) who owns the lands adjacent to the area and to the east. Such mining would not affect the surface wilderness which we propose. The hard fact is that as long as copper is available at unit mining costs comparable with current open pit levels, nobody is going to put up the millions to prove that there is some copper under more than a mile of strange mixtures of five different volcanic rocks that tend to defy drilling.

United States Senator Harrison Schmitt, being both an astronaut and a geologist, as well as just thoroughly understanding public opinion in his home town Silver City, expressed concern about the Wilderness Act cutoff date of January 1, 1984, after which no mineral patents within a national forest wilderness area would be issued except for valid claims existing on that date. We were able to point out that under Section 4(d)(2) of the Act that:

> the Secretary of the Interior shall develop and conduct in consultation with the Secretary of Agriculture, such areas shall be surveyed on a planned, recurring basis consistent with the concept of wilderness preservation by the Geological Survey and Bureau of Mines to determine the mineral values, if any, that may be present; and the results of such surveys shall be made available to the public and submitted to the President and Congress.

Note the word "recurring." This proviso is not affected by the cutoff date. It is not expected that the secretaries could delegate such surveys to commercial operators.

The Wilderness Study Committee has several times tried to suggest that, instead of permitting the construction of temporary roads to drill sites in

Wilderness Areas, the assignment of large cargo helicopters (owned by the federal government) be made to haul the drill rig in and out. Then, if the holes indicate commercial-level values, an appropriate road could be authorized. The operating cost of the helicopter, to be borne by the drilling company, should in most cases be considerably less than the cost of drill-site roads, all costs (environmental) included. The carrying capacity of the largest cargo shoppers in the early 1970's was in the order of 20,000 pounds or ten tons. Drill rigs are not transported all in one piece, anyway, and few weigh as much as seventeen tons.

In the late 1950's, the town of Hot Springs, some 25 miles to the east of the Black Range as the raven flies, put on a great promotion to attempt a convulsive rejuvenation. They were able to engage a certain Ralph Edwards who had a Radio and TV Show called "Truth or Consequences" to help them get national publicity for the affair. They even changed the name of the town to Truth or Consequences.

One of the feature events of a couple of weeks of orgy was a Jeep race that took off in the rough country surrounding the town. Each year since, various degrees of off-road vehicle (ORV) races are held, either starting or finishing in Truth or Consequences, or both. Some fabulous machines and tales of "derring-do" have resulted. Very few first starters have won the race or even placed. It takes practice. So it was inevitable that such ORVs would begin to show up in the Gila Wilderness and Primitive Areas, and in the Black Range.

In the early 1970's, the four-wheel-drive vehicles became much more capable and much more expensive. They started to show up on the mountain flanks at much higher altitudes. Dune buggys also entered the fun. Various kinds of motorcycles began to infiltrate our back country. The enduro-bike was a highly-geared, powerfull machine that did not tear up the countryside if driven with skill. Some other bikes, often called trail-bikes or dirt-bikes do have to be ridden faster than the enduros. They tear up wet soils and have been known to machine grooves straight up hillsides. The erosion patterns which sometimes result have characteristic features.

A couple of families from El Paso decided that it would be fun to drive down the Gila River from its junction with the Cliff Dwelling National Monument Road. They drove down the river bed through the Wilderness and bogged down close to the west side of the Wilderness Area. The Forest Service Supervisor required that mules be used to snake the FWD's out of the river. It cost the families an appreciable towing charge as well as a heavy fine.

President Richard Nixon signed an Executive Order on February 8, 1972, to "ensure that the use of off-road vehicles on public lands will be controlled and directed so as to protect the resources of those lands, to promote the safety of all users of those lands, and to minimize conflicts among the various uses of those lands." Each National Forest in the Region issued draft ORV Management Plans in 1976. We were not too happy with some of them because closures were not proposed on all of our proposed wilderness areas. Consequently, we appeared at the public hearings, meetings, open houses, or listening sessions as they were sometimes called. We also wrote letters and talked to the Forest Supervisors. So far we are not completely certain whether our comments did much good. We are not happy with the final result, either, but we made some headway.

The ORV Management Plans were interfered with to some degree by a Roadless Area Review and Evaluation process that followed quickly on the President's Order. This USFS Southwest Region issued its first announcements in March, 1972. New Mexico made "The Chief's List" with many more areas specified on the inventory than most other states. Our friends in the Forest Service were quick to point out that they must be more observing than their compadres in other states. We, of course, responded that they had more to work with (as de facto wilderness) than the foresters in other states. Some of our proposed areas did not make it onto the magic list. You will probably hear about them later.

Subsequently in 1977, Roadless Area Review and Evaluation No. 2, RARE II, another survey of the same kind, started but this time the inventory process sounded as if it has more liberalized criteria for roadless areas. For example, it defines Roadless Areas: "An area of undeveloped Federal land within which there are no improved roads maintained for travel by means of motorized vehicles intended for highway use." As far as the Black Range is concerned, there is generally an ORV closure, but it is complicated when you try to follow the Forest Service Map and descriptions. Their RARE II area inventory surely includes more than enough to encompass our proposed Aldo Leopold Wilderness.

Our initial (Black Range) Aldo Leopold Wilderness Area had a number of exclusions based upon our early interpretation of what should be in the area and what should be out. It was estimated to contain 231,737 acres in November, 1970, whereas the Forest Service proposal was for 181,967 acres. They were even purer than we in our determinations. Subsequently, much more field work and reassessment of the natural restoration of some of the old wagon tracks and Jeep trails changed our boundaries again until on our November, 1975, map we proposed an area of 315,300 acres. And on February 4, 1976, we submitted our recommendations to Senator Haskell of the Senate Interior and Insular Affairs Committee. The additional 83,463 acres were generated by some very dogged investigators mostly along the eastside of the North Star Road. I have sampled most of the large additions and they are surely wilderness.

In summary, we have done our work in preparing a good Aldo Leopold Wilderness Area proposal, it has been transmitted to the appropriate Congressional Committee, the Wilderness Society has been advised, and it should be clear to get some legislative action. The mineral survey is completed also. Perhaps it will take Senator Schmitt to get some action.

TRAILS AND ROUTES IN THE BLACK RANGE

A great get-acquainted hike starts at the limited parking lot at Emory Pass Vista. It is about two-and-a-half miles (maybe three miles) generally north along the ridge to Hillsboro Peak Lookout. An old road was started in that direction and then it was closed. That road has tempted ORVs of various kinds if I can read muddy tracks correctly. Within a mile or so, the barriers seem to give them the idea that they are not wanted. The Vehicle Closure signs are vandalized quite frequently.

The grade of the trail is gentle, but you climb almost 2,000 feet in elevation. During midsummer the odor of balsam is strong, blowing upward off the western slopes. I was always wary of lighting a match (or a lighter) when it smelled that way. It must be close to an explosive gas.

It is tempting to follow the trail on northward to Granite Peak. It is about four miles an generally downhill. Granite is about 1000 feet lower than Hillsboro Peak. There is no water on the route so far. Getting back to the car before the late afternoon rain can be fun, particularly when the lightning is licking around the top of Hillsboro Lookout. Kent Carlton spent a summer up there and said that the tower was well grounded.

You have travelled about 14 miles and climbed or ascended a total of about 6000 feet by the time you get back to the car. You have had vistas on both sides of the Range. The country toward the north gives you a glimpse of Reeds Peak.

If you are backpacking, you may find it interesting to climb over the Apache Peak about one or two miles to the north-east of Granite. East Curtis Spring about a mile north of Apache Peak is further from the trail (uphill) that it is shown on the maps. The Quad Map is more accurate than the 1974 Class A Planimetric Forest Service Map. We still had some fairly deep drifts in mid-May the first time we hunted for the spring (unsuccessfully).

There is another Apache Peak two and one-half miles northest of the Apache Park in Sections 10 and 11. It is east of the remains of the Old Spanish road which is now marked Forest Trail 307. Some prospect mining was done in the mid 1950's in that locale; and the U.S.G.S. Report 41 indicated that little ore evolved.

A longer trip north of Hillsboro Peak extends to Victoria Park Mountain. My notes are a maze of trail numbers because of some renumbering of the trails that summer (1959). We had plenty of water for the canteens along the trails and we even caught a couple of small fish in Las Animas Creek. That night we thought we saw a couple of lights in Hermosa but next morning we concluded that it must have been car headlights in the vicinity. My compadres complained about the distance back to Emory Pass (some 17-18 miles) and the seeming nearness of Hermosa.

We half-heartedly drew lots to see which one of us would drive the car around to Hermosa but could not get a taker. However, we agreed that the next time we came to Victoria Park Mountain, it would be from Hermosa. My trip notes say that the altimeter read an almost identical elevation for Victoria and Hillsboro Peaks. Another comment is, "If you don't mind verticality, the nearest road to Victoria Park Mountain is on Seco Creek about five miles northeast." On a later trip in the late 1960's, Milo Conrad and I saw a deer near Seco Creek tank.

Reeds Peak and Diamond Peak are for me the Black Range epitomized. I like the route westbound from Hermosa up Rattlesnake Creek to the Ridge Trail. The other way up from the west is interesting because you can drive to the Continental Divide on the North Star Road and follow Trail 74 northeast about eight miles to Reeds Peak. Incidentally, Reeds and Hillsboro Peaks are supposed to be the same elevation.

The trip to Diamond Peak from Turkey Draw (to the north) is a pretty steady pull of about eight or nine miles unless you climb up onto the divide trail east of James Brothers Spring. Then it is at least 10 miles but the scenery is better. I guess I like to return via the divide trail but to come up Diamond Creek Trail. Remember that the low country around the Aldo Leopold Wilderness is mighty hot during midsummer. Its saving grace is that it does rain nice warm rain until you get up to about 9000 feet. Then it can be "hail in July."

There are dozens of trails in the Black Range that lead up to the high country. Each has its character and surprises. Although there is plenty of water, several times I've been forced to go a couple of more miles to get water that hasn't been fouled by cattle.

On only one trip did I have enough time to wander without any regard for trails. The country generally between Diamond Creek and South Diamond Creek is full of game and wildflowers. If you get lost, you can always go downhill to the North Star Road to the west. The birds, particularly the flycatchers, along the South Diamond Creek are worth the trip even if the cattle beat up the creek bottom every summer.

CHAPTER 5:
Banco Breaks
Defacto Wilderness

Banco Breaks is 40 miles airline northwest of Albuquerque and 20 miles northeast of Mount Taylor in that corner of Cibola National Forest. It is most easily approached by turning off State Highway 44 onto unpaved Road 229 some 19 miles northwest of San Ysidro. A branch of the road climbs southwestward up onto the Chirato Mesa. Banco Breaks are the eastern slopes of that mesa. Get a copy of the Cibola National Forest map to aid in roadfinding; the quad map of the area will help understand the breaks better.

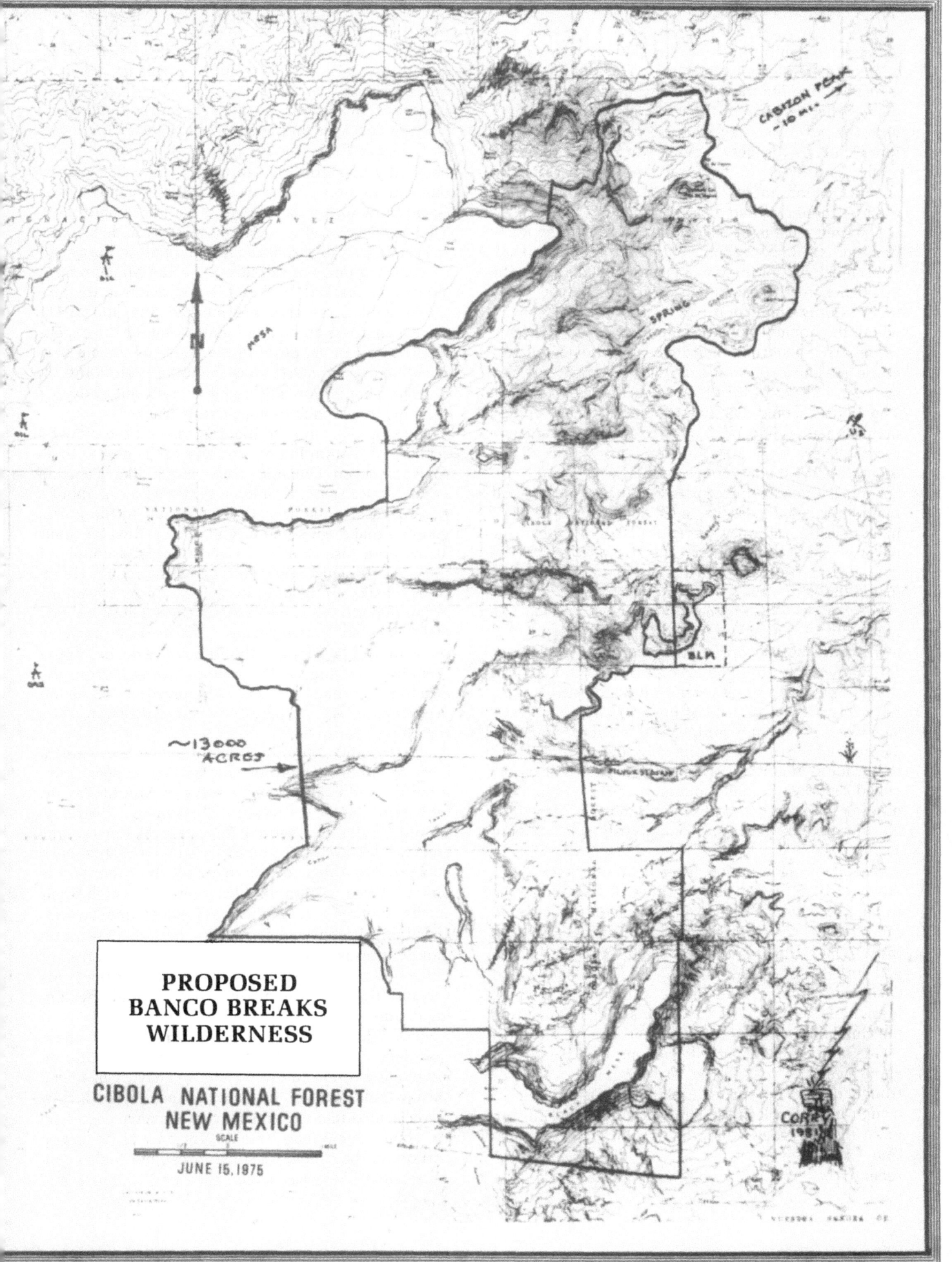

Repeated lightning strokes struck the extreme north edge of the mesa above the house. The night had been a restless one for the small band of beleaguered Indians. The bushes and the rocks glowed in the dark with the glow discharge that we now call St. Elmo's Fire. Then, as the slow moving storm front came out of the southwest, down from the eastern slopes of Mount Taylor, mixed rain and hail pounded their roofs — the dawn had a saffron hue.

The time must have been about A.D. 900 when they first fled to their redoubt, about three and one-half miles north of the rim of what is now Black Mesa. The Spanish named it El Banco de la Casa. Even today there is only about one way to the top of the mesa where the ancient houses remain.

The driving storm penetrated every crevice of their crude masonry. It went through the brush and clay roofs and soaked everything, even their bowstrings. The houses could barely accommodate a standing man, and they had only one room. A few had two rooms. There were only a dozen houses at most and one or two of them were storerooms.

Even if their enemies managed to get up on their mesa, they had to pass through a narrow and low door in a massive masonry parapet that still blocks the narrow ridge leading to the tiny houses. The defenders, in retreat, were at a momentary advantage inside the doorway.

Perhaps it was the early Apaches or even the marauding Comanches from the plains who struck terror into these people.[1] It happened several times for many centuries. The crucial door or opening in the parapet has a lintel beam in it which surely must have been replaced at least once in all of that time. The wood is probably juniper and is almost petrified. These frightened beings probably looked off toward their sacred mountains which their Navajo successors called Tso Dzil (big tall mountain) or Dzil Dotlizi, turquoise mountain.[2] It marks the southern border of the Navajo universe. We uncermoniously call it Mount Taylor.

Our proposed Banco Breaks Wilderness Area cowers off in the northeast corner of the Cibola National Forest which extends northeast of Grants for 40 miles or so — as the raven flies. By truck, it is like 70 miles. The study area is about 25,000 acres of the rugged breaks and bottoms of Tapia, Salado, and Chamisa canyons. Guadalupe Canyon is a small branch of Cañon Tapia, and has a spring not far from the Guadalupe Ranger Station.

Guadalupe Spring gets cleaned out by a cloudburst about every 50 years, or at least its holding pond or trough does. The spring trickles into a pot-hole or trough in the rock in the canyon bottom that fills up with algae. Perhaps underneath, the water is good. The Forest Service used to clean it out but more recently has simply carried in the needed water during the brief periods of occupancy of their trailer.

Access to the north, west, and south sides can be accomplished by driving in from the northeast. About 19 miles northwest of San Ysidro on State Road 44 is an unpaved State Road 279 which goes through the ghost town of San Luis and crosses the Arroyo Chico west of Cabezon Peak. By staying on the road which is hesitantly marked "To San Mateo" in a few places, one can get up onto the mesa on the Ignacio Chavez Grant (now under the Bureau of Land Management). That road generally wanders southwest, has many misleading forks and branches going off to many cattle watering tanks or salt licks. The San Mateo road is sometimes marked "57" and the branches to the proposed wilderness area are marked 194 and 194A. Take a compass and a quad map along for the experiment. You can get close to the edges of the big canyons below to start your mountain climbing in reverse. That is, you have to climb back out of the big canyons to get back to your car or truck.

You can hike out onto Black Mesa and see the wild scenery of the Rio Puerco country to the east with its rows of seven volcanic plugs much like Cabezon Peak. Mesa Prieta is the long, timbered mesa about a dozen miles to the east. If you look off to the north, you can make out some brightly colored water tanks at the Juan Jose Ranch in Cañon Tapia, a couple of miles off. Richard Silverstein owns the ranch. He installs clocks in beautifully polished cross-sections of gnarled old trees, in his spare time. Those we saw were slabs about two inches thick made to hang on the wall. But let's look at the Banco Breaks in its contemporary setting, as if we were seeing it from the outside, perhaps from Albuquerque or even Washington, D.C., where the critical decision of its future will be made.

The Cebolleta Mountains are about 40 miles northwest of Albuquerque but can hardly be seen from town except as apparent foothills of Mount Taylor, which dominates the western horizon on a clear day. Mount Taylor is a sacred mountain to the Indians and to the uranium miners.[3,4] The Indians have believed since their beginnings that the Mountain is one of three geographic locations at which their spirits emerge from their religious underworld. Uranium mining was started in the late 1940's and took the forms of both shaft and open pit processes. Since that time, about 1200 square miles of the lands surrounding the Mountain have been overlain by mining claims.

Mesa Chirato is on the eastern edge of these Cebolleta Mountains. The broken edges of the Chirato tumble down into the Rio Puerco valley. It has been hard to build roads on those broken edges. The largest roadless area that remains is what we have been talking about, our Banco Breaks. Not only is its largest portion on the Cibola National forest, but it also contains two BLM areas which they call Chamisa and

Banco de la Casa. The whole area is in the order of 38 square miles. There were no mining claims or leases in this rugged area in 1979.

The Banco Breaks have defended themselves against the extensive drilling which has taken place on the adjacent Forest Service and BLM lands primarily because they are roadless and rugged by comparison to those lands closer to Mount Taylor.

The Roadless Area Review and Evaluation process, in its RARE II phase, required that the Forest Service make a resource analysis and assign a rating to the area. The potential mineral values assigned by the Forest Service were 89% for uranium, 30% for coal, and 78% for oil/gas. The Wilderness Attribute Rating Score (WARS) for the Banco Breaks area was 24, well above the average for the state. The Forest Service, despite the high mineral resource potentials, recommended that the area be given "further study" before the decision was made to either declare it national Wilderness or Non-Wilderness. The Wilderness Study committee was satisfied with that recommendation because we believed that the economics of the development of the resources of the area would prove our conclusions.

The Bokum Mine at the town of Marquez about 10 miles south of the Banco Breaks along the same general escarpment is a shaft mine very recently completed. The uranium horizon is at about 3,500 feet. The ore body underneath the Marquez Mesa (a part of the larger Chirato Mesa) to the west is being drift mined. These drifts are tunnels originating at the shaft. They do little damage to the surface of Marquez Mesa, well above the town and mill/mine site. The State Environmental Assessment Office has placed some kind of holding order on their putting into operation a mill tailings settling pond by reason of its potential contamination of the downstream water table. Even before the court hearings and resolution of the matter, a large tailings pond near Church Rock broke and discharged radioactive water and materials into the Rio Puerco drainage which goes westward from Gallup.

We had hoped that, if any uranium mining were to be done in the future in the Banco Breaks, a similar shaft and drift mining process from the eastern perimeter would leave the surface similarly untouched. Those that looked at the "potential" ratings in Washington could not know that such a possibility would be most economical and probable, although the Regional Forester knew it.

The coal beds in the vicinity are too deep for strip mining and the grade of coal is generally too low to support shaft mining. Some possibility may exist for coal gasification in situ, one of these centuries. But that is what Wilderness is for: to marshal our resources for the future, among other things.

The oil/gas potential is about the same picture. there are no producing wells in the vicinity but the surrounding areas have been drilled extensively in some places through the uranium horizons into the generic oil/gas formations. There are so many hundreds of square miles in which the oil/gas showings are so much better that economical wells are a long way off. Again, forebearance of needless developments should have been the conclusion of a Further Study program if it had been given an opportunity.

The area is an island of wildlife, so far undisturbed by the poaching of deer and elk accompanying the drilling crew roads outside the area. There are mountian lions, bears, and raptors included with a plentiful mix of smaller varieties of wildlife. It is no lush rain forest, but the rugged area has provided safe refuge for the mountain desert wildlife long after it has disappeared in the developed areas around it.

Suddenly, in mid-April 1979, the President switched the label from Further Planning to Non-Wilderness. The Office of Management and Budget had looked at the Forest Service recommendations all across the nation and juggled some of the results. Admittedly, when our lower San Francisco Canyon (near Glenwood) was simultaneously switched into Wilderness, we were pleased with the dealer. However, it began to feel like a shell game.

The contiguous BLM areas were degraded in their temporary classification as a result of the President's action. One such area (Banco de la Casa) contained a potential National Inventory Site (archaeological) which could only be accessed from the National Forest Land adjacent. This site is the one described in the lightning-sequence at the beginning of this chapter. The Chamisa (BLM) Area to the north of the Guadalupe constitutes the balance of the geographic entity we know as the Banco Breaks.

The price of progress will come very high if this area is forced into non-wilderness development. It surely will be the hardest three percent of the whole 1200 square miles to develop. Can this area be rejudged with some real economic factors plugged into the analysis? A road adequate for drilling rigs would be a drain on agency funds because the Banco Breaks are so broken. Why not mine the other 97% first before public funded roads are forced onto this refuge of wilderness? Or mine it from its perimeter.

We have tried an appeal in many of these same terms. Representative Lujan forwarded it to the Forest Service and we received an answer from the Chief to the effect that (you) "should be aware that the designation of areas for uses other than wilderness does not mean that all of these areas will be intensively developed." By the time you read this, you might check to see that history has repeated itself. Somehow a Forest Service road will appear in the area, constructed with public money, for the benefit of the oil/gas drillers or miners. The game will have been poached off. However, before that happens, I am going to hunt the area with my bow for both elk and deer during the next legal hunting season. If I get one, we can haul it out on Richard Silverstein's pack horse which will stay in his pasture until then.

TRAILS AND ROUTES IN THE BANCO BREAKS

Deer hunting has been good on Mesa de la Vereda Piedra Blanca as recently as the early 1970's. Some deer hides and other remains attest to some poaching. An old road or rutted trail goes about a mile northeast of Guadalupe Spring on Mesa Blanca. The road has been closed for several years, but somone gets onto it with his four-wheel-drive once or twice per year. Try backpacking overnight and sack out near one of the big clearings. The deer will come up out of the canyons and the coyotes sing all night if the wind is fairly calm.

The northern 6,400 acres of our proposed area (the old Grant part) is BLM territory. There is a rudimentary road southeast of Ned Tank which goes out to the canyon wall. One can readily drop down into the Chamisa Canyon and possibly get a deer or bear in season. The problem is to get the meat back up the steep canyon walls. A packhorse out the bottom is a possibility, but the road around the bottom, in the Rio Puerco Valley, is no easy matter either. Chamisa Losa Spring does not run year round. However, when it does, it has a clatter of birdlife, including wild turkeys.

The road which runs generally southeast about one mile to the northeast of the steep plug, Cerro del Ojo de las Yeguas, is the branch which goes down the Rio Puerco Valley. That is a fair-weather road that leads ultimately to Richard Silverstein's ranch and to the vicinity of Banco de la Casa. All told, there must be a good dozen gates on that road to open and close. Park in the draw just to the north of the ranch houses and head off southwest from the ranch and climb up onto Black Mesa. It is wilderness all of the way. We have packed in overnight several times in mid-winter, sacking out on the mesas at the 7,800 or 7,900 foot levels without any snow. Then again, it has been impossible to get up onto the Black Mesa from Cañon Puente with snowshoes and skis in other years by reason of deep drifts of frosty powder snow.

Hay Meadow Canyon is immediately south of Black Mesa. You can drive down the canyon if the gate is not locked and come out on the Marquez Mesa road. The road has not had any maintenance for years, and it takes a good four-wheel drive vehicle. If you get hung up crossing one of the dry washes, you could be there a month. There is one sidehill sashay which traverses a sandy-clay bluff which gets impassible if the dew is heavy. It is probably easier to walk the route than drive it.

If you drive out onto the mesa finger which overlooks Salado Cañon on a branch of Forest Road 57, you will come to a water tank which is fed by a hydraulic-ram pump in the adjacent cañon bottom. The ram can be heard for quite a distance, but the deer do not pay any attention to its noise. The water up the cañon from the ram inlet is good drinking water if you get it where it emerges from the ground. Wild currant bushes make it hard to get that close.

Finally, after you are through exploring our surprising little area, you will probably head out northward on State Road 279 again. The high bridge across the Arroyo Chico can make interesting crossing in a foot of water. If you stop, you have had it. Then, as you feel that you are home free and practically in sight of the Cuba highway, there is a really slick spot of bentonite clay (like drilling mud) along one ridge that that makes even four-wheel drive cars spin sometimes. If you are lucky, the bentonite will drip off your car in your driveway for months every time it gets wet. I hope NM 279 never gets paved. It is one of the few adventures left! It also helps to isolate the Banco Breaks.

CHAPTER 6:
Wheeler Peak National Wilderness

Wheeler Peak is about 13 airline miles northeast of Taos, and just to the immediate east of the Taos Ski Basin in the Hondo Basin. State Road 230 leads to the ski basin and the wilderness trail heads. Wheeler is the highest peak in the state and is one of the many high peaks in the Sangre de Cristo Mountain Range. Maps are available in the Taos and Questa ranger stations.

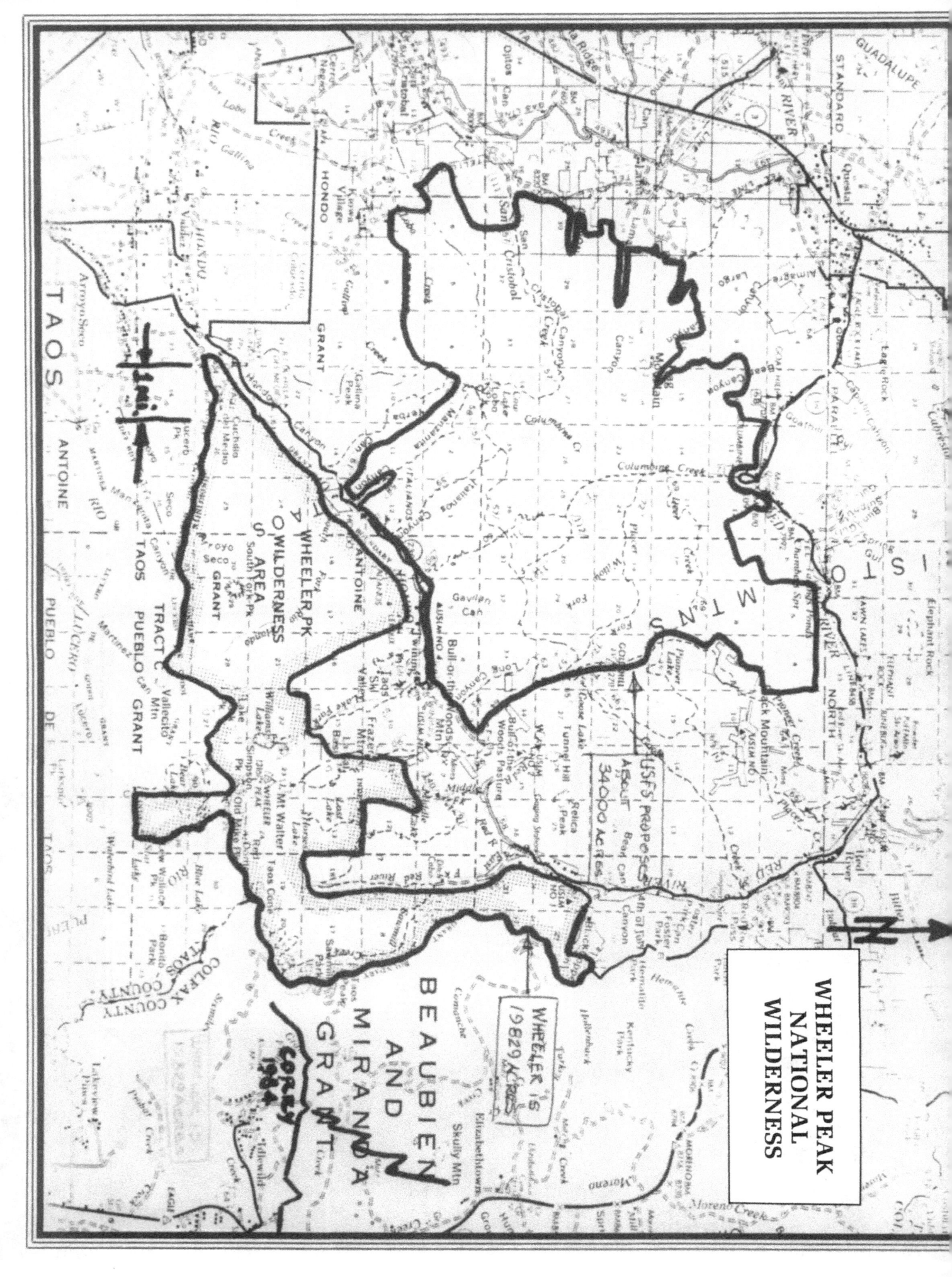

Man's activities have swirled around the clump of mountains which contains Wheeler Peak, the highest mountain in New Mexico. Many prodigious tasks have been accomplished in the area; many not altogether happy ones.

A small straggling group of people fled upriver from Central America long before Americus Vespucci arrived on earth. They had been persecuted by the Mayans and, subsequently, the Aztecs from time immemorial. There was probably an alien idea — or ideology — in many of their heads. There must be some place on this earth where they could be governed only by themselves. That idea kept them on the move.

Their ancestors had come across the land bridge out of Asia and the migration southward over the millenia was driven by survival. Food was scarce, lodging in a wildly fluctuating climate was difficult, and the competition with the fauna and flora made tomorrow uncertain.

When they settled in Central Mexico, they discovered that, when the natives weren't restless, the volcanoes were. Then that idea of freedom to govern themselves kept goading them on. All of this is a Caucasian view of what happened. It is based upon little except word-of-mouth folklore of the Taos Indians. They were supposed to be following a bird north.[1] I think the idea for a bird and that for freedom must have been the same in their folklore.

So then came los conquistadores (1540); then, the uprising and expulsion of the Spaniards and Mexicans (1680). These Indians had settled in over the centuries and held some annual visitations and retreats to the headwaters of their little stream that ran through their town. We call the stream "Rio Pueblo de Taos" and its headwaters, "Blue Lake."

A couple of hundred years later, after they had almost become used to the people who were farming in Martinez Canyon, they decided to intermarry with them as a means of solving their problems. In the interim there were officious looking and sounding people showing up with paper scrolls with golden seals, saying that "Antoine Leroux owns this land."

Others appeared, saying that the foothills north of the home lands "had been bequeathed to Antonio Martinez by the King of Spain." Another piece of parchment was shown to the local magistrate, saying that Lucero de Godoi had the timber and water rights east of Manzanitas Canyon. These overlapping Spanish and Mexican Grant claims were by no means unique to the Taos watershed areas.

Just to the east of Taos a dozen miles, for example, a French trapper, Carlos Beaubien, settled on some land granted by New Mexico Territorial Governor Armijo in 1841. His partner, Guadalupe Miranda of Taos, was also named. Then Lucien B. Maxwell came onto the scene in 1849, married Beaubien's daughter, and subsequently bought out the Miranda heirs for $3,000.[2] So, the Maxwell Grant extended from Red River Pass on the north to well below the site of Eagle Nest Lake on the south.

As the soldiers from the Civil War were returning to the Territory, they brought a wave of "friends" with them.[3] In 1865 the first house was built in Virginia City which became Elizabethtown in 1866. It was about five miles north of the present-day Eagle Nest, and not far from Baldy Mountain on the west side of the Maxwell Grant. Gold was discovered in that same year, and Elizabethtown had about 3,000 people in it within a year.

A ditch was dug and constructed, starting in 1868, on the East Fork of the Red River near where Sawmill Creek comes into it, and extended 40 miles to a series of dredge ponds in the Moreno Creek Valley near Elizabethtown, to float a dredge called "The Eleanor." If you walk the ditch out, you will find it was a monumental job. Every small creek and drywash on Baldy Mountain was also dug out to bedrock and panned or sluiced for gold and silver. In 1950 there were still ricks of wood stacked up and down the old roads on Baldy where they had been abandoned when the wood-fired stamp mill was shut down during World War I. Prospecting continued in the Baldy Mountain vicinity until after the stock market crash in 1929. I bowhunted deer on the Mountain as a guest of the Mutz Brothers in 1950 but did not get one there.

Red River was combed thoroughly for gold during the late 1800's, as were all of the streams in the Wheeler Area. The French trappers had been running much of the whole mountain area for beaver and other pelts, for almost 100 years before then.

The Caribel Mine on Pioneer Creek near Black Mountain, a couple of miles south of the present town of Red River, operated in the 1880's, acquired a stamp mill in about 1896, and was still in spasmodic operation until about 1922. When gold went above $400 per ounce in 1979, mining started again, but on a relatively small scale. The Klondike Mine, about two miles southeast of Taos Peak, had a good vein of sulfide gold ore that pinched out early in the century.

Closer to Wheeler is the Amizette or Twining Mining District at the headwaters of the Rio Hondo. One of the most spectacular dumps remaining is that at the Bull-of-the-Woods Mine on the ridge north of Frazer Mountain and Wheeler Peak. Al Helphenstine, a prospector, had a wife named Amizette in about 1890. He spent a lot of time away from home but named his claims after her. In about 1895, William Frazer found copper and gold further east in the Hondo Canyon toward Williams Lake. Albert C. Twining, a New Jersey banker, put up a $300,000 smelter which would not work on wood and coal hauled in from Madrid. They could not adequately flux the ore to keep it fluid enough to process it properly.[2] Subsequently, most of the high-grade ore was either shipped to El Paso or to

New Jersey for smelting. The prices may be getting high enough to give it another try in the 1980's or 1990's. We know a lot more about drift and slope mining now than we did then.

There were some pretty good drift mines in South Fork and Italianos Canyons near the bottoms of those canyons as they enter the Hondo.[4]

Taos grew and became a settlement famous for painters and other artists, primarily because of the beauty of the surrounding mountains and the continuously occupied Indian Pueblo. Another contributing factor was the patience and good-humored tolerance of those same Indians who came up the Rio Grande long before Coronado. They ran out of patience once, you recall during the Pueblo Revolt.[5,6]

Many kinds of people were attracted to the frontier and for various reasons. One example is that of a banker from Purcell, Oklahoma, by the name of Alfred D. Hawk who decided at age 45 to come to New Mexico for his health. He first settled in Elizabethtown at about the turn of the century. He soon acquired the land now occupied by Red River Town, Sunshine Valley, and the Del Monte tract near San Cristobal. He sold part of his Del Monte tract to D.H. Lawrence, the famed author. Many of the Hawk offspring were variously instrumental in the development of the habitable lands in the vicinity of the Lobo Peak foothills. Walton Hawk is a doctor of veterinary medicine who lives in the San Cristobal area and is one of our experts on our proposed Wheeler Peak Wilderness Addition boundaries.

Guides and outfitters took large numbers of tourists, including painters, up onto the high ridges from about 1900 to 1925. There are tales of lightning strikes and the resulting deaths of some horse caravan members.

The U.S. Forest Service was given charge of certain Public lands within the confines of the Carson National Forest after the mining phase had largely passed. They worked quietly before World War I trying to heal the damages inflicted on the land during the mining era. The automobile and truck came upon the scene and more people started to use the forests, streams, and mountains than ever before. Old mining roads now had new uses, called "recreational." The Sunday driver now wanted smoother roads.

The Forest Service entered a cooperative agreement with the Taos Indians on September 6, 1933, which required protection of the purity of the water in the Rio Lucero watershed and provided for continued grazing of Indian livestock within a part of the area without fees.[7]

The Taos Ski Area started growing up the hill to the south of Twining in 1955. I had been up to Williams Lake sometime in 1950 or 1951. My recollection was that there was good looking ore on the road in several spots before the road dead-ended in the swamp above Twining or Amizette. It looked as if somebody had thrown several wagonloads in some mudholes in the road. At that time it was thought that Wheeler Peak was not as high as south Truchas Peak in the Pecos Wilderness. Surveys were done in the 1952-1953 period which established Wheeler as about 60 feet higher than Truchas and Costilla Peaks.[8]

That first time at Williams Lake, I remember becoming disinterested after catching two little fish and could not resist the climb up to the Peak. My fishing buddies thought I was nuts for climbing that rockslide when I could be fishing. The cairn on the summit had been kicked over by someone and a coffee can smashed flat still with paper in it. There were bunches of note paper under every loose rock. Now there is a big pipe with a tight cover for a cairn.

The first time I went skiing at Twining I had to park a half-mile below the place along the road because of the crowd. That was in 1956. The lift lines were long and the main lift was shut down intermittemtly to let a gearbox or something cool down. So I spent most of the day climbing, but the hill was worth it and the snow was great. From the first, Ernie Blake has had a continuing problem to keep his facilities in step with the crowds his area attracts.

The Wheeler Peak Wild Area was established in 1960 and it became a National Wilderness area in 1964 at the time of the Wilderness Act passage.[9] Its main claim to fame was its smallness — 6051 acres.

The ski area became more and more famous for its variety of runs, its consistently good snow, and its long season. The Rubezahl trail runs some seven miles from the top of Number Two Lift, plunging to the east and around to the north down the west slopes of Lake Fork Canyon and back to Twining — or the bottom of the chair lift again.

The road up the Rio Hondo Canyon was widened and paved in the late 1960's, much to the concern of many of the property owners along the Hondo below Twining. The bulldozers pushed some large boulders, several of them over six feet through, into the stream. Before the furor died down, they were named Hassle Rocks after Gene Hassell, the Carson Forest Supervisor at the time. The raw cut-banks along the road were not promptly planted by the contractor and many minor rock slides resulted until the belated plantings took hold.

During the mid 1950's, it was a good hike into Blue Lake up the Rio Pueblo de Taos, but the fishing was spotty. I had just learned to cast a fly some distance offshore with a spinning rod and a plastic bubble partially full of water. While I was trying it, a young Indian came up in back of me and seemed spellbound with the process. I asked him if he wanted to try it and looked around somewhat nervously before he said yes.

We talked for a short while after he tried the fly casting, but he cut the conversation off short when I asked him where all of the olive bottles and cans and lids that littered the place came from. Several of us from the Albuquerque Game Preservation Association had hauled out several dozen burlap bags full of the bottles and trash for three years. The bottles were in the water to a distance of 10 to 20 feet from the shore and generally were not broken, but those on shore were broken and hard to pick up. The Fish and Game Department did a similar cleanup during each summer after the snow melted.

The Forest Service must have thought the littering and abuse of the lake had gone far enough after they saw the shambles in September of 1970, because they closed the trail to the lake just before Christmas. The Taos Indians were irate. They started a series of legal maneuvers which terminated in their obtaining title to the Blue Lake and the trails leading to it. The Taos Pueblo Land-Blue Lake transaction then included all of the land from the Lake up to the Old Mike-Red Dome Ridge, the complete watershed. The claim was based upon the Indian's traditional religious use of the Blue Lake and its environs. The organized fishermen were furious. Very few were ever permitted to go into the Lake after 1971, but occasionally the governor of the pueblo will ussue a permit during June and early July, but not later. Their big ceremony is sometimes in late July or in August at the lake. My son, Kent, and I, on August 14, 1971, saw a large group of Indians around the Lake (via binoculars) commemorating their Blue Lake acquisition. We were on Lew Wallace Peak at the time.

On March 20, 1973, the Forest Service established a permit system for the Wheeler Peak Wilderness with the exception of Trail Number 154 to Blue Lake.[7] Nobody seemed to like the permit system which was put on the San Pedro Parks and Pecos Wildernesses at the same time. There was a public hearing at Taos in 1974 at which someone from the Regional Office of the Forest Service replied to a question from the floor to the effect that the permit system was being used to make use-frequency studies, not as an over-use control measure. Many of us in the Wilderness Study Committee reacted adversely because we thought that a permit system for that purpose was importune or surely not a reasonable use of the administrative device. The counting process could be a by-product, we thought, but not the main thrust of the use of the permit system. In any event, the permit system has no roots in the Wilderness System by Law.[10]

Let it not be thought that the Indians have a monopoly on littering lakes in the area. In 1972, by summer's end, the cans around Goose Lake were extensive. A couple of us cleaned all we could reach in the water with long wire hooks, but the paper and other trash in the open garbage dump to the east of the lake was a shambles. The bears had been sorting it out and the flies were bad.

Goose Lake and Middle Fork Lake were both fished heavily by Texas tourists staying in Red River. They rented Jeeps and got a kick driving them up to the lakes, particularly up the switchback road to Middle Fork Lake. A couple of the turns were too sharp for even a Jeep so there was one stretch on which one must back up to the next turn to go forward again. Coming down, the process had to be repeated or you would have to back down at least a half a mile.

Whatever the source, the Forest Service could not keep up with the trash at those two lakes, and most of us backpackers avoided them whenever we could. That was the year when the State Parks and Recreation Department decided that they could not keep up with the trash in the State parks so they removed the trash cans and put up a sign about taking it with you in your car. There is still a lot of trash, but it is better than it was. We no longer see such large mounds of cans and cartons in the State Parks. It is either being carried out or thrown further back into the brush out of sight.

The South Fork Roadless Area has been hard enough to get into and has remained wild. The canyons are choked with brush and the canyon walls are precipitous. The ridges are often clear but they are not continuous. I made one trip down the main draw from the ski area to the Rio Hondo where the creek comes out near the "Taos East" condominium. It is mostly bushwhacking of the kind in which one practically lies down on the brush before it gives way.

There is a silver and gold lead on the ridge immediately southeast of the South Fork and Hondo junction. An old mining road went up the hill and fairly extensive open cut, shaft, and tunnel (drift) mining was done.[4] The north slope looking downward to the Hondo has one avalanche chute after another along its face. One of these lesser chutes seems to aim at Bill Stevens' spectacular cabin alongside the creek.

The Taos Indians talk of having "traditional use" claims to the South Fork area. We may have a tussle to get it enacted as an addition to the Wheeler Peak Area for that reason. There was talk of putting a ski run down the South Fork canyon at one time in the 1971 or 1972 period. Someone claims he skied down the canyon one of those years. I doubt it, since I had a hard enough time coming down one rainy day in midsummer. It is four miles of jungle.

While the power line for the ski-lift was being put over the Bull-of-the-Woods Pasture from the Red River Canyon to the northeast, the open swath cut for the power line must have been inviting because there were truck tracks going down it. I had a full new set of brake linings on a dune buggy which I had built. A friend was with me who had no more sense than I, so we pointed downhill from the "Pasture." Since I had a skid plate under the engine and a short 80-inch wheelbase, it only made raucous screeches when we drove over the occasional tanktraps left along the right-of-way. We did get down, but the thought of having to abandon the machine entered our minds. One difficulty persisted. The gas tank was in front, over the front wheels. The engine was in back, over the back wheels. At an idle, the fuel pump had problems with hoisting enough gasoline uphill to the engine, even if it was an electric pump. So, when the engine started to cough, we had to stop and rev up the engine. I tried going down with the key off but in trans-axle low and it worked on some of the lesser grades. It worked better to get it in reverse and churn the wheels backwards. Too late, one has thoughts. It would have been better to have a rope and some kind of a spider to let the strand out slowly or not to have driven down at all.

All of this was not too old in a couple of minds when we first heard of a rebirth of a glorious plan to make a Grand Circus Route that included a proposed road over the top at the Bull-of-the-Woods Pasture and down to Red River so that mobs of people could "come to Northern New Mexico and ski at Red River and at Taos Ski Area in one Grand Circus Route" tradition as in the Alps. The road would come out of Forest Service funds and would, of course, be an all-weather highway over the top at 11,500 feet. You can imagine all of the wandering switchbacks on the canyon hillsides north of the "Pasture" to use up all of that elevation. Over a period of a year and a half, the grand illusion persisted as a solid Forest Service plan.

Letters were written by our Road committee and much public reaction finally persuaded the USFS to delete the high road from the plans. This seemed to be an ill-fated Loop Road concept that had its counterpart in the Sandias and at Elk Mountain. Bill Stevens blew the whistle on the abortive concept. Consequently, the high road from Red River to Taos Ski Valley was officially abandoned in 1974. Chalk another one up for the local citizens in the Hondo Canyon area. They seem to have unfailingly good judgement.

The then Regional Forester, William D. Hurst, was not so final in his letter of January 7, 1974, to William C. Schaab, the attorney for the Taos Indians at that time. He said, "To superimpose a New Study Area over this would violate the long range planning principles, as well as the trust of the people of New Mexico and the American Taxpayers whose tax dollars have gone into the highway construction already completed." The "already completed" part went or goes up to Twining, for the apparent sole purpose of providing all-weather access to the Taos Ski Area. We thought we were simply identifying a prime roadless area — which it is — without that power-line swath, and we get accused of "violating a trust." Actually, neither the Sawmill Canyon-Ditch Cabin Area nor the Gold Hill (Columbine-Hondo) Roadless Area completely circumvent the high road between Red River and the Taos Ski Valley since much of the road would have to follow the present road up the south slopes to the "Pasture" on Pattison Trust Lands and down the north slopes in a sort of snake dance. It is true the two Roadless Areas meet at about the power-line swath on that north slope. Better reasons for the Loop Road or the High Road will have to be generated if such an expensive undertaking is to be reconsidered.

More dynamic road forces were at work in 1974 as well — a Draft Environmental Statement for Taos Ski Valley Expansion to include a Kachina Village upstream from Twining towards Williams Lake. Ernie Blake and Company, as well as the Pattison Trust, wanted an access road through the intervening Forest Service land. Our response was that if the access road were given, an access agreement via the Bull-of-the-Woods mine road to the north end of the Wheeler Peak Wilderness Area should be one of the conditions. After all of the flak of public reaction to the Draft E.S. had settled back to earth, Bill Snyder, the Carson National Forest Supervisor, said no road to Kachina Village.

In 1975 and 1976 there were times when the Bull-of-the-Woods road was closed by the Pattisons and in 1977, it sounds as if a repeat may be in store. It seems to be open during the week and closed on weekends only to reverse fields the next time one inquires. In 1979, there is now a new private road on Pattison land west of Frazer Peak.

Farrell Perdreauville of Trout Unlimited loaned me his file on the Sewage Plant issue of the Taos ski Valley. The pertinent facts are that, after ten years of operation of the ski area, a sewage plant was installed in 1967. It had a design capacity of 32,000 gallons per day which was estimated to be adequate for an approximate equivalent population of 350 people. However, the performance of the facility has been degraded by the high altitude and low winter temperatures at the location, and by inadequate operation and maintenance practices. Many lodges and condominiums have been added since 1967 and new lifts have been installed. In 1974, overnight accommodations were available for 900 people, and the annual skier days exceeded 100,000. The plant was built with 75% federal funds, 12.5% state, and the balance, private funds. The Twining Cooperative Water and Sewer Association in 1974 was obligated by the Federal Water Pollution Control Act to obtain a permit from the U.S. Environmental Agency (EPA) to discharge into the Rio Hondo.

On August 16, 1976, the EPA issued an administrative order citing specific violations of monitoring, operational, and planning requirements.

A group of landowners downstream at Arroyo Hondo are urging the Association to operate the plant properly, to build a more adequate plant, and to stop using "taxpayers' money to incur their private profit." They say, "The people of Arroyo Hondo will continue to oppose the expansion of the Taos Ski Valley and the taxpayers' subsidy of private business interests there." (Taos News, April 14, 1977).

The New Mexico Environmental Improvement Agency said in their June 20, 1977, letter to Trout Unlimited that:

1. A full time operator was hired to operate and maintain the plant.

2. No new hookups will be made until the present facility is upgraded or a new one is built.

3. Upgrading construction is underway (in time for 1977-1978 ski season) as a temporary measure.

4. A new district is being formed which will be eligible for federal funding.

To all of these tribulations around the perimeter of the Wheeler Peak area, we must conclude with a new understanding of "Ah, Wilderness!"

One evening in mid-March, 1977, I received a call from one of the men from the Questa USFS Ranger District to the effect that Secretary Bergland of the Department of Agriculture had requested the Attorney General of the United States to render an opinion of the legality of the secretary of Interior's (Andrus) "readjustment" of the Wheeler Peak boundary to exclude Bear Lake and its watershed all of the way up to the Crestline of the Wilderness.

The Federal Register of April 11, 1977, contained the "Order Clarifying Boundary," and it was issued and signed by Secretary Cecil D. Andrus.

We sent a letter on May 16 asking for a transcript of the public facts. We received a number of letters which belabor the following points: The Secretary of Agriculture asked the Attorney General to review the validity of the Order by which some of the Wheeler Peak Wilderness was transferred to the Taos Pueblo Indians. The Indian claim was that an erroneous survey in 1893 misplaced the boundary of the Antonio Martinez Grant which was acquired by the United States in trust for the Taos Pueblo in 1941.

It is my understanding that the Department of Justice confirmed the opinion. A new Survey was made during the summer of 1977. When we defeat someone at war, we spend the rest of our lives giving him reparations in many forms.

TRIPS TO TAKE IN THE WHEELER PEAK AREA

A good trip for a starter is up the Lake Fork of the Rio Hondo to Williams Lake. Sometimes the road to the meadow above Twining is open and sometimes it isn't. Either way, there is a sign (unless somebody did not like signs) aiming you southeast — up the canyon. Yes, it is the same canyon that the famous seven-mile Rubezahl ski trail comes down from the Number 2 Ski Lift — Kachina Basin. Lift Number 4 is a shorter.

The one time I was at Williams Lake in a July long ago, it was gently raining. Somebody had made a fire, and the smoke was hanging about lazily above the water. Tiny New Mexico-sized trout slurped salmon eggs; they disdained flies hauled out onto the depths by a plastic ball cast with a spinning rod.

The next time I was near there, Joe Threadgill, a western writer, had his van stuck in the aforementioned meadow. Bob Watt, a Los Alamos physicist, Bill Stevens, and I were looking at boundaries of some future additions to Wheeler when we ran into a harried Joe. The van came out with a tug and his daughter was saved the inconvenience of another night out with her swain. Bob Watt, our first Chairman of the New Mexico Wilderness Study Committee, could surely drive his four-wheel drive Jeep Wagoneer. He managed to get us into road heads that were scarcely roads, with help from a "tilt indicator" that he had made. But we had to hike from there on.

Drive to the Caribel Mine, for example, from Red River. On some maps it is called Black Mountain. Follow the tracks up the mountain to the north of the old Caribel Stamp Mill. The road goes past some old bunk houses and turns into a trail to Pioneer Lake. The tracks generally keep going on up to Gold Hill. The Forest Service has tried several times to put up a no-motorized sign on that trail. It seems to be down more often than it is up. There is good water for your canteen as high up as Pioneer Lake.

Leave your car in the Columbine Creek Campground. A mile upstream over some pretty bridges, you should pass the fork to the Deer Creek Trail. Continue up Columbine Creek Trail to the Lobo Peak Ridge. You have at least a couple of options. The Placer Fork takes off the main trail to the east about a half mile above the Deer Creek Trail. It hits the ridge trail about a mile southwest of the summit of Gold Hill. Whether you go up Columbine or Placer Fork or Willow Fork, you will hit the ridge trail. Then turn left! If you don't you'll end up down in the Hondo Canyon to the south of the Lobo Peak Ridge Trail.

Signs have a way of disappearing. The Forest Service tells me that bears tear them down. (Some others must have something to do with it. They unscrew bolts — with their claws and teeth?) However, if you watch carefully for the intersection, you may find the vertical post which had a sign on it at one time. Somebody on a horse had a contract to drag a wheel which measured something. Then he picked out a sign which said Flag Mountain 4 miles thataway. Then three cigarettes later it was 5 miles to Rio Hondo. The next year the porcupines had eaten the signs. Now they are screwing the signs on the Corten square steel tubing with non-reversing bolts. I'll bet the bears take rocks and deface the signs. Interpretive signing, says the USFS pamphlet. Why don't we interpret that the public (bears) does not want signs?

Flag Mountain. Drive southwest of Questa on the south side of the Red River on the gravel road about a mile and a half. Then a road takes off up the mountain (drywash) to the southeast in the vicinity of Lama Canyon. You will find many places in which the Moly Corporation has set up and drilled exploratory holes. The next time you drive by Questa, look over toward the southeast and you will see how the road has wandered the western escarpment of the mountain.

Drive as far as you can and start walking. Mark

your map where you think your car is parked. You may hear a dozer making the road to another drill site. Watch over to the northeast from the highest ridges as you top out. Those big scarps of bare rock and open swaths in the timber to the north of Columbine or west of Red River are Moly Corporation areas. If you listen carefully, you can hear the big dragline engines unless they are drowned out by the noise of the jets, or the nearby dozer, or even the wind.

There is a trail on the ridge that goes southward to Lobo Peak. If you have someone to meet you, you can drop down the switchback trail in Cristobal Canyon; and, if you can, solve the sometimes locked gates late in the afternoon in the foothills. Some of the gates lift off easily from some hinge pins without disturbing the chains and big padlocks. But do close the gate as the sign says.

The Lobo Peak Trails. A nice trip up Yerba Canon to the northwest of the Rio Hondo just a quarter-mile downstream from the Taos East Condominium (near the junction of the South Fork) is possible even after the heavy snows have started. When you top out, you are only about another quarter mile to the top of Lobo Peak. It was here that I had a strange experience.

I no sooner had made the peak at about 3:00 p.m. that Saturday late in November of 1976 when a wave of nausea washed across me. It was clear to me that my closest friend, Phil Tollefsrud, was in some kind of a crisis. That young man was such a strong prototype of a Viking that he put out megavolts when he died in an Albuquerque hospital that afternoon.

The trail goes east to the next canyon called Manzanita. The snow was about knee deep in the timber but some deer had recently gone down the trail in front of me. It was 3:45 p.m. when I started down. The sulfur taste and the nausea were gone with a few mouthfuls of snow. In spirit, Phil and I ran down Manzanita together like a couple of Basques. When the snow thinned to only five or six inches, the euphoria disappeared. The last mile from the small clearing to Bill (Steven's) cabin at the mouth of Manzanita on the Hondo was a twilight of abject loneliness for an old man. Bill understood and said very little on the drive home. Sonja, Phil's wife, called me with the sad news shortly after I got home that Sunday evening. The coroner's report ultimately read: "probable cause of death — Leptospirosis." He possibly drank some contaminated water in Wyoming the week before while on a hunting trip. He was impatient with my caution in always treating "wild-canteen water."

The Gavilan Canyon Trail. The trail only starts up Gavilan from the Hondo. Then you get lost. There is a giant, massive rock formation above you and you don't care. You decide that you should go back to the car and get the map. Your ten-year-old son wants to stay and climb rocks.

The map shows the trail going up the branch canyon to the west of the rocks and we finally found it, a rain shower later. Some beautiful soaring switchbacks take us up onto the Lobo Ridge trail. Something like a mile and a half to the west we found one of those bare posts (bear posts?) on the wrong side of the trail. I was sure it must be either Italianos Canyon or Manzanita maybe? My notes talk about columbines and Johnnie-Jump-Ups in bloom. There was at least one poison ivy leaf that touched my son's hand that afternoon. We had no Calamine lotion nor washing soda. Much washing with soap and water eased it up.

I'm sure a photographer would prefer to ascend Italianos and come down that Gavilan branch in the late afternoon to get a shot of the sun kissing Wheeler goodnight up past those vertical Hawk Rocks (Gavilan Cliffs).

South Fork short circuit. Get a permit from the district Ranger at Questa to go to the top of the Number 2 Ski Lift. Politely ask Ernie Blake or the owner (operator) of Taos Ski Valley for his (her) permission to go up the road to the heading. Resist the temptation to follow the ridge around to the south. Plunge off straight to the west and dig your heels in. Do not cross over the ridge to your north or you will wear out your billfold dropping into the Hondo and maybe even starting a rock slide.

That ridge looks inviting — the one that heads west. I have never tried to follow it down. I know the canyon drains into the South Fork. Practically all of the game trails are on the contour. You seem to know instinctively that you should not go down. There are only a few places in which you have to lie on the brush to get through.

When you get into the bottom of the canyon, it gets easier — if the flies are not thirsty for salt that day. The trip is an unbelievable three miles! All down hill. Absolute wilderness.

South Fork of the Rio Hondo — a route, not a trail. Do the same permit procedure. This trip was on June 25, 1977, with Bill Stevens and his son, Richard. Peggy Stevens drove Richard's truck back down the ski lift road. It is much less comforting to drive down it — even with four-wheel drive — than to go up.

We stepped out at 9:00 a.m. at 11,700 feet elevation or so, climbed up and contoured around the west side of Kachina Peak to the south of old Number 2 Ski Lift. Without snow, the "bowl" looks pretty rough for skiing. In that saddle just north of Kachina there is a shelter, not like an Adirondack, for the weary. It had four students from New Mexico Tech debating whether a nearby rock was Amphilbolite or not.

Our course was set slightly downhill to the base of the rock field at the western face of Lake Fork Peak. One piece of good advice is to stay separated by 10 yards or so and cross such boulder fields horizontally. The angle of repose is in the order of 40 degress. Some of those beautiful, lichen-covered dollops are loose and teetery.

One navigates by sight, not compass or trail. It was almost due south, however, about a mile and a half from the truck (horizontally) when we first bottomed out. Lake Fork Peak was straight up to the east and South Fork Peak was somewhere over to the west. A little stream trickled out of a spring. And there were the remains of an old cabin, circa 1900, nearby. Only the tumbled-down chimney and a couple of notched logs gave it away. The first sign of habitation was a skeletal tin can near the stream. We found no aluminum beer cans or snap tops. That tin can vintage was some 60 years previous.

We noticed considerable bear sign as we descended. The Hudsonian flora yielded slowly to scarlet pennstamens and skunk cabbage. There was some elk sign due west of the old cabin site as we next dropped down to the South Fork Creek a half mile.

South Fork starts in an avalanche chute northwest of Vallecito Mountain. It tasted as if it had ice cubes in it. There is only one description of following that wild cateract down to the main Hondo. Bushwhack! One follows an occasional game trail but they tend to contour away from the stream, and you find yourself too far above the stream the next time you see it.

We had our fly-rods with us and Richard caught a beautiful 12-inch native trout in one of the few holes in that tumultous thread of water. I hooked something smaller which promptly snagged me under an overhang. That trout was brilliantly colored — orange-red — a prime cutthroat.

As you take turns finding a way along the stream, you are forced from one side of the creek to the other by the tangle. The spruce changes to mixed aspen and willows to aspen and scrub oak, then to a sumac combination. The columbines and Indian paintbrush and hairbells were not quite a hazard to each step, but maybe every four.

The deer sign picked up as the bear sign diminished. The coyote sign was skimpy. There were many birds along the creek but few squirrels or chipmunks contested our passage. It started to grumble up near the Peaks in back of us but we only got a sprinkle. The ticks, which were bad two weeks before, were about spent for the season.

A trail route (someday) above the creek some 50 or 100 yards would make a delightful transit of a pristine wilderness. We made it down to the Hondo at the Taos East condominium at 6:00 p.m. We estimated some six (horizontal) miles and a drop of some 3,500 feet in altitude.

On August 18, Harold Walling and I were dropped off by Peggy and Bill Stevens at the top of Number 2 Ski Lift. We ran the ridges southward to Kachina Peak and on south to Lake Fork Peak. Last year's snow was still on the north slope of Vallecito Peak where we found a trail.

It soon became clear that we could not follow the ridge around to South Fork Peak. We camped for the night in the first timber patch immediately southwest of the Vallecito Peak in a branch of Martinez Canyon, probably on Indian land. There are very few spots flat enough for a sleeping bag. The BLM boundary survey of 1977 located the markers around the South Fork Basin along the ridgetops by helicopter in such a way that it is very hard to stay off Indian land on a cirque transit of the peaks.

The next day we went along the ridges northwest of Vallecito Peak by first making a wide swing around the headwall west of Vallecito and back onto the ridge before we topped out on South Fork Peak. The views down into the basin were so distracting that it induced us to dawdle overlong over our maps. Details in the basin are not exactly like the map shows the features.

We descended to the mouth of the South Fork by making a compass bearing line down the steep ridge from the lesser peak northwest of South fork Peak. Two hours of going down that grade makes one wish for resharpened heels or even to turn around for a change and back down. At the bottom, the weather cut loose for about 30 minutes. We were soaked when we arrived at the car near Taos East condominium (the south fork junction with the Rio Hondo). It was a beautiful two-day trip.

The Wheeler Peak Grand Cirque Trip took Phil and me seven days of loafing and we enjoyed every step of it. I'm going to mix in things about backpacking gear vintage mid-1970's so you can see how primitive we were back then.

The route approximates 36 miles with a divider and map. We probably did 40 miles, horizontally, My pack averaged 35 pounds with three quarts of water. We started only slightly above Bull-of-the-Woods Pasture on Saturday in mid-June 1974 and circled around from Frazer to Wheeler to Old Mike to Taos Cone to Taos Peak and down Sawmill Park to Ditch Cabin.

The route then went the 50 miles around by car to the top of the Pasture again, over to Goose Lake, Gold Hill, down Deer Creek to Columbine Campground and home. If you are not interested in a round-by-round description of the trip, skip the rest of this chapter; some of it is how to backpack. Besides, I may have been made giddy by the altitude and the pleaure of being with my best friend in spectacular country.

My notes, or trip report, say "Wheeler Peak Week." We drove to Cottonwood Canyon Motel across the road from Cottonwood Campground west of Red River and parked the truck. We drove Phil's four-wheel drive up past Bull-of-the-Woods Pasture and parked between the mine and there. Some dozen or more large timberfalls blocked the road at that saddle just north of the mine.

That evening we made camp in La Cal Basin in a tongue of trees by the snow brook. The tundra along that ridge from Frazer Mountain was just beginning to wake up. My son, Kent, had taken some close-up picutes of the tiny blossoms up there one July day in 1971. Some of the blossoms measured little more than a millimetre in diameter. The scale of things makes our Vasque Red Wing boots look gigantic.

We could have gone above timberline that first day, but decided to camp out of the wind. It was the take-it-easy day, the altitude acclimating one. Six miles between 11,000 and 12,500 were enough to start. We saw a buck deer in velvet grazing below us. That night, the coyotes serenaded us. A couple of owls talked about something for an hour or two. It was probably my orange tent that was their conversation piece. Phil generally disdained my five pound tent (2-man) and used his two-and-a-half-pound shelter-half.

The wind and rain seldom drove him inside but sometimes the mosquitos did. The oversized polyurethane foam sleeping bag I had made along the Gil Phillips-Ocaté lines was luxurious in that tent even if it did weigh five pounds in the stuffing bag. I built a compressor into the stuff bag and, when it was lashed for the trail, it was hard as a parachute pack. I used a French sleeping bag liner and another for a cover, both of which must have been specified for a Charles DeGaulle; I am six-two and one-eighty and I still rattle around inside even with the top noosed up to a three-inch hole. Anyhow, my pack has to go outside if man number two has to get in the tent.

We were topping out of La Cal at sunrise that special Sunday morning. My morning prayers came easily and aloud. We had breakfast with the sun's rays shining up at us from below. Phil's Svea stove was balky, but my quiet alcohol stove did our coffee water at 12,700 feet with no problems. My first meal was a couple of high-protein cereals and some powdered milk in a couple of plastic bags and raisins sloshed with some canteen water. That is the only breakfast that does not abandon me by ten o'clock whether at work or on the trail. We talked about that snowshoe rabbit we had seen just at timberline and how he had missed getting caught by those noisy owls and coyotes last night. He was still white and the snow was gone down there.

Even if it was mid-June, where the trail was snow-covered by a couple of cornices, we could see that we were the first ones to cross recently. The cairn register on Wheeler is a six-inch pipe with a cap screwed onto it and there were three years of registrations documented.

We had no lightning that trip to run us off the ridge as it had when Kent and I had been there previously. We had a couple of squalls of corn snow before we cleared Simpson Peak and dropped down to Bear Lake. The switchback south of Old Mike Peak leads to a jutting ridge that permits one to see one of the two Blue Lakes. You can also see the steep switchback trail on the east side of Old Mike Peak.

We dropped down the 4.6 mile trail to Bear (or Lucero) Lake. A couple of Taos Indians on horses were coming out. They said "snow too deep in trees on trail; go around rocks." There seemed to be about three lakes but we finally found the "true Blue." The Eastern brook trout, being a char, did not need a stream to spawn. They took Panther Martin lures and we had all we could eat for dinner and breakfast.

My ensolite closed-cell pad was luxurious, even against those rocks under my sleeping bag. It weighs ten ounces and reaches from the shoulders past the hips. The pad rolls up into a five-or-six-inch diameter cylinder and goes into a stuffing bag on top of the pack. I put my tent poles and stakes, my beret, and wind shell jacket inside the rolled pad to keep it from collapsing.

The last things I heard were Phil swatting mosquitos, the beaver splashing around among the spawing fish, and something like a loon calling out. Once I woke to hear the deep reverberation of a porcupine chewing on a disreputable outhouse. No wonder the Indians complained about that structure in their testimony on the Wheeler Peak Proposed Management Plan.[7] The whole matter was probably resolved by the recent ceding of the Bear Lake Area from the Wilderness to the Taos Indians.[7] Since you can't go to the Lake anymore, you won't have to climb back up that 1,500 feet to the ridge by Old Mike Peak.

Just as we topped out on that ridge, a 50-60-mph blast of cold wind laced into us. I had on my nylon windbreaker, but Phil was in his shirtsleeves. He solved the problem by plunging over the cornice which was a good 60° slope. I followed him — we were like two beavers on a slide. The trail switches about three times in that one-hundred yards, and we came down on the trail below just as if we knew it was going to be there. Our seats got wet but we were out of the wind just as it started to hail. Our Vibram soles were a lifesaver as we punched holes in the snow cornice trails down Old Mike toward Red Dome Peak toward the east.

The wrap-around suspension of my pack really helped get the load of my pack into my legs since the only tabs attaching the belt are at the points of the hips on each side. The shoulder straps stabilize the load without pulling down on your shoulders as they used to.

I began to feel my 60 years when we had to punch holes in timber drifts. We found where the Indian horses had floundered in the snow which was deeper than their bellies. That was on the south side near Bear Lake. Again, on the northeast side of Red Dome the drifts would not hold me and my pack up. Every other step went to the bottom.

We sacked out that night just below the saddle west of Taos Cone. The only flat place was up there in the saddle but the wind was climactic. A slight trickle of water started in a seep several hundred feet below us — on Indian land. But we still had two quarts each. The snow was above us and a mile back. It would be easy to get dehydrated up there.

Lipton used to make great dinners called Stroganoff and Ham Cheddarton. They were both economical and tasted great when you added the prescribed tablespoon of margarine and a cup or so of water. They provided all of the calories, protein, and starch. Top that off with a small can of cocktail fruit and a cup of coffee and you had it made. The only trouble was that housewives did not buy them at the supermarkets and Lipton stopped marketing them. My letter about selling them through the backpack stores was answered by some one who said forget it. Since then, as long as we have to carry the water into most of our New Mexican back country, we carry some of it with us in cans of stew, hash, etc.

Taos Cone does not seem like much of a cone when you are on it. There is a crater-like hole which may have led to its name.

We could see out to the east unimpeded, now. A teepee burner north of Eagle Nest Lake was putting out a pall as far as we could see to the northeast. The Angel Fire ski-run clearings were visible even from that distance. There was a massive bald ridge northeast of Taos Cone that was inviting. Instead of jumping off without a hang glider, we went down the east side until we cut the trail.

The trail changed to an old wagon road about one and a half miles before we got to Sawmill Park. It pays to locate the probable trail location from above because there are many old "wood roads" near the boundary of the Maxwell Grant. The Sawmill Park trail is a string of sighting posts or stakes that must have been great from horseback once upon a time. We saw elk, deer, and a lot of birdlife in the grassy side canyons. Phil saw two ptarmigans just southwest of Red Dome Peak.

The fish were tiny in the little stream, but I caught an eight-inch trout for an appetizer for dinner. The second-growth trees were starting to invade the park margins. We even saw a porcupine shuffling along the trail. He couldn't make out what we were so he sniffed our boots and kept going.

There used to be an old Jeep trail into the bottom of Sawmill Canyon, but the USFS put in a new trail over northwest to Ditch Cabin and discontinued the road. We ran into fresh blowdowns and much green litter in extensive areas without squirrels. As we descended to the 10,000 foot level, it became apparent that there were preferential directions of the blowdown. It was probably the same storm that closed the Bull-of-the-Woods saddle road when we first started.

We stayed overnight near the old site of Ditch Cabin, and Richard Stevens met and drove us the 50 miles around through Red River and back up to the Pasture. On the way, we had a steak dinner, a shower, and reprovisioned for the next segment of the trip. We could have hiked from Ditch Cabin down the East Fork to Middle Fork and up the powerline or the West Fork trail. We had earlier cached our reprovisions at Bill Stevens' cabin.

The trip from the Bull-of-the-Woods Pasture to Goose Lake was uneventful, if scenic. On the ridge above Goose Lake, Phil suddenly stopped, dug out his camera, and went into the low junipers. He got pictures of some bright eyes in the deep shadows. They belonged to several snowshoe rabbits (true hares) which were not white this time.

Another (bear) post marks the top of the trail on the ridge top above Goose Lake. Skid down here, it invites. We camped on the green meadow on the south side of the lake as far away from the road as possible. Enough fish for dinner — the put and take kind — responded to the bubble-and-fly routine. An electrical contractor from Red River and a family from St. Louis, all fishing with marshmallows and chunks of lead, were ecstatic. The garbage dump east of the Lake had been cleaned up a little, and there were cans in the water where Cindy Simmons and her new husband Joe and I had swamped them out so carefully several years before.

The next morning I awoke to a strafing attack by some airship that trilled as it dived. Four or five hummingbirds seemed to take bead on my flame orange tent from the cliffs up there and did a minor sonic boom on it. The dew made everything almost as iridescent as the chest of one of those dive bombers that sat jauntily on the feather in Phil's parked hat. Phil was up on the cliffs watching a pair of peregrines trying to fake him away from their nest. While I watched him with my binoculars, I heard a cony. I crawled up on the talus slope in my yellow nylon sleepers with my binoculars and watched a family of rock morts — coneys, or pikas. Breakfast was late that day. The marmots and Phil played tag. One marmot slid down a snow patch three or more times. A raven searched out the crannies of the cliffs to see if he could locate the clamoring falcon chicks.

That was a Friday and the human animals showed up early, too, in their Jeeps. They fished for half an hour and left — for Middle Fork Lake? A family of kids showed up about 9:30 a.m. and really populated the place. So, we took off bushwhacking up the hill to the northwest of the lake. While I was resting, a grouse took off with its explosive, heart-thumping ruckus. One could rest by merely extending an elbow and you were lying down (up?)

We almost topped out on Gold Hill when a young Jeep herder (on foot!) passed us. He had been hired in Red River to bring a fishing family up to the lake and, while they were busy, he just decided to run over to Pioneer Lake a couple of miles north to see his buddy who had just packed in another family on mules. Then we heard a trail bike coming up the trail from the Claribel Mine direction. We saw tracks on the trail, but the noisy bike stopped somewhere below us.

There was an old cabin northwest of Gold Hill near

Columbine Hondo due north from Lobo Peak.

the spring at the top of Deer Creek. We picked a grassy spot a few hundred yards to the north and settled for the night. Phil's Svea backpack stove had just been turned off. I saw him do it. The blowtorch noise persisted. We did a double-take. A large sailplane with a small turbojet engine was not more than two or three hundred feet above us. The wing looked to be almost a hundred feet tip to tip, and not more than two-feet wide. He hissed off to the east and did a lazy 360° over Pioneer Lake and continued eastward. (It later checked out to be a Santa Fe M.D. who had the first turbine in this country on a sailplane. He got killed in his ship in the spring of 1977 — probably doing the same thing.)

My notes say, "All day long we heard blasting going on at the Taos Ski Valley, three or four air miles to the south. Phil mentioned that he heard the night shift dragline engines at the Moly Corporation mine (north of us) last night at goose Lake." We heard them that night, too, from the head of Deer Creek, both engines and blasting.

An old fire topped out on the Deer Creek ridge and immediately killed a whole forest right at timberline, close to 12,000 feet. It is now a gnarled, bare, ghost forest, and even a relic forest. We only had three or four pictures left and we could have used another role of 36. Phil brought back a sprag of the dessicated wood that looked like some eery, giant sheep's horn, polished and petrified.

The new trail westward, down the Deer Creek, is about a quarter-mile uphill to the north of the creek bottom. It is in the timber all the way and delightful. But my feet began to smart. The Scholls innersoles had lost their springiness and my socks had lost their loft. A change of socks and a rest with the feet in the air above your head "helps drain them" for another five miles. I have since learned to make innersoles out of those indoor-outdoor carpet tiles and they work better than the $5 ones worn by policemen and nurses.

My down sweater came in handy every night and then made into a great pillow in its stuffing bag. My parka served well most every day except that it was still a bit short when draped over my pack, even with the extension fold unsnapped. The rain ran down it, wet my legs in back, and even my fishnet drawers underneath.

My last lunch tasted good. On the first day I generally take a sandwich and some fruit. After that, on successive days I eat a small can of fish steaks (usually herring in various sauces) for protein and a can of shoestring potatoes for starch. A candy bar or a bit of fruit like an orange tops it off. It only takes five minutes to make coffee or instant tea to go with it.

We haven't made an open fire for years. It takes too long, makes a mess, and is a misery to cook over. My alcohol stove (not a Sterno job) even simmers a deer liver slice beautifully. The open fire in winter time is a real pain, even a snare and a delusion!

There is only one more essential piece of gear which I haven't mentioned. It is a thin pair of buckskin gloves, great for rock climbing, nice for cold days, and indispensable for bushwhacking in scrub oak and tornillos. Sometimes we hike in shorts but that can be bloody in our mountain deserts. It was nice to change to a thin pair of moccasins or sneakers each night around camp. A beret is good for cold nights with your head out of the bag. Incidentally, the nylon sleepers work well in a sleeping bag. You can even turn over without taking the bag with you. A squeeze-bottle of anti-perspirant makes sleeping inside the bag tolerable. Then, if the wind comes up or it gets too cold for your bag's rating, you can slip your down sweater (your pillow, remember) on without getting out of the sack. It adds 15-to20 degrees warmth to wear your clothes in the bag. But I now have a down bag (three pounds) with most of the loft on the topside and it works great. So I sleep with the nylon things on even in the dead of winter trail-skiing into Williams Lake.

You can read about the Horseshoe Lake and Lost Lake Trails in guide books. There were too many people and too much rain when I went in there. Somebody had a nervous dog in the next camp.

There is more to see in the Wheeler Area than I have covered. Discover it for yourself and think of some of us who have worked for so many years to get Wilderness legislation for the whole area. I hope, as you read this, it no longer will be the smallest wilderness in the whole country because we managed to get the South Fork, Sawmill, and Ditch Cabin additions; and that the Gold Hill (or Columbine-Hondo) Wilderness is enacted before it is permanently disfigured by more "development." Yell out an "I-CO" from the peaks and I will answer you back, so listen carefully.

CHAPTER 7:
Latir Peak National Wilderness

Latir Peak Wildeness is about five miles northeast of Questa in the Carson National Forest and about 30 miles south of the Colorado-New Mexico border. It is a truly alpine wilderness in high peaks, meadows, and ridges. It is in the Sangre de Cristos Mountain range. Get your wilderness map at the Questa ranger station on the road just east of Questa.

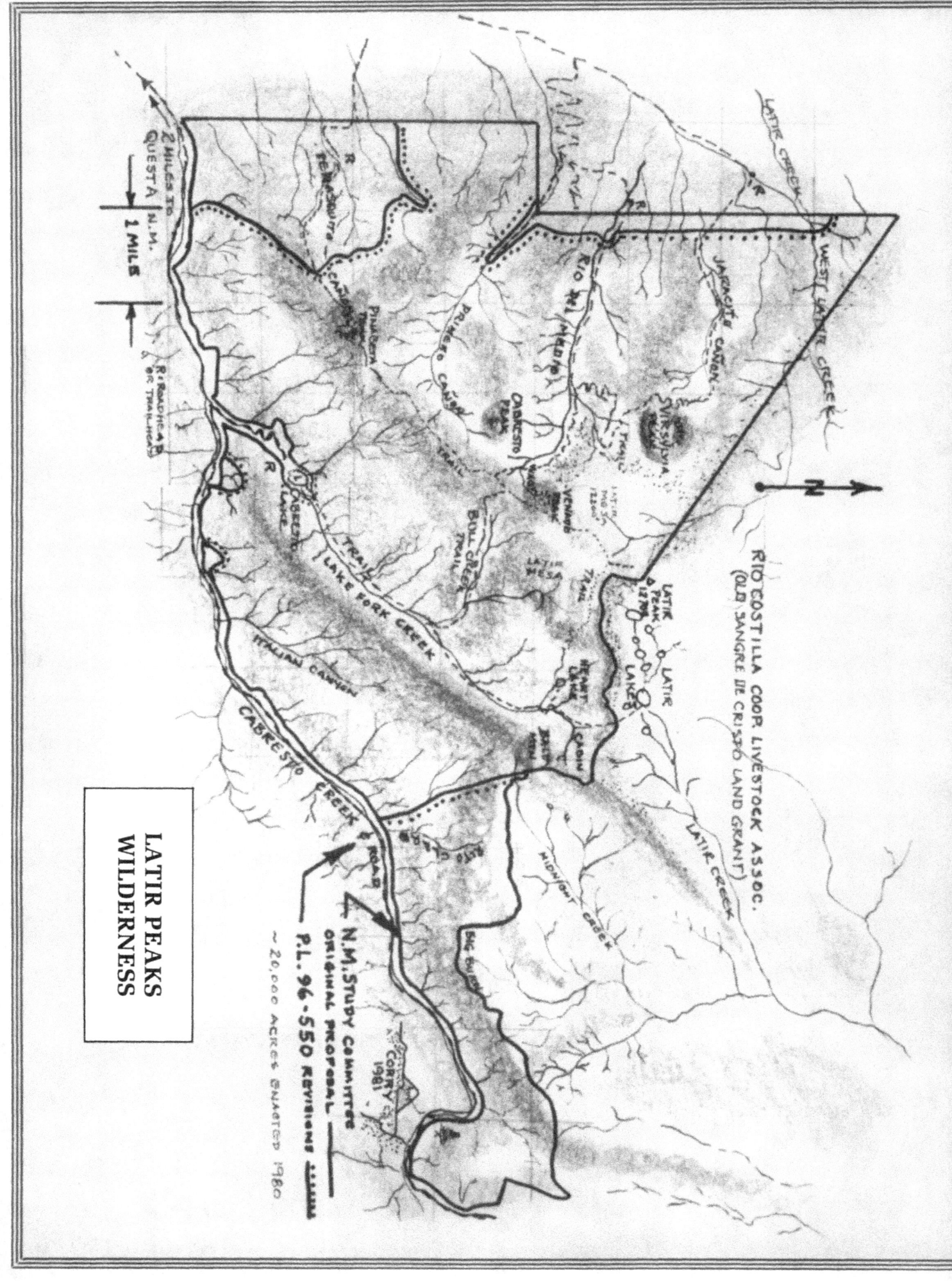

The day was one of those late fall golden glade times when the afternoon sun was not impeded by the few remaining aspen leaves on the tall white trees. The three brown horses stood out sharply against the yellow carpet of fallen leaves and gleaming tree trunks. Eagle feathers tied to the mane of the larger bay fluttered gently as a vagrant breeze blew leaves into the creek.

Nothing disturbed the medicine men in their deep contemplations. A few glowing coals on a huge boulder gave off a pungent smoke for every pinch of powder sprinkled on them. These shamans met in this spot each year to discuss the fortunes and problems of their peoples; one from the Taos people, one from the Dulce Apache area, and the other from the Yankee Mesa people (east of what is now Raton). Hunting had not been adequately rewarded for their tribes that year.

The meeting place was the mouth of the Rito del Medio west of Piñabete Peak, a special and mystical location for the spiritual leaders for centuries before the bearded men appeared with their cattle and horses. That year they were to decide that the plains Indians to the east would have to hunt deer and elk in the western areas because the buffalo herds had dispersed northward beyond their respective territories — some said because of great clouds of grasshoppers on the grasslands. Others said horseback hunting brought the changes.

A century later, a mestizo sheepherder camped for the night next to that ancient boulder. Later he told his patron that he had unusual dreams about snakes in the dark that gave off fire when he hit at them in the blackness. The patron located a mine and a small arrastra there, but of little success. The gold and silver would not amalgamate with the cinnabar in the pit.

The mountain men found a series of beaver dams in the location many years afterward. The arrastra center post protruded above the surface of the main dam. They tied their traps to the post and rubbed it with castor to attract their prey. The old chain abrasion marks on the post were scarcely noticed by the trapper. But he did notice that his trap came up with a glint of copper color on it. He later told Kit Carson, but he could not remember exactly where it was that it happened.

Later decimation of the beaver led directly to the decay of their dams. And a series of fires originated for clean-up on the ranches down below swept across the mountain face and denuded the water retaining brush and forbs on the steep slopes. The heavy cloudbursts gutted the canyons and piled dead trees in the lower reaches of West Latir Creek, Jaracito Canyon, Rito del Medio, Rito del Primero, Piñabete and Peñasquito canyons. The main canyon mouths looked like they were piled with jackstraws. Ranchers burned these accumulations to allow their cattle to get up the canyons to graze.

Prospectors soon discovered that the cloudbursts had uncovered a number of highly mineralized leads. There are some footnoted in the records of the Amizette Smelter fiasco (see Wheeler Peak Chapter) that indicate some ore sacks from Rito del Medio had been brought in for processing by a miner. When the furnace charge solidified, one can imagine that the miner's ore sacks remained stacked until they rotted.

Typical of many streams in our arid mountain deserts, the several creeks emanating from the west side of the Latir mountain clump flow out some distance from the canyon mouths during the spring snow melt. They quickly recede as the season advances and soon sink into the gravel bottoms of each canyon water course. This is the process of formations of the obvious alluvial fans starting at each canyon mouth. In the late 1800's, there was a concerted operation by some of the ranchers and miners to excavate and pan those dry washes all of the way down to the Rio Grande. The placer mining activity apparently paid its expenses because of the extensiveness of disturbances remaining. Cloudbursts and floods in the 1940's and 1950's eradicated more obvious evidences of the handwork.

A couple of miners from E-Town (Elizabeth Town in Colfax County) spent the summer of 1876 in Peñasquito Canyon prospecting some of the exposed leads resulting from those earlier cloudbursts. Rumor had it that they had been fired for high-grading over in E-Town. They had a grubstake and spent a day or two in Cerro at the cantina when they came out for supplies. They could not speak Spanish very well so communications were not entirely satisfactory. Cerro at that time was larger than Questa. Several times they tried to meet with the County clerk and Recorder from Taos when he was staying overnight with relatives in Questa but there is no record of their having done so.

Melaquias Segura, an old timer in Cerro, told his nephew in later years that he remembered the miners bringing some ore sacks to town on pack-mules. He said the ore sacks were made of elk hide and that they smelled. Somehow the claim got filed and ownership passed through several hands until the Archer mine was being worked by at least a dozen men in the early 1880's. The ore was purported to be gold and silver in quartz with much iron pyrites and galena interspersed. The old dumps show the characteristic copper salts which they probably considered as waste.

Several other small mines, all less extensive than the original Archer Number 1, were worked in successive years. There appears to be a maze of changing ownerships in the old Taos County records. This could be the result of having showy ore that could not be smelted economically or it could be that each owner made his fortune and quit while he was ahead (uncharacteristic of miners). The dumps look like those up at the Bull-of-the-Woods Mine in the Twining

District (see Wheeler Peak Chapter).

A miner from Los Alamos named Lindsay and his brother from Oklahoma located and filed a number of claims in Rito del Medio and Primero Canyons during the late 1960's. It is our understanding (in the New Mexico Wilderness Study Committee) that the claims were located for the purpose of mining radioactive minerals. Northrup[1] indicates that there are 49 minerals known to be radioactive, some 34 which contain uranium or thorium as major constituents, and 15 contain only minor amounts of these elements. All will pulse a Geiger Counter but the latter 15 only weakly.

The Lindsays must have tired of walking because a bulldozer suddenly appeared in Rito del Primero. A road was constructed up that canyon in the summer of 1969 and over into the Rito del Medio Canyon the next summer, but without the permission of or notice to the Forest Service. The operator of the bulldozer bragged too much in a Questa bar. Somebody alerted the Forest service as a result.

The Forest Service had a mineral survey of the claims made in 1970 and concluded that they could not be valid claims. Consequently, the Forest Service required the quasi road builder to close and erect barriers on the road, which he did reluctantly. One of our honchos on the area, Armen Chakerian, soon found the road in his crosscountry travels and was mightily perturbed. Armen and an environmental reporter from the Albuquerque Journal (Phil Nicklaus) went into the area and wrote a feature article on the occasion. The article was lauditory of the Forest Ranger's action (See *Albuquerque Journal*, September 28, 1975.)

During the summer of 1978, someone on an Enduro Bike (a type of motorcycle) managed to get around the barriers and cruised the ridges of Piñabete and Cabresto Peaks. Those are surprising machines in that they can traverse even large boulder fields. However, after watching one do it, I'd rather walk. At least they don't cut grooves or ruts on the steep hills as many of the so-called trail bikes do. Fortunately, none of these machines, including snowmobiles, are condoned in National Wilderness.

Since the price of gold jumped from about $200 per ounce in 1979 to over $400 and silver more than tripled as well during the same period, prospectors have started to comb the hills again. They assume, perhaps, that mining and prospecting costs have not inflated correspondingly. The cost of four-wheel drive and off-road vehicles has only risen about 30-40% in the same period but gasoline costs have tripled.

Two men from Cerro, Señors Segura and Gallegos, correctly filed a notice of intent with the Forest Service to construct about 200 feet of road to the old landing at the Archer Mine (in lower Piñabete Canyon) to truck out a 10 ton shipment of ore to the smelter in El Paso. If the ore will process and pay the inflated costs, we may have an operating mine on the western edge or our proposed area. The folks in Cerro have been good neighbors to our big mountain.

Before we leave the west side of our mountain, let me report a strange experience a couple of us had when we were walking out a probable west boundary. It was in the mid-1960's during the period when the Taos, Arroyo Seco, Questa, Lama, and San Cristobal localities were undergoing an influx of young people going back to the earth. They were variouslsy called commune groupees, hippies, and flower children among many other sobriquets by the earlier inhabitants of those small towns.

It was our habit to drive as close to the Forest boundaries as the backroads would permit and walk them out from there with map in hand. Surprisingly, we came upon an ancient truck apparently abandoned along a faint two-track road. There was part of a crate on the bed of the truck which was stamped with the trademark of the Indio Date Company or perhaps Mecca Date Processors. The truck bed was mahogany and there were cane or rattan inserts in some partial sidegates. It had solid tires. The exposed engine looked like it was out of the ark. Those clues jogged my memory of similar trucks in the old date orchards in southern California during the 1930's.

Not far from the old truck was a fanciful house, something of octagonal shape made out of green logs and having many good sized windows. Visible inside was a large main room with a stream and waterfall cheerfully splashing in the sunlight. Unfortunately, nobody was home. We wanted to congratulate them for their selection of such a beautiful setting and execution of such an unusual and unexpected house. We never did get back to get acquainted.

An Alaskan visiting the Molycorp Mines to the southeast of our proposed Wilderness is purported to have said that this part of the Sangre de Cristos was the best he had seen since leaving the Far North. For sheer verticality he should have come up onto the Latirs, not far to the west, about a dozen miles.

As a means of helping you get acquainted with this wilderness redoubt, let's start at Cabresto Lake from our parked car. Above us to the west is Piñabete Peak, at least 3000 feet up and not more than a mile away. Lake Fork Creek trail Number 82 climbs the stream toweard the northeast. It is five miles to Heart Lake. The algae bloom in September of 1978 gave the lake an emerald green hue. None of the half dozen parties camping around the lake had caught any fish. I suspected that the bloom had depleted the oxygen and either killed or driven the fish downstream.

Heart Lake is heart shaped, like that of a real heart, not like a valentine. It is an altitude of 11,600 feet. Latir Mesa is a great tableland above the lake at the 12,000 foot elevation on trail Number 85. The trail, being in the Hudsonian zone, is not a worn tread in some parts but more nearly a route. The trails are heavily used. However, above timberline (approximately 12,000 feet on Latir Mesa) the trails are marked by rock cairns and poles on the tundra. Keeping on route could be a problem between cairns if the weather were socked in since there is no dominant trail tread. In clear weather there are peaks all around you can locate from your map and compass bearings.

On top of Latir Peak (at 12,760 feet) just north of the National Forest boundary on Rio Costilla Cooperative Livestock Association land, one can see the half dozen Latir Lakes to the east and considerably below. The Latir Rock Cairn is on the boundary. Within five minutes all three of us saw some ptarmigan, a large bear, and a full grown wolverine. The ptarmigan are wary but if a group of hikers splits up and takes separate routes the birds can sometimes be observed looking at your friend several hundred yards away but well hidden from him however exposed to your view. Once they detect you, they will disappear in an instant even though there seems to be little cover in the rock field. Sometimes, if you sit quietly in camouflage with your binoculars, you can outwait them in the early morning hours if you are in good ptarmigan territory.

A party of five people with a large black dog (a Labrador, I think) camped above us the night before and went over the saddle from Heart Lake to the Upper Latir Lakes in the morning just as we were leaving camp to climb up onto the Mesa. We heard the dog barking furiously at the approximate time of their arrival at the lake. Just as we topped out on Latir Peak proper (north of the cairn), a large bear was coming out of the col from the east between our summit and a minor crag 100 meters to the north of us. The animal appeared to be fleeing something in back of it.

The bear probably saw us at the same time we saw it. We were less than 50 meters from it as it plunged over the escarpment to the west. Our attention was almost immediately distracted by a smaller animal that seemed to be traveling approximately the same route and it also was looking over its shoulder as it loped along. At a distance of about 75 yards, I managed to get my binoculars on the animal as it dropped down the scree slope to the northwest. All three of us agreed that the smaller animal was a wolverine. It appeared to be a full adult and completely at home on the rock slopes.

Both animals were observed as they travelled down across the open rockslide slopes to the northwest of us toward the basin between us and Virsylvia Peak. The bear was in sight for about five minutes and the wolverine's route took it out of sight in less than a minute. The Game and Fish Department Chief in Albuquerque (Jack McDowell) thought it was probably the first sighting of a wolverine in the state. We believe both the bear and the wolverine were flushed out of the vicinity of the Upper Latir Lake by the big black dog that was so noisy a short time before.

Two more unique wildlife sightings are worth reporting. Dave Saylors owns some 40 acres along Cabresto Creek on the southern edge of our proposed Wilderness. In the late 1960's, he photographed some ptarmigan on top of Latir Peak. That proved to be the first sighting of the birds in the state during the last sixty years. Not long after that, several of us have seen them on the summits of the various peaks near Wheeler Peak as well.

Dave was snowshoeing one January day in 1972 or 1973 near his property in the canyon bottom. Paralleling him for about a mile at distances of 70 to 100 yards or so was a wolf. The animal was far more massive than the coyotes he had observed many times. The sighting is credible for me, because my son Doug and I believe we saw a mature male wolf while we were fishing in the summer of 1956. It was not in the Latir area but on Santa Barbara Creek near Llano about 50 airline miles south of Latir. Frank Hibben, our famous archaeologist and big game hunter[2,3], at the time said that it was impossible. Subsequent observation of wolves in zoos and in movies made in Alaska, Canada, and Isle Royal have convinced me that we were within 10 feet of a true wolf. He just casually glanced at us as he forded the stream between us. Doug thought that the wolf might snag his line, he was that close. I recall a dog or two sounded off upstream from the scattered car camps along the road.

The huge, mountainous territory to the north of Latir is a story in itself. The folks in the vicinities of Costilla and Amalia banded together in 1942 and bought the 90,000 acres of land between the Colorado border and Latir. About 180 families took part. The experiment has been successful so far based upon what little public information has been released. The September 1979 issue of the *New Mexico Business Journal* carried a story about a proposed new ski area. The company's name is the Rio Costilla Cooperative Livestock Association.

The area includes practically all of the Latir Creek and Rio Costilla watersheds including the nine Latir Lakes. It is bounded on the east by the Vermejo Park Ranch, on the north by the Colorado border, and almost extends to Ute Peak on the west. It contains most of the land in the historic Sangre de Cristo Grant.

The land has many known natural resources and probably much more not yet discovered. The timber, cattle forage, wild game, minerals, and recreation make the area a mountain wonderland. At present, the recreation is largely limited to the snowless seasons. Let's look on our adjacent Wilderness to the south of the Rio Costilla ranch. I will call it a ranch for convenience, and not because there are many others like it.

Previous timbering operations were poorly done, probably on a shoestring; many trees were felled and abandoned because they split or cracked when cut. The slash was left in a tangle. The logs were apparently dragged to the loading ramp without trim-

Latir Mesa. Versylvia in background.

ming the branches first. This tore up the forest floor and induced erosion and its subsequent siltation of the Rio Costilla. Some of the trees were pushed over by a bulldozer and then some of them were highgraded out of the piles. In at least one area stumps about three feet high remain. I'm sure the Association now will permit only the most modern and conservative logging practices.

As one drives and walks up the Rio Costilla, you get the impression of traversing a cleft in a huge mountain mass. The canyon is narrow, the boulders are large, and the stream is powerful. There are a few places where cattle have beaten up the canyon bottoms. That condition has been circumvented by opening up cattle waters higher up the mountain sides away from the main stream. Some parts of the timberline country on the ranch were overbrowsed by sheep in the 1920-30 time frame. Those areas are now hard to identify because they have recovered so thoroughly.

The elk herds in residence and occasionally some from Colorado must seem to the owners as providing too much competition for the cattle, particularly in the northern parts of the ranch. Conversely, several guides and outfitters do a large business when the elk population rises. The elk seem less skittish on the ranch than they do on the outside. There is probably less poaching on the ranch than on public lands, perhaps because the ranch lands are better protected. If the Game and Fish Department and the Forest Service had 200 people to oversee 100,000 acres they could perform as well as the owners.

I have not explored much of the entire area in only four brief trips into the ranch. The wildlife appeared plentiful both from the quantity I have seen there, and also based upon the extensive sign one transects while hiking. It should be expected that the Latir Wilderness Area will benefit from this fine pool of wildlife as it gets partially displaced by scheduled developments on the ranch. It surely has many wilderness dependent species on the more remote parts of the ranch at present.

I could not find much in the public records about the mining activities on the old Grant or the ranch. The Sangre de Cristos upthrust of Precambrian rocks tend to indicate a series of horizons for pegmatite mineralization. The Cedros prospect on the ranch has shown feldspar-rich pegmatities which may contain concentrations of other more valuable minerals deeper in the veins. There could be some Quaternary and Tertiary Age granitic uplifts (Cenozoic Era) eventually discovered where the Precambrian is shattered and faulted near the headwaters of the Rio Costilla. Some of the same strange molybdenite concentrations in the magma which is under the Molycorp's stamping grounds might occur also under the ranch lands. Another such ore body could be expected to drastically change the atmosphere of the ranch.

Sometime in the past, probably in the late 1800's, placer miners dug up the gravels in the West Latir Creek for 200 hundred yards some distance above the southwest boundary of the ranch. They must have gone to bedrock, judging from the sizes of the boulders they dislodged in the process. The treatment looks similar to that in the canyons on the south side of Eagle Nest Baldy Peak. Since there do not seem to be mine dumps up above, they probably found the "Mother Lode".

The mother lode for the Association will probably be their ski resort by-products. This will provide a year-round income in that seasonal recreational activities, properly advertised, could sustain accommodations for several thousand people. That influx should increase the number of people exploring the ranch backcountry and could spill over onto the Latir Wilderness. The ranch road network would be improved to facilitate movement of visitors. And that would surely improve the access to the north side of our proposed wilderness and possibly increase the control problems for the Forest Service.

In many ways the ranch is attractive as is the adjacent Vermejo Park Ranch to the east of it. The Pennzoil Company had purchased it from a Mr. Gourley in the mid-1970's. The State of New Mexico talked about acquiring the ranch at that time, bit the price was out of its reach. Rumors about the possible acquisition of the Vermejo by the National Park Service have not been given much currency although it is of that caliber. The price now approaches that which bought Alaska from the Russians. Much of the Vermejo is beautiful de-facto wilderness and would be a wonderful addition to our national heritage of enacted wilderness.

The dominant activity to the south of the Latir Area is the Molycorp mine west of the town of Red River. On a quiet night on the southern flanks of Piñabete Peak you can hear the big trucks rumble about five airline miles away. When the wind is coming directly from the south, one can hear the big engines distincly. Their big open pit appears to be at least 1000 feet from the upper end of the cut on the mountain to the bottom of the pit. The lower lip of the pit allows trucks to haul the ore out of a much shallower bowl but still onto very steep grades to their mill. It is a very thrilling ride the first few times. The night time operation is an unearthly visual experience. Make an appointment to see it.

Their mill concentrates the ore and the molybdenite is shipped in 800 pound barrels to the nearest railroad in Alamosa, Colorado. The tailings are piped down the Red River in a slurry to the extensive tailings ponds you can see from State Highway 3 west of Questa. The lines cross the Red River several times. The big pipes seem to break right in the middle of the stream and drop a fatal load into the water almost every year.

I have a theory on what causes the line ruptures, or at least contributes to the leaks. As the slurry moves through the pipe, it generates an electrical current that is drained off, or grounded at areas of contact with the moist earth on which the pipes rest. However, where the pipes are suspended above the ground for any great distance, such as when they cross the river, larger currents exist in the lines. This electrolytic system causes increased corrosion at those locations. The highest point of stress in the line is midway between the two suspension points on each side of the stream. Put both the electrolysis and the tensile stresses together and you have a designed-to-leak system. Better supports and more grounding would reduce the breakage.

When the slurry leaks into the stream, the finely ground tailings suffocate the stream bottom life and the fish starve or migrate. The sand emulsion also tends to coat their gills. The first few spills contained chemicals toxic to the riparian habitat. The Red River Fish Hatchery downstream has been adversely affected several times. The points on the slurry line which have repeatedly failed should be alarmed so the valves could be closed for immediate repairs.

You can get a panoramic view of some of the surface disturbances from the Columbine Campground west of Red River town. An even better view can be had from the ridge due east of the campground. That view should not change very much after they change back to shaft and tunnel mining by the early 1980's.

At some point, one of their tunnels might emerge along Cabresto Creek if their ore body extends much further north. That could have some adverse effect upon the adjacent Latir Peak Wilderness Area, particularly if they put in another mill to process the ore coming out of the tunnel. There would be no more wolves on Cabresto Creek.

The legislative status in 1979 was as follows. Our proposed (New Mexico Wilderness Study Committee) 1975 Omnibus Bill included a 26,600 acre Latir Peak Wilderness. The 1972 RARE I Chief's List (U.S. Forest Service) had the area as 18,600 acres. After little action derived from RARE I, RARE II was fired up in 1978 with an accelerated timescale and some more systematic rating processes were included. The original RARE II Forest Service studies added up a figure of 25,960 acres for Latir in 1977. The harder they looked at it the smaller it became until, when the final RARE II Forest Service Recommendations were made to the Administration in early 1979, the area submitted was 24,600 acres. The public response at the earlier meetings indicated 394 for wilderness and 51 against, an 89% public opinion as a pro-wilderness expression. It did not address the specific size.

One of the typical last minute ploys exercised by some of the anti-wilderness forces was a farce. It was claimed by an unnamed person that there was 18 MBF (18,000 board feet) of timber in the eastern portion of the proposed Latir Peak Wilderness Area. Congressman Manuel Lujan was apprised of the supposed fact. I also heard about it. Representative Lujan reacted to the effect that he had no difficulty with endorsing the western end of the proposed area, but not the east end.

I contacted the Questa Ranger's Office to see if somehow we had missed a patch of merchantable timber. He assured me that we had not, that the only timber that was potentially feasible to remove resided in a few stringers in some of the canyons branching north from Cabresto Creek. Furthermore, he indicated that those stringers were not eligible for timber sale because of the incident stream and watershed damage. He also took the occasion to extend an invitation to our Senators and Representatives to make an escorted visit to the area. A call and letter to Mr. Lujan restored him to his original position of full endorsement. If the opposition had been only an month or so late, their tactic might have worked with drastic effect on this area.

Early in 1979, the Atlantic Richfield Company issued a statement of conflicts with RARE II recommendations. In their Summary of RARE II Conflicts they said that they are "extremely concerned about the escalation in the rate of federal land withdrawals from multiple public use. And, most lands under investigation for withdrawal contain minerals as well as geological structures favorable to oil and gas." They then went on to tabulate the RARE II areas containing conflicts for base metals, uranium, oil/gas, and geothermal, and then graded them as critical, significant, or moderate. Latir Peak area, RARE Tract No. 3031 was marked critical for both base metals and oil/gas.

I made a comprehensive study during February and March, 1979, as well as pulling all of my notes and prior analyses together on all the areas on which they had made their conflict statements. My mining background stood us in good stead.

LATIR PEAK WILDERNESS TRAILS AND ROUTES

I have reviewed my trail and route notes and compared them with Herb Ungnade's book.[4] His trail information is more complete than mine, so use his recipe this time. When I get on top of those long, bare ridges, I seem to forget about the trails anyway. If the trail is going in the direction I want to go, I follow it. If not, I don't. I find that I conscientiously rock hop to avoid walking on the tiny and tender tundra plants.

Water in the Latir high country is another matter. If there is some snow in patches, your problem is solved. If not, you will probably find out what I did. The maps show streams in the canyons but in most instances there was not enough flow to fill a canteen for at least a quarter mile down hill. The water should be treated before you drink it.

CHAPTER 8:
Apache Kid National Wilderness

The Apache Kid National Wilderness is about 40 miles southwest of Socorro in the San Mateo Mountains and about 35 miles northwest of Truth or Consequences. The easiest approach is via the trail heads at Springtime Recreation Area about 10 miles west of I-25 Highway. Get your wilderness map at the Forest Service offices in Albuquerque, Magdalena, or Truth or Consequences.

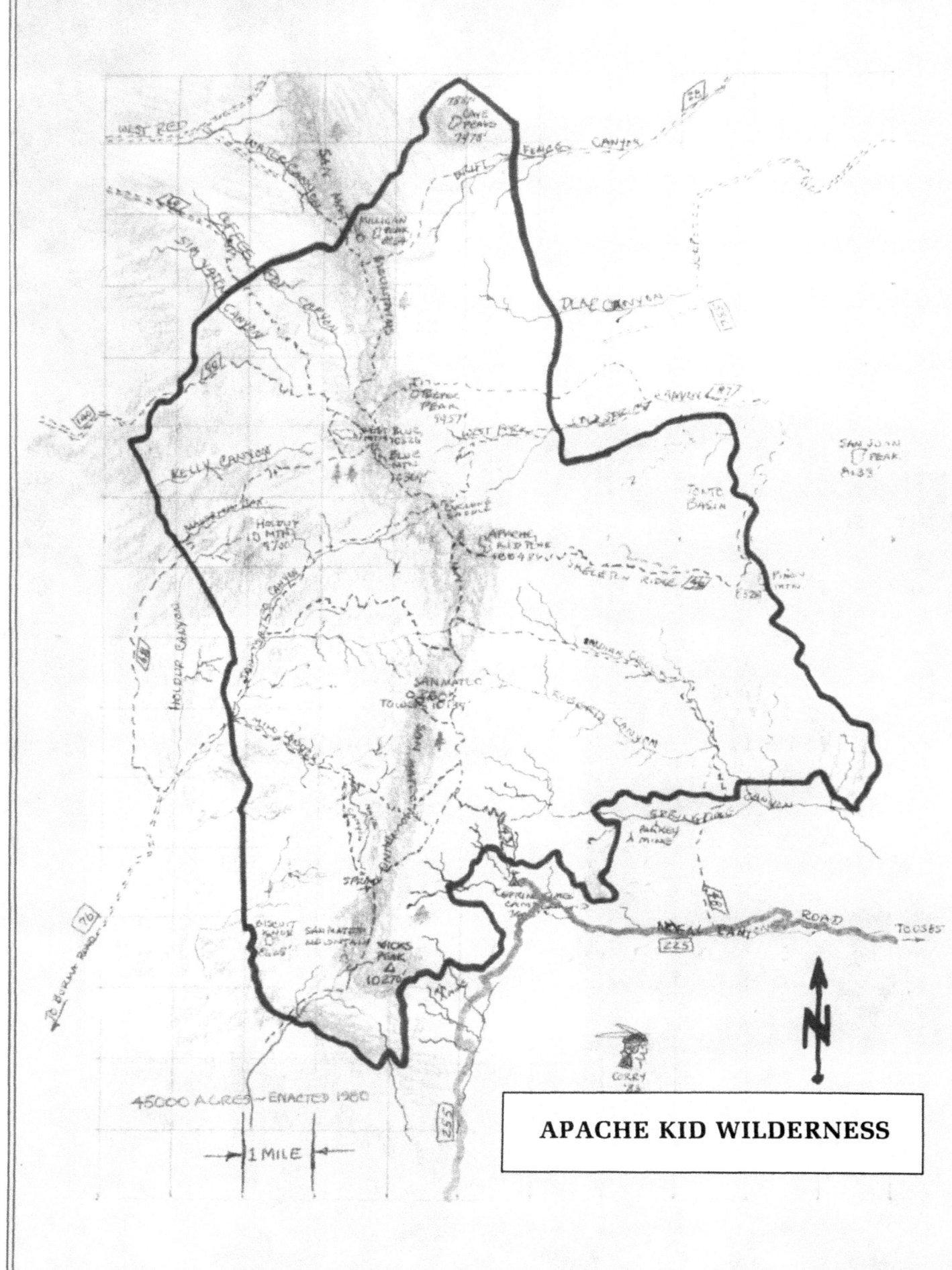

A band of hunters was scouring the dry washes on the west side of the big river that early spring day in the mid-1500 AD period. They expected to find a buffalo calf newly dropped by its mother in those sheltered draws near the river that are the first to green up as the season changes. The larger watercourses still ran with the last flush of the melted snows. Along the river, flocks of birds greeted spring.

These men were sensitive to all that was around them. Hunters did not operate alone because of the animosity of neighboring tribes and the centuries old habit of capturing slaves. They noticed something disturbed the birds upriver into great massed swirling flights. The hunters scattered to concealment. From the sound they thought it might have been three or four elk or buffalo but usually birds did not take flight at such transits.

Light tinkling sounds joined the plodding thuds of hoofs. At first sight the oncoming animals looked like antlerless elk in the brush. Then they saw men on the backs of the animals — their first sight of horses and riders. Two Spaniards, probably soldier messengers from Coronado's encampment at Tiguex upriver (near present day Bernalillo) were making a forced march to the Spanish settlements in Mexico. This scene, including its unique odor which remained after the Caballeros passed, dumbfounded the Indians.

Soon the Indians in the confluence of the Alamosa Arroyo and the Rio Grande became used to the occasional passage of mounted horsemen in glinting jackets, helmets, and even saddles with polished buckles. There was little Spanish activity after Coronado went back to Mexico in 1542[1], until around 1600 when Oñate was well settled in his "capital" near the present day Espanola. The horse trail followed the west banks of the Rio Grande from the present day Hatch upriver to the vicinity of San Marcial.

There were four expeditions in the latter half of the 16th century and those travelers carried baggage on pack animals and ox-drawn carretas, the massive two wheeled carts. The horse trail was not practical for wheeled transit. The only other route was later named the Jornada del Muerto. It went due north from the vicinity of Hatch some 90 miles (or 35 Spanish leagues) to the ford at Cantarecio (later Ft. Craig).[2]

Oñate's records indicated a great deal about the ordeal and described the location of the spring at Perillo by a dog of that name. The Indians along the way were hospitable enough but Oñate put on sham battles to show he meant business. Uneven treatment soon alienated the Indians, as patient as they were.

There are few actual accounts of the many difficulties of the transit of the Llano Esteril or the Jornada del Muerto, possibly because it is a common characteristic of the mind to forget the unpleasant experiences and remember only the happy events. But the Indians managed to make the passage uncomfortable in many different ways over the next 250 years. When the Spaniard was beset too hard, he usually chased the miscreants into the San Mateo mountains to the west. The mountains were not named then but the Indians thus introduced the bearded men to our Apache Kid Wilderness Area.

Those infrequent forays west of El Camino Real (Royal Road) are not documented but they proved that mounted men could easily cross the Rio Grande at any season of the year except flood times. Many of the less prepared caravans of travellers were saved from thirsty deaths because they could send horsemen to the west side of the dry riverbed to get potable water at the many seeps and springs along the way. They also discovered deep grass on the gentle slopes between those blue mountains to the west and the big river. The earlier cattle drives north during the 1600's generally traveled west of the river for that reason. The Indians helped some of the stragglers get lost in the arroyos that led to the mountains.

Throughout the 1600's and until mid-century 1700's, the Alamosa River ran reliably most of the way eastward down to the Rio Grande. Although there were no pueblos along its course there was sporadic Indian occupancy in some locations along its banks. With the coming of the white man there was a sweeping disappearance of game in the valleys. Indian subsistence hunting was diverted to the mountains and our San Mateo mountains were able to withstand hunting pressures well until the Spanish and Mexican herders started to run their sheep and cattle in them. A few ranches, generally used as summer headquarters, were located along the Alamosa. The Indians would burn them every winter in resentment of the intrusion. The Alamosa valley became denuded by overgrazing, fires, and weather changes, and the river flow decreased, probably due to these changes in the watershed. Yet the forage on the Vicks and Peñasco Peak vicinities continued to support cattle grazing and some wildlife.

At the time Oñate first went upriver in 1598, there were no towns along El Camino Real except a small settlement at Alamillo. It was on the west side of the Rio just south of Rio Salado junction about 10 miles north of the present day Socorro. This was the general location where Oñate put on his sham battle to impress the natives that were too friendly to suit his ideas.[2] There were some permanent buildings in Alameda and the Sandia Pueblo was fully occupied. The good grazing at Alameda helped cattle herds recover from trips upriver while the main party proceded on to Santo Domingo and later to the first "captial" at the Yuque and Yunque pueblos at the confluence of the Chama and the Rio del Norte (not yet named Rio Grande).

With all the battles being fought upriver and the flurry of church and mission building that took place in the first quarter of the 1600's, there was much traffic on El Camino Real. However, only small settlements evolved along the way. The towns of Socorro, Albuquerque, and Santa Fe emerged and grew for their own separate reasons. The Indians kept up their harrassments of the wagon caravans in the Socorro vicinity.

When the big Indian uprising took place in 1680, it was anti-climactic in the region surrounding the San Mateo mountains. As the Spanish settlers retreated to El Paso del Norte, the Indians simply stepped up their harassment including the fouling of the springs on the escape route. Corpses hanging in the chapels and the few remaining unburned buildings did little to cheer the retreat of the Governor and his entourage. Governor Otermin and his people were delayed many days at the usual river crossing at Fray Cristobal by flooding of the Rio Grande. This was at the north end of the Jornada del Muerto, the infamous location of Indian ambushes for almost a century.

De Vargas and his soldiers returned to Santa Fe in 1692 and started restoring the kingdom. The Apaches did not make any condescending agreements with the valley Indians or the hated Spanish. Some of the Indian men who had come of age during their 12 years of peace in the central river area and other scattered locations away from the De Vargas thrust joined the Apache raids. These Apache onslaughts apparently were directed not only at the Spanish,[2] but at the appeased Indians, and even the Mexicans below El Paso del Norte. Many of these renegades had been captive miners during the earlier Spanish occupation and took out their resentments partially by obliterating the mining sites in ingenious ways, including rockslides.

Records show only a slow return to normalcy during the 1700's. The Royal Road and its problems returned to areas surrounding our Apache Kid Wilderness neighborhood. Socorro grew and a couple of rudimentary bridges erected at the Fray Cristobal crossing washed out in major floods. Some Spanish mining was started again in the area of Magdalena. Governor De Vargas assigned a contingent of soldiers to cool down the Indian highway men but made the mistake of stationing the troops in Socorro and occasionally near the Hatch vicinity. Nightlife in Socorro made the troops unresponsive to the fast hitting raids near there and the Apaches enjoyed well armed cavalry raids on the token forces of road soldiers at the Hatch end of the Jornada. The San Mateos managed to provide game provender and refuge for the Indians. A few wild Spanish cattle lived in the high country and made extra sport for the hunters.

One of the soldiers, Pedro Armendariz, was more conscientious and effective than his compadres at the road soldiering task in the early 1800's. He was later the alcalde (mayor) of Santa Fe. Consequently, he was granted a large tract of land of his own definition by the King of Spain. The land extended northward on both sides of the Rio Grande from Hot Springs (now Truth or Consequences) to San Antonio just below Socorro. It was about 25 miles wide at its broadest east-west point. One of the provisos of the grant was to subjugate the raiding Indians along the eastern boundary, El Camino Real. In 1825, the Indians drove him off the land.[3]

Meanwhile, Mexico had thrown off the Spanish yoke in 1821 and New Mexico became a northern state of Mexico. The Indians, including the Apaches, did not accept the change in ownership of their lands once again. They raided heavily in old Mexico for a decade or more. When the Treaty of Guadalupe Hidalgo was signed in 1848 by the United States and Mexico after the Mexican War, one of the conditions given the United States was the impossible responsibility of curbing the Indian raids in northern Mexico originating in Texas, New Mexico, and Arizona.

Mining was on the upswing when New Mexico became a Territory of the United States, Congress read the message and decided that the U.S. Army should establish Army Posts and forts in the new territory.[4] The big Indian War of the West was at home in New Mexico. The Spanish must have sighed with relief, along with the Mexicans.

One of the first posts to be established was Fort Conrad in 1851, two miles upriver from the old location of Fray Cristobal near that much-used crossing of the big river. It was on the west bank, at the northern end of the still-used Camino Real. The bog in which it was located grew fine vegetables but was a poor building site and was a breeding ground for mosquitos. In three years, the Fort had fallen apart and was moved four miles south to a more suitable location and named Fort Craig.

In February of 1860, small bands of Indian raiders managed to keep two companies of the Mountain Rifles and several of the local civilians in a continual uproar. The troops had some success in recovering stock, but one group of men under Captain Manuel Chaves had a sharp fight with about 100 Indians and lost all their animals. They returned to Fort Craig on foot. The following year, the mail was attacked in the Jornada del Muerto south of the post and had to fight its way to the safety of the walls.[4]

The Civil War came on before all of the forts and Army campaigns were able to subjugate the Indians. Some of the soldiers swapped sides and started to fight each other. The battle of Valverde was won by General Sibley's Texans on their way north, to be defeated upstate largely by overreaching their supply support. The Texans' line of retreat was along the eastern flank of our Apache Kid Wilderness mountain fastness. The Indian scouts told the officers at Fort Craig several days after it happened.

Soldiers from the fort ranged far and wide looking for meat for the troops. They were having trouble paying the rent to the Armendariz heirs and successors, and consequently could not readily buy beef from any of the local ranches. The result of such hunting was the decimation of game on the San Mateo mountains and the further alienation fo the Indians who had been sustained by it.

The U.S. Army realized it would be more economical to feed the Apaches than to fight them. In the first peaceful breath after the Civil War, some officer made that beneficial suggestion and negotiations started. The Apaches agreed to go on a Reservation of Ojo Caliente on the Alamosa River just to the west of our Apache Kid Wilderness (San Mateo Mountains). The Army built a fort or a post in the middle of the Reservation and started the food distribution. Depending upon whom you listen to, neither the Army nor the countryside could support 2000 Apache stomachs. Many Apaches went back to their White Mountains. About 450 were transferred to the San Carlos Reservation in Arizona. And in 1879, hunger and lost promises drove the Apache leader Victorio and his band of Chiricahuas, accompanied by a few Mescaleros, to attack the garrison at Ojo Caliente. Eight troopers of the 9th Cavalry were killed, 46 horses captured, and Victorio escaped to Mexico. In 1882, the post was abandoned — the experiment a failure.

A gold strike in 1882 was made on the eastern slopes of the San Mateo Mountains due west of Fort Craig about 27 miles by current roads at the present site of Rosedale. Within a few years, a 750 foot shaft was driven. A mill filled much of the descending gulch below it with tailings. (See the Mount Withington chapter for other aspects of mining in the area.) Despite the nearness of the military, Indian interferences with at least two gold shipments were entered in the Fort Craig records before it was decommissioned in 1885.[5]

Fayette A. Jones, a mining engineer in the territory, was almost killed by an "Apache Kid" in late 1892 in eastern Arizona.[6] This was the same Jones who made a railroad survey in 1893 from Maxwell City to Taos. Jones was also President of the New Mexico School of Mines in 1898-1902. He had apparently prospected the San Mateos from end to end before then.

The railroad was constructed in 1880, and passed by Fort Craig. By now the old El Camino Real ceased to exist. A wagon road paralleled much of the railroad. Both were subject to many washouts before the turn of the century. And the railroad generated many rapid changes. It hauled in the mill equipment for the Rosedale mill. Further haulage of the equipment from San Marcial Station to Rosedale was a monumental task for local muleskinners.

Train robberies became the new style of harassment. Indians were blamed for more than they did because of the often fanciful costuming of the holdup men. (See the Ladron Mountain chapter.) The bulletin board at the San Marcial depot had a Man Wanted poster constantly displayed with pictures of Indians purported to be train robbers.

My dad once told me of his impressions of an adventure which he had as a 15 year old. His father had died when dad was 10, and his six younger brothers and sisters depended on him to help his mother support the family. They were in Great Falls, Montana for a couple of years and subsequently in Butte, Montana, where dad became a (child) miner and his mother the proprietor of a dressmaking shop. Ready-made clothing had not yet arrived. Dad worked in Colorado mines (it was a deep depression period). He decided that he would go to New Mexico to see his uncle, William C. McDonald at White Oaks, and perhaps get a job in the mines there.

So in the early summer of 1895 the train stopped at San Antonio, New Mexico about 11 miles south of Socorro. Two young men swung off the high step of the chair car, each with a beaten-up suitcase. Both wore celluloid collars and string ties. They walked across the road from the depot and rented horses from a Mr. Hilton who had a stable and rooms for rent in a two-story building.

Dad's companion was his second cousin, a 16 year old nephew of Mrs. McDonald. Mr. Hilton knew both W.C. and his wife Frances. (Hilton was Conrad Hilton's father. Conrad is the founder of worldwide hotel chain.) The livery stable man looked at the city dudes with their patent leather shoes and had his doubts. His employer had told him to load up a pack horse with a shipment of supplies for Bill McDonald in White Oaks.

The unlikely riders, leading the packhorse, were immediately initiated as the trail led directly to the swollen river. Dad recalls that everything got wet because the horses had to swim part of the way across. Then they had to unload everything and dry it out, including their box lunches bought from the butcher on the train. It was overnight and 70 miles to go.

The country is at the upper end of the Llano Esteril of the Jornada wastes. Our youthful travelers did not know how to properly repack to keep things from falling off. But they managed to follow the faint trail to Carrizozo. The route at that time swung north of Broken Back Crater and Little Buck Peak at the north end of the malapais, the big lava flow. Dad said the grass was up to the horse's belly much of the way and that it rained several times in the two days. The suitcases almost dissolved. (Read the El Capitan chapter for the rest of this story.)

Land titles continued to generate problems into the twentieth century and Land "ownership" was contested by Indians who fought among themselves for territory, generally because of hunting needs. When the Spaniards moved in, the Indians fought them for land rights and to resist becoming slaves. The Spanish grant made to Armendariz was partially sold off to Hugh Smith and Thomas Biggs in 1849.[3] He or his heirs sold some of the land near Hot Springs to Mexican interests in the vicinity of Elephant Butte Dam backwater. The U.S. Government refused to pay rents consistently on the Fort Conrad and Fort Craig lands but after the Civil War bought the Fort Craig land from the heirs or assigns.

Can you imagine the turmoil caused by railroad agents appearing to buy contested land up and down the Rio Grande for the right-of-way? The Treaty of Guadalupe-Hidalgo was supposed to clear all of the titles. In the early 1900's and well into mid-century, long after state and county government and taxes became a way of life, many Spanish land grant heirs would not pay taxes on the apparently fallacious assumption that they were exempt from state and federal laws on their own undeeded lands. The sheriff's sale for taxes became more the rule than the exception. When the men came home from World War I, much of the land surrounding the San Mateo mountains was sold for very little.

The Lincoln County wars reverberated at least as far west as the Rio Grande. They are treated in passing in the Capitan Wilderness chapter. If anyone won in those wars, it was the lawyers. My own ancestor, William C. McDonald of White Oaks, prior to his mining career had been a lawyer. He left his native New York state to seek his fortune in the west. Somehow the combination of his success at mining and his early training in legal matters made it possible for him to acquire the McDonald Ranch which included those lands east of the aforementioned Armendariz Grant and the Jornada del Muerto. Holm Bursum of Socorro developed the ranch lands to the northwest of the McDonald Ranch extending to the river on the west. The big lava flow was on the McDonald Ranch.

McDonald and Bursum ran for Governor of the State of New Mexico; McDonald won and became the state's first Governor in 1912. Previous ones had been Territorial Governors. Lt. Governor E.C. de Baca succeeded Governor McDonald in 1916. One of the few McDonald accomplishments recorded in the state annals was that he built a governor's mansion in Santa Fe. I think it was mostly his wife's doing — but his money. The state was not that solvent at that date.

Closer to the Apache Kid Wilderness Area is the Joe Pankey Ranch. He acquired and developed those then grassy and watered parts of the Rio Grande valley from the San Mateo Mountain eastern foothills eastward to the river in the early 1900's. In the Fall of 1979, an Exhibit of Photos, Books, and Artifacts entitled "Land and Cattle, The Story of a New Mexico Rancher," first opened on Ocotber 25, 1979, at the National Agricultural Library in Beltsville, Maryland. Joe Pankey and his family are depicted in this travelling exhibit put together by the Education Bureau of the Museum of New Mexico with pictures by Jack Parsons. One can see the era of the cowboy wax and wain in the articles of the exhibit. One artifact not shown is the trail bike which is replacing the horse on many of our ranches.

Old highway US 85 was an outgrowth of the old road which paralleled the railroad in the first half of the century. When my family and I came to New Mexico in 1947, we traveled the highway frequently. It was a two lane, blacktop road and was noted for the series of dips crossing those usually dry arroyos which the "old ones" so avoided with their carretas. US 85 followed the old horsetrail on that west side of the river. Automobile speeds in the 1950's were in the order of 75 to 85 miles per hour. At such speeds, the dips could produce great surprises when even small flash floods came down an arroyo from the San Mateos. It was only a dampening experience unless the water washed boulders onto the road in the dips. The boulders belonged to Joe Pankey west of the highway. When Interstate I-25 Freeway was put in during the 1960's, it skirted the Pankey Ranch. The Interstate eliminated the scores of dips and the adventures of flash flooding. The Tequilla Run to Juarez became a milk run. One now just sets his cruise control to 55 mph and plugs Spanish music into his stereo.

An unearthly light, brighter than day for an instant, temporarily blinded the deer and cattle that black night of July 16, 1945, on the whole east side of the San Mateo Mountains. The first atomic bomb was exploded on the McDonald Ranch (the Trinity Site) about 40 miles east of Old Fort Craig. This was not the same McDonald from White Oaks who later was the first Governor. But the Governor was long dead by that time and his widow had remarried a gentleman named Truman Spencer. Some of the ranchers noticed their cattle subsequently had grey patches of hair against the brown and black backgrounds, and they wondered about the bomb.

The first time I was in the Apache Kid area, sometime in the early 1950's, before I started making trip report notes, I recall seeing a winking chain of lights down in the valley on the old highway. We were in our sleeping bags on San Juan Peak from which we could see lights up and down the valley from Socorro to Elephant Butte dam. We concluded that the car lights were winking because they were going up and down through those numerous dips. The headlight dimming, so frequent on two land roads, possibly contributed to it. That same night we saw a test missile fly overhead from Green River, Utah, to the White Sands Missile Range. Since the San Andreas Mountains are in the way, we could not see the impact point, which looked like it was on Fort Bliss instead of White Sands. The rocket trail was persistent along its trajectory in that black sky.

The Wilderness Act of 1964 stipulated that roadless areas over 5000 acres were to be inventoried for possible Wilderness Area Enactment. The U.S. Sports Fisheries and Wildlife Administration, then in charge of the Bosque del Apache Wildlife Reserve which extends along the river from a mile or so below San Antonio downstream to the old site of Valverde, immediately started their process. In 1966, they held public hearings and submitted recommendations to congress. The enactment of the Bosque del Apache National Wilderness followed in rapid order. The outdoor organizations were not organized to respond to the challenge. Consequently, we discovered that we now have a National Wilderness containing parts of the old El Camino Real, Old US 85, the I-25 Freeway, the railroad, a powerline, and a natural gasline. There is a north-south corridor to accomodate most of these "marks of man." Subsequent enactments have been better advised.

Our Wilderness Study committee recommended a 99,000 acre Apache Kid Wilderness to Congress in place of the 132,700 acre area which the Forest Service recommended in their Roadless Area Review and Evaluation (RARE II) process. Our reduced area does not include the several peripheral areas in which there are many service roads in various states of disrepair. Generally, our recommended areas are larger than those indicated by the Forest Service, so this is a notable exception to that rule.

Stories were circulating in 1907, as rumors do, about an Indian who had an unpronounceable name showing up in unexpected places like Chise, Chloride, Winston, Kingston, Cuchillo, Mogollon, Mimbrês, and Pinos Altos. He would hang around for a couple of days, bum a few meals, a drink or two, being very picturesque and dramatic about it. Something would always turn up missing, like hams from a spring house. It wasn't too bad until 1908, when he started taking horses and an occasional calf. By 1909, he had a name. The Apache Kid. Was he the same one who ambushed Jones? An Indian girl who spoke some English came into the small town of Luna and bought groceries with greenbacks. When she left, she also was leading a lamb with a rope — and it was objecting. The story has many gaps in it but Tony Wolfe has done a creditable job in piecing it together if you can ever find a copy of his manuscript. In any series of events, the Apache Kid was supposedly shot somewhere near Cyclone Saddle by an irate Black Range rancher whose horses he was reported to have stolen. The young (Indian) lady wept copiously and with reason. There are many versions of this story. I have not heard Joe Pankey's version of the story but it is probably more factual than romantic.

Whatever the facts, we have given the Apache Kid's name to our horse-sized Wilderness Area. I have never ridden a horse in the area, however. One can do it all on foot but do not escort too many dudes into the area. If you do, you might be harassed by the ghost of an irate Apache Kid or the old Texas longhorn steer with the lion claw marks on its back which some hunters have claimed to have sighted. Any moment I expect to hear about someone seeing the Apache Kid on a big old longhorn steer riding the Skeleton Ridge trail amidst bolts of lightning.

You've probably noticed that all the history seems to have happened east of the Apache Kid area. And surely most of the human activity has. That brief period in which the Apache reservation was at Ojo Caliente on the Alamosa River near Monticello was an exception, possibly because the Rio Grande river has dominated, or at least strongly influenced, men's lives throughout the centuries. The river even showed its independence and unruliness in 1929 when it washed out all of the town of San Marcial, the bridges on the railroad, and highways. An earlier San Marcial was wiped out in 1866.

The telephone company wanted to put a microwave tower on Vicks Peak early in the 1970's. We managed to convince the Forest Service that it should not be permitted on the basis that there were other less expensive alternative locations for the facility.

Hopefully, all of the foregoing activities will make your wilderness trips in this vicinity more interesting; perhaps you will wonder with me how the Apache Kid Area remained an island of wilderness over the five centuries of these vigorous endeavors of man.

TRAILS AND ROUTES

Something woke me up that quiet night in late February, 1973. Perhaps it was snow slipping off my tent. My watch showed about 3:00 a.m., and my flashlight revealed snow in great feathery flakes. Phil's shelter sheet was sagging in the middle with the weight of a fluffy six inches of fresh snow, but he was snug and dry under it.

Our camp was in a clearing just northwest of Teepee Peak, north of West Blue Mountain, at something over 9,000 feet. It was a snowshoe trip out of West Red Canyon on the northwest corner of the Apache Kid Wilderness. The snow was four or five feet deep on the flat — but there was not much flat. It had a breakable crust but the snowshoes worked well on it. My Bearpaws seemed to stay up better than Phil's red, plastic Ojibway style ones. We could not find a good snowbank or drift for a snow cave, so we "slept on top." You could take about two or three steps on the crust around our camp and then go down to your waist on the next step, without snowshoes.

The next morning we awakened to find mountain lion tracks encircling our camp. The track had little snow in it, so it must have been after 3:00 a.m. The lion came no closer to any of our gear than 10 yards or so. We had not seen any deer tracks above about 8,000 feet the day before. We later found the lion had followed our tracks up the trail from down near the Hardscrabble Spring Trail Junction.

The second night we camped along the Crest Trail in only about a foot of snow near the Cowboy Trail Junction on San Mateo Peak. We saw a polar orbit satellite that night and wondered if it were ours. We could make out some lights of Socorro and could oc-

Fog in Springtime Canyon — Apache Kid Wilderness.

casionally see lights on the interstate to Truth or Consequences below us toward the east.

We made it from our camp to the empty lookout tower the next morning without packs or snowshoes, something about a mile round trip. A packrat was busy inside the tower house. It sounded like somebody making batter for flapjacks (it was before our breakfast). We could practically smell them cooking. The rat was sunning himself and thumping his tail when Phil climbed the steps to look inside. But the door was locked so we could not run it out.

We were very hungry when we got back to our camp. It was that morning that we made up a limerick about red-in-the-morning and grit-it-the-granola, or something. It snow-showered all of the way back to the car at Red John Box. We saw turkey tracks in West Red over our tracks of a couple of days before.

Some big gully washer must have come down West Red Canyon in 1972. It gutted out the road through Red John Box. I haven't been back through that way since to see if someone had a dozer in there to try to fix it. It looked impossible to rebuild then. At any rate, you can generally drive up the Canyon as far as the Box which is about two miles from our wilderness boundary. A detour now swings around to the north.

Cyclone Saddle was named by some miner after the trees had been blown flat in a swath half a mile wide. I saw it on a Fort Craig map dated 1855. At least I saw the name, but the map showed the San Mateos and the Black Range practically joining. Hike five miles north of Springtime Trailhead on Trail Number 43 to get there. Some claim the Apache Kid is buried there.

Mining: There is none within the Apache Kid. A lot of prospect holes must have been fruitless. There are no mining claims nor inholdings within the area.[6] The Pankey Mine is on the southeast side of the area.

Grazing: Ruben Pankey has a permit and the Weltys had another in the mid 1970's. Most of the better grazing is in the canyons along the west side, but it is limited. The deep grass is gone. We have seen some cattle in the high country meadows during midsummer; they may have belonged to Joe Pankey, Ruben's father. The brands were indistinct.

The road recipe from San Antonio to Springtime Campground is as follows: drive 23 miles south of San Antonio on interstate (I-25) to exit 115. Take the east service road southward to Forest Road 225 which is about six miles south of Nogal Canyon on old US 85. Ten miles west takes you to Springtime Campground. The trees seem to be suffering from chlorosis because they are so pale.

The trail goes up to the Crest in about a mile and a half and wanders round on top, both north and south on the ridge. During good years of rain and snow, the Crest Trail down (south) toward Vick's Peak gets indistinct. Strangely, the Crest Trail almost stumbles into several springs. However, my boys and I became badly dehydrated because the cattle had trampled the seeps, and the kids wouldn't drink the muddy water doctored with halizone tablets. The next time on top, several years later, it was a riot of flowers.

An interesting trip for three of us (without my boys) was in one November in 1968 or 1969. One drives from Monticello north about eleven miles toward Vick's Peak. There was the fork to a twisting trail called Burma Road. The road meandered generally westward in the twilight above some deep canyons. After we cleared the worst of the switchbacks, we started north along a steep hillside only to be stopped by a tree across the road. It was dark by the time we had cut the tree clear of the road; another couple of miles and we arrived at the end of the road.

The next day we hiked past Cook's Cabin at daylight and were up Milo Canyon to San Mateo Spring by about 11:00 a.m. We had intended to follow the Crest Trail north past Apache Kid Peak to Cyclone Saddle but we got lost somehow in Smith Canyon. We got separated and decided to head back to the car. Two of us headed west to try to cut the San Mateo Canyon Trail but we ran into one heading down much sooner. It was really a downhill trail: steep, slippery, and full of switchbacks. It dumped us right into San Mateo Canyon. While we were catching a breather, Jim came down the Canyon Trail in high gear. He was lost and scared. We all sacked out right there.

The next day we took our day packs and went up the Canyon Trail northeast to Cyclone Saddle and to the Blue Mountain Cabin. We finally figured how we had become confused on the trails the day before. We had a map that did not show the trail west of Twenty-five Yard Spring. Much chastened, we went down the Maverick Canyon Trail to the head of Upper Holdup Canyon. Somewhere in this vicinity I saw some ore on the trail. An ore sack must have broken as a mule was going around a switchback in the trail. I never did see a prospect hole up that high on the mountain. Then we bushwhacked down Holdup until it ran into our familiar San Mateo Trail. The car was about a half mile away, but with a flat tire. Even if we got back to Albuquerque by 10:00 p.m. that Sunday night, we admitted that we had covered too much ground without good maps.

A more leisurely trip was up Indian Creek Canyon. The trail head is about three miles east from Springtime Campground on the road but it was not marked with signs that you could see from the car. The trail skirts the foothills and finally takes off up Indian Creek. We ran into two different herds of deer. This time (in June, my notes say) we saw a lot of bear signs around Twenty-five Yard Spring. We sacked out just east of Apache Kid Peak below the switchbacks on Skeleton Ridge Trail.

The second day, it rained off and on. We didn't move camp and just did a "pasar el rato" down to Piñon Mountain and back in our ponchos. The third day we returned down the Roberts Canyon Trail and ran into a real prospector with a burro. He talked with us at least 30 minutes but afterwards, on the way home in the car, we could not agree on what his name was and what he told us. I think it was Griegos and he was hunting buried treasure instead of prospecting. There was some question about what was fact and which was fancy.

Our proposed Wilderness Area is about 99,000 acres. It has a surprising number of trails in it for the limited number of people we have seen there. One summer, a young man and wife team were the fire lookouts on San Mateo Peak. They said we were the only people they had seen in a month. For some reason, unknown to anyone we have asked, the trail up Drift Fence Canyon on the north end is heavily traveled at least up to about Cave Peaks. Few people seem to go all of the way up to Milligan Peak and the Crest Trail. Conversely, the Coffee Pot Canyon Trail seems to be used only by lion hunters. Anyway, the whole area is surely Wilderness — with a capital W. However, it is the only one of our wildernesses in which we have seen a Forest Ranger. He was Bud Brunner, stationed in Magdalena, a real horseman, a gentleman, and one smart hombre. Fred Richter and Jim Culbert, both with the Forest Service in Magdalena can tell you about little used trails in the Apache Kid mountain fastness. There is far much more in the area than I have seen and it has been a whole new experience every time I have been in it. It is the only one in which I have been temporarily lost. Be sure you have an extra day's food supply.

CHAPTER 9:
Mount Withington National Wilderness

Mount Withington is about 25 miles southwest of Magdalena at the north end of the San Mateo Mountains. It overlooks much of the Plains of San Augustin to the west and northwest. It stands completely separate from the Magdalena Mountains toward the east. Blue Mountain in the Apache Kid Area is almost due south and at eye level from Withington. The Mount Withington fire lookout tower is at 10,116 feet elevation. State Road 52 leads southward from U.S. 60 across a small corner of San Augustin Plains and up onto a steep alpine forest land. Get a Wilderness map at the USFS Ranger Station in Magdalena.

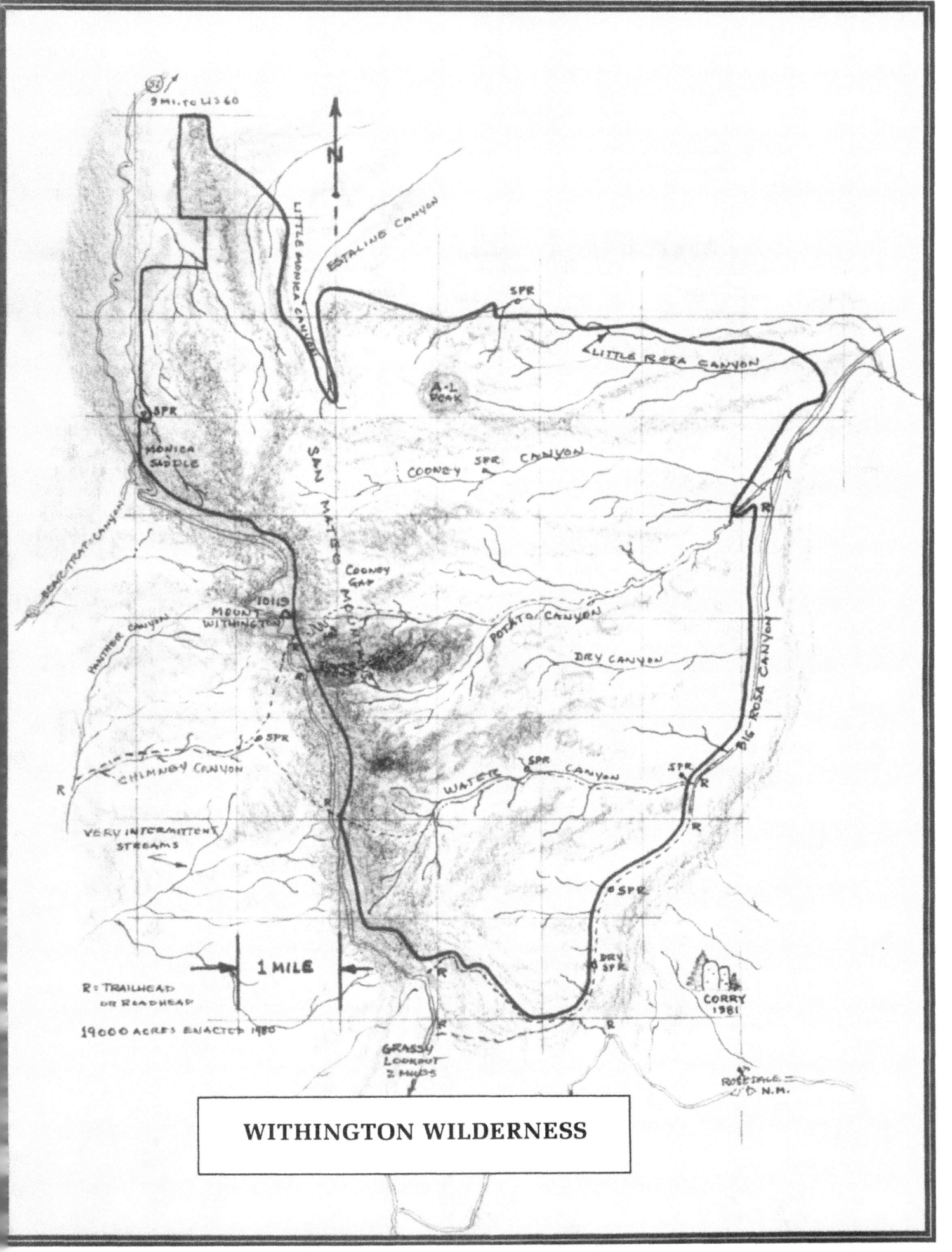

Mount Withington is a surprise in many ways. It is the highest peak in the northern extension of the San Mateo Mountains. Since you can drive to the top with a passenger car, the steepness of the hillsides you contour on the road is unexpected. The beautifully formed trees on these steep hillsides must have lots of water and fairly regularly. The canyons contain unusual rock formations awaiting your discovery.

The first time I saw the top, in 1961, it was covered with military trucks and trailers, antennas, festooned wires, and wooden cable reels. The Arthur D. Little Company of Cambridge, Massachusetts, was the lead organization for an international team of scientists doing lightning research. Bernard Vonnegut and Charles Moore were the project leaders. I met specialists from Japan, Britain, Belgium, France, Italy, and one of the African nations. They were variously measuring the space charge, the pressure changes, the wind velocity, the temperature and humidity, the magnetic gradients, the spectral density of the clouds at VHF and UHF frequencies. They were also making time-lapse photos of the onrushing storms.

They had the clouds trained that July day. The first storm cell arrived on schedule from the Black Range to the southwest (now the Aldo Leopold Wilderness Area.) The time was 10:45 a.m. Bolts of lightning flickered out of the anvil of the dark cloud that seemed less than 1,000 feet above us. Hail followed close behind. Charley (Moore) had some "lightning traps" rigged so that he could photograph the bolt as it hit the peak near us. They had bright, new, garbage cans with camera lenses looking out through holes at the "traps." These cans served as Faraday Cages to isolate the cameras from the static electricity. Film inside unshielded cameras can become light-struck by such a phenomenon.

Later in the day, whole strings of storm cells came and went, appearing to trigger one another. It rained in gushes and then hailed deep enough to pile up on some of the north slopes of Water and Potato Canyons and photograph like snow. The wind cranked around from several directions as the cells passed by on their way northeast. It almost seemed orchestrated.

One of their experiments was to attempt to control the space charge in large volumes of atmosphere to see if precipitation could be induced. Vonnegut was the originator of using dry ice in the clouds to induce snowfall and was an early experimenter with silver iodide to seed rain clouds. The process used at Withington, however, was to string stainless steel wire from peak to peak, making huge arrays miles in length. The wire was paired with nylon monfilament and fed out of helicopters from large reels, then secured on the peaks and tensioned into a catenary curve that satisfied the elevation requirements. A generator was connected and cranked up to charge the array with about 35 kV of negative ions.

The theory was that the negative ions would be stripped off the wire by the aerosols and carried downwind many miles. The charge of the ground plane beneath these negatively charged plumes would be driven positive a thousand feet or more below. This orderly arrangement was intended to induce coalescence of raindrops (as in the laboratory) and precipitation on demand. When I suggested they shoot a rocket like the Connecticut Yankee did, they cringed. Withal, the rain refused to obey. Their studies are beautifully documented.

My own theory differed from their hypothesis. Whereas they believed that lightning was a precursor of rain and was instrumental in the formation of the great gushes associated with some summer storms, I contend an opposite view. Of course, the fact that I am a mechanical engineer thoroughly untrained in weather phenomenology, had little to do with our friendly jousting.

My theory is a highly contrived one that goes like this: the laws of conservation of energy require in my mind that, when the millions of tons of water fall from a cloud formation, say a mile down to the earth, the kinetic energy gained must be converted to potential energy in the atmosphere, perhaps in the upper parts of the clouds. Then when the imbalance of energy grows to high enough proportions, that potential energy must equilibrate through lightning strikes. I had made photographs and obervations for years previous in which I had seen lighning striking ahead of the storm front from the leading cloud anvils at promontories jutting upward to establish virtually a massive spark gap. Of course, I assumed that the particulate matter in the clouds, around which the water vapor must have been coalescing, probably jumped as much as I did when a bolt discharged. So it rained harder for a short time. And that's my theory.

The Lightning Project people had been flying through the active clouds and measuring the apparently critical parameters for several years previously, so, of course, they could wag their heads in disbelief. A couple of years later, they moved the project over to the Langmuir Laboratory on Magdalena Baldy under the auspices of the New Mexico Institute of Mining and Technology. The single storm cell onset is not as tidy on south Baldy but the storms are almost as predictable during the peak of the rainy season in July and August.

Meanwhile, the Mount Withington test site has nicely recovered and you can still watch the whole process from your car. It is well to stay inside the car during a storm instead of standing up on that mountain like a lightning rod.

All that rainwater and ozone and nitrogen fixation — or something — grows beautiful trees, grass, and wildflowers. And the wildlife seems to repond as well. Do treat their little mountain gently. It will remain one of your favorite spots.

The Roadless Area Review and Evaluation precess (RARE) was started in the early 1970's and culminated in a list of roadless areas selected for wilderness study by the U.S. Forest Service called "The Chief's List." The Regional Forester's recommendations were pared down after the Agency reviewed the line inputs. The Chief's List, published in November, 1973, did not contain our Mount Withington area.

Elsewhere in this book you will learn of the discord generated by that series of action. Briefly, the earlier endeavor was labeled RARE I, and a subsequent process called RARE II was launched in June, 1977, by the Forest Service. It can be fairly said that the Forest Service reopened the study becuase of public dissatisfaction with RARE I. A more sophisticated methodology for evaluating the main factors for composite consideration and comparison with other areas was used by the Forest Service. Our New Mexico Wilderness Study Committee adapted to the new set of signals and maintained its public inputs to the RARE II process.

Our continued insistence and consistency apparently paid off in 1979 in that the Regional Forester recommended that Withington be a candidate for Wilderness enactment. The whole environmental population is far from satisfied with the process. Those specifics will be related elsewhere as they come closer to conclusion.

The Atlantic Richfield company (ARCO) now not only a worldwide oil company but a natural resources developer, rose up in some indignation at the RARE processes, the Alaska National Interest Lands Act, and the BLM Wilderness Review and proffered: (ARCO) "is extremely concerned about the escalation in the rate of federal land withdrawals from multiple public use." ..."Such withdrawals obviously limit federal acreage accessible for energy and mineral exploration and development." They went on to list areas in many states in which they classified conflicts as critical, significant, or moderate.

Mount Withington was listed by ARCO as critical for base metals. I made a mineral occurrence analysis summary in March 1979 which was titled: "Comments on Atlantic Richfield Co. RARE II Conflict Statement." It leads off as follows:

The concern of Atlantic Richfield in New Mexico rings with a hollow note. It does seem strange that without core drilling, the specific .6% of our State, or 5% of our National Forest recommended for Wilderness becomes so important in the overall balance.

ARCO has selected 10 areas recommended for Wilderness as being critical for base metals. Let us examine these areas in the light of the past and recent eagerness of the mining industry to freely use and explore these areas.

Withington contains no operating mines or prospects in 1979. The only active mining area near the Withington Roadless area was at Rosedale, a small mining town that existed from 1882 to 1937. The gold and silver lead was composed of broken stringers which were mined painstakingly over the years to produce a total of approximately $300,000. All that remains is the tailings since the buildings and larger structures were removed in the late 1950's and early 1960's.

A few prospect holes exist around the lower reaches of Mt. Withington. An outcropping of galena in Bear Trap Canyon has been periodically scratched at by prospectors over the centuries. Some fluoride appears to be associated with the galena. Potato Canyon has some pieces of selenium float mixed in with extensive weathered smithsonite and shale fragments. Here again is a mountain with some evidences of mineralization around its lower reaches outside the roadless area apparently without sufficient economic quantities to induce development or much notable assessment.

The analysis went on to make a similar specific statement on the other nine areas which they named, and on an additional six areas recommended for "Further Planning" in RARE II. We (the New Mexico Wilderness Study Committee) sent copies to all of the parties that were likely to be contributing to a final decision on each area in the hope that these facts

Giant Potato in Mount Withington Wilderness.

would be considered along with those opinions held by ARCO. We await the final enactment by Congress on this surprising little area.

TRAILS AND HIKING ROUTES

The road arrangements make it possible to take some one-day hikes downhill through an interesting de facto "pocket wilderness."

Park your car at Bear Trap Camp Grounds (8,000 feet elevation) and drive another one onto the Peak. Now, on foot, drop down the right canyon and you will come out at the first car. Do your navigating with a good compass and believe your contour map. It is steep, but there are no surprising cliffs on that west side. A buck I shot ran down the mountain that way with an ever so slightly misplaced arrow in him. We found him in the canyon a half mile east of Bear Trap Camp, nicely cooled out and ready to field dress.

Park the car in Little Rosa Canyon to the east of Withington, somewhere below its junction with Big Rosa Canyon. You can turn west off State Road 107 in several places. Again, use the quad map and mark where you left your car. Drive the other car to the top of the peak, and a little farther this time toward Grassy Lookout. Park at the head of Potato Canyon or Dry Canyon and take off on foot downhill generally in the canyon bottoms. There are lots of birds, small game, and interesting geologic formations. Interesting is the sound and experience of walking on slate for a couple of miles. It gets noisy. When you head down any of those canyons to the east, if you just keep going downhill you will end up in Big Rosa Canyon and subsequently in its branching Little Rosa Canyon.

You may find that you should not go down some of the grades into Little Rosa Canyon from the east with your car. You might have trouble coming back out of them, if it rains. Walking an extra mile or two can keep you out of such trouble.

The trip down Water Canyon works the same way except you have to drive farther south on the Grassy Lookout road, or come up from the old ghost town of Rosedale on Forest Road 330 from State Road 107. The tour down Water Canyon to your car is in the neighborhood of 10 miles, all pretty dry. Somebody with a bulldozer got tired trying to push it up the mouth of Water Canyon and quit right there, only 100 yards up the canyon. You would never expect the tangle of boulders and trees it left. A mile or two up Water Canyon is the wrong place to shoot a deer. A friend of mine (not a bow hunter) got one in there, dressed it out, and hung it in a tree. He asked me that night to help him get it out the next day. I had to work but another friend helped him. A lion pulled the deer down from the tree and dragged it a quarter-mile up onto a hillside. By the time they found it, the coyotes had worked it over, too. My friends brought out the horns and a few tattered steaks.

Forest Road 73 no longer goes down into Big and Little Pigeon canyons from the Grassy Lookout Road. some deep washouts on the arroyo crossings in the summer of 1972 made the road impassable. Somebody got through with a trail bike because we found a smashed bike wheel in one of the washouts.

The hike west from Grassy (where you left your first car) into Little Pigeon can get confusing even if you swing around just south of Bay Buck Peaks. The finger canyons are not all shown on the quad map and you can easily end up in Whitewater Canyon instead of Little Pigeon where you left your second car.

If you want a rough trip, drive as far up Forest Road 98 from State Road 107 as you can and mark the map with the car's location. Then go up to Grassy Lookout with the other car through Rosedale. Hike back from Grassy. It's tempting to follow the "cattle road" which swings north of Horse Mountain in Exter Canyon but stay on the south shanks of Horse Mountain and you will find the road (98) where you parked your car. We have never had any trouble with vandalism of any of the cars in the San Mateos.

Cooney Canyon on the north side has some interesting rock formations in it. Drop off — and I do mean drop — from Withington Peak to the north and get into it. My notes and memory are a bit vague about some brush-busting we had to do to get down to the car. I have heard that there was a trail crew in there recently. Check with the Magdalena Forest Service Office first.

Here's a bear story in closing. It was in late March and we were driving back to Withington from Grassy or Rosedale on Forest Road 138 about mid-morning. The road coming up to Withington from State 52 was still snowed in so we came in the Rosedale way. At the head of Potato Canyon there was a wire fence along the road on the east side. A blond bear, the cinnamon phase of brown bear, was ambling up out of Sanchez Trough Canyon on the west side. She saw us, did a double take, ran up the hill, and crossed the road about a hundred feet in front of us.

The bear was apparently just out of hibernation and skinny. However, the hide she had was for a lot bigger bear. It really moved separately from the animal which was streaking for the fence. Magically, as if in an Arabian Nights movie, the bear rug flattened out and went through the wire fence without missing a stride. I have often wondered what she sounded like skittering across those slate slides in Potato Canyon.

One pastime you should never overlook when you go up on Withington is to count the VLA antennas out on the San Augustin Plains. These (very-large-array) radio telescope antennas look out into space more deeply than any others on earth because they are arranged in a huge Y-shape, each leg 13 miles long.

If I could be an old bull snake, and could pick my haven of horny toads and quietude, I would settle blissfully on the slopes of Mount Withington. Please treat us gently.

CHAPTER 10:
Sierra Ladrones Defacto Wilderness

Ladrone Mountain is the isolated peak some 45 airline miles southwest by south of Albuquerque and about 14 miles due west of Bernardo on Highway I-25. The road mileages are much greater since they wander extensively. It is about 20 airline miles to Socorro southeast from Ladron Peak. Get a map from the Bureau of Land Management in Socorro or Albuquerque.

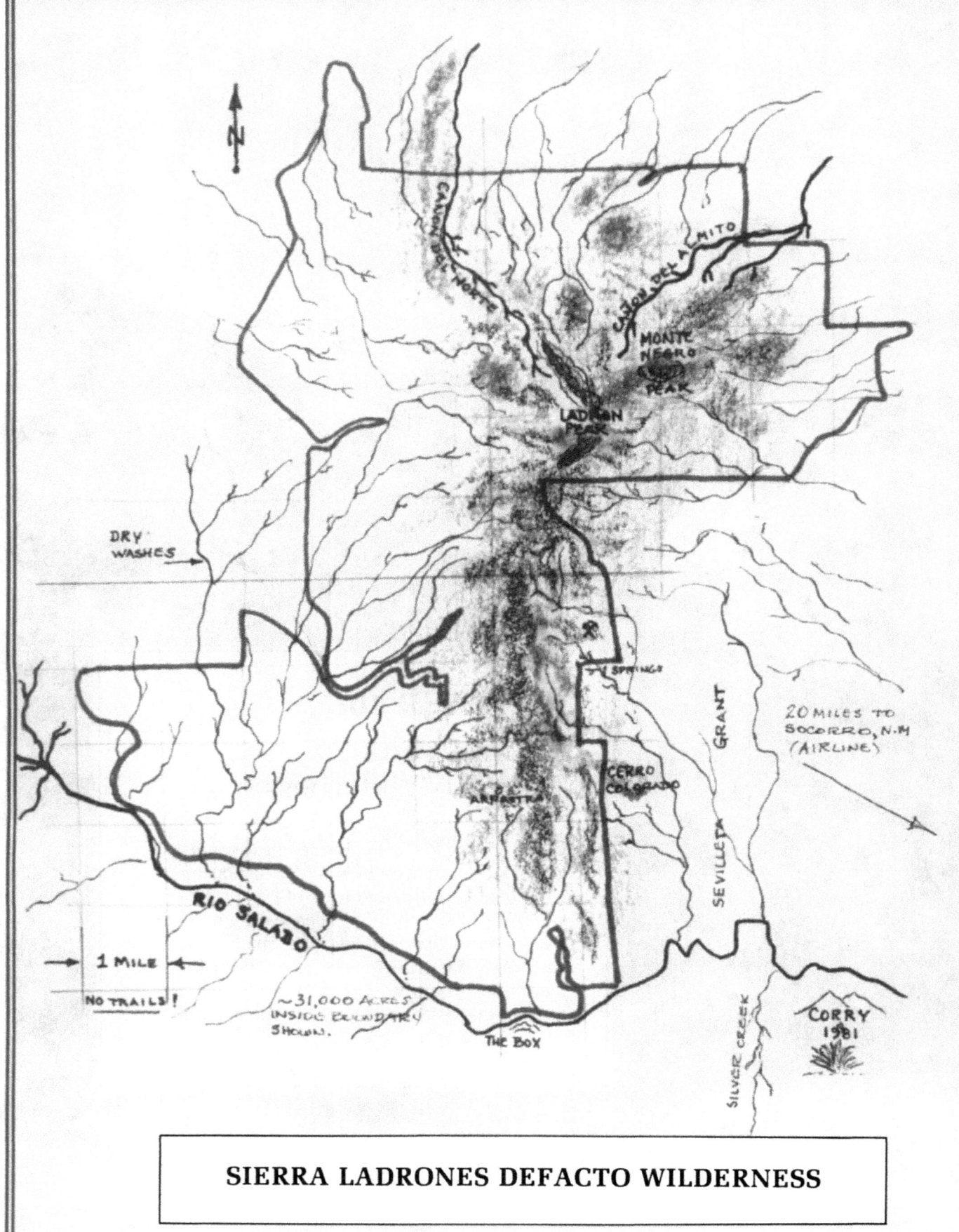

SIERRA LADRONES DEFACTO WILDERNESS

The sighing of the wind in the tornillos along the Rio Grande was accompanied by a new and strident sound. In 1650, great carretas, wooden-wheeled carts pulled by oxen, made their way northward from El Paso del Norte to Santa Fe. They announced their coming with a shriek of dry wheels on worn axles.[1] The wheels were as tall as most men and they vibrated agonizingly even after their axles had been lubricated with tallow.

The Indians at Pueblo Teypana, just upriver from the future site of Socorro, heard the carretas on the little-used Camino Real. The south wind carried the sound for up to 15 miles. Los Indios had learned to vanish from sight as these wagon trains drew near since Spanish tempers were on edge from the constant axle noise and heat of the jornada.[2]

Some of their kind had parted company with earlier wagon trains and now lay in wait with a few renegade Apaches in the breaks near the Rio Salado. The numerous arroyos running into the river slowed the train progress and required much pushing by all hands.[2] At such times the ladrones (robbers) would descend upon some of the carretas and steal supplies, weapons, clothing, wine skins, and horses.

The ladrones fled to the mountains to the west. The mounted soldats chased them a short way but gave up. Many such events have taken place throughout the centuries since.[3] Even the posses of the late 1800's failed to deter the robbers. The principal reason was that the Sierra Ladrones were too rough to tolerate any horses but stolen ones.

Most attacks seemed to have been launched from the old ruins of Tutahaco, just north of Teypana Pueblo, even after Socorro was a town.[4] The Camino Real was moved to the west side of the Rio del Norte (Rio Grande) through Socorro just before the Pueblo Revolt in 1680.[2] But Apache and Navajo renegade harrassment was scarcely interrupted by the Pueblo Revolt. The reconquest of 1692 simply changed characters by the addition of Mexicans to the Navajo and Apache ladrones.

The Sais family settled near the present location of Bernardo immediately after the reconquest.[5] Infrequent raids by highwaymen continued. The last recorded robbery was in 1910 near the Bernardo crossing. A fatal mistake was made in that some of the loot belonged to Wells Fargo (a custodial shipment). The Santa Fe Railroad and the Wells Fargo Company put a bounty hunter on the job. It took him almost two years to locate and dislodge the culprits from the Sierra Ladrones. A final shootout took place on the Grants Malapais, a huge lava flow fifty miles northwest of the Ladrones. Nothing was said about recovery of the bullion except that the case was closed.[6]

Toward the end of World War I, in 1917-1918, angora goats were introduced to the Sierra Ladrones by one of the ranchers on the west side of the mountain. They prospered until the mid-thirties when the springs dried up. This was the same era as the dust bowl years a few hundred miles north and east. The mountain was badly overgrazed according to some of the recollections of Haas Tinnin, a well driller for General Campbell who owned the Sevilleta Grant to the east of the mountain.[5] By 1948, when I first climbed the two peaks, there were still some characteristic overgrazed brush patches but the springs were running again.

An arrastra is a dish-shaped pit lined with stones; the early Spanish ground their ore in these pits. A horse dragged a heavy stone on a chain back and forth and sometimes on a pole over these pits. Such an arrastra in the Sierra Ladrones was covered up by Indians during the Pueblo Revolt. There were Indian stories about being conscripted to help turn the pole when the horses died. (Little wonder they obliterated arrastras throughout the region).

When public lands were divided between the railroads, the Forest Service, and the Bureau of Land Management, some early BLM managers were surprised that such a big mountain was in the Socorro District. The northwest corner of the Sevilleta Grant is on the bare rock of the ridge first south of Ladron Peak. The peneplain surrounding the mountains rises imperceptibly to 6,200 feet in elevation around the flanks of the mountain.

Ladron peak, 9,214 feet in elevation, is the higher of the two peaks in the range. Monte Negro Peak, approximately a mile airline toward the northeast, is slightly lower in elevation and separated by a thousand-foot-deep notch. Strangely, a section of state land rests between these two rugged peaks. There is a small stand of ponderosa and a few Douglas fir within the notch. It is a chancy hands-on, non-technical climb from Monte Negro to Ladron Peak. There is no water above the 8,000 foot elevation, to our knowledge, except in a trick-tank on Monte Negro.

The trick-tank is the variety which has about 75 square meters of neoprene rubber as a water catchment liner. The drainage is into an underground basin which is piped to a trough with a float-feed system. The whole catchment is enclosed by a high-wire fence. The Monte Negro tank is used by deer and other wildlife exclusively. This tank was constructed in the the late 1960's by the BLM; materials were carried to the site by helicopter so there was little ancillary damage.

Another trick-tank is located on the west ridge of the mountain at about the 7,800 foot elevation. It was constructed with the aid of a bulldozer with the blade up. Evidence of the route taken by the dozer was still apparent in 1976. Some random cattle usage of this tank is evident during the summer.

The New Mexico Wilderness Study Committee began to get interested in late 1968 in the possibilities of getting National Wilderness enactment for the

Ladron roadless areas. We discoverd that several people in Socorro were interested in the mountain. Paul Krehbiel, a teacher at New Mexico Institute of Mining and Technology, surfaced as the most outstanding proponent. He and Phil Tollefsrud struck it off and soon had a good map of the proposed wilderness area.

In 1971, a couple of Public Planning Meetings were held by the BLM in Socorro. We were able to make known our first recommendations for a proposed wilderness. The BLM said that they were having thoughts about a primitive area designation — a designation requiring sensitive management to retain the primitive character of the land.

Our wilderness study area proposal included an estimated area of 16,020 acres of BLM land, two sections of State land (1,280 acres), and 5,500 acres of the Sevilleta Grant. The Grant lands passed into the management custody of the U.S. Fish and Wildlife Service (USFWS) in 1972 from the Campbell Trust via the Nature Conservancy acquisition. A provision was made by the grantors that the land be managed as an indigenous wildlife refuge. Administrative access by automobile to an existing microwave tower (two miles south of the Lazy C Bar J Ranch in Section 3) is permitted by the USFWS at Bosque del Apache Refuge south of San Antonio.

In 1971, the New Mexico Department of Game and Fish proposed in ibex release in the Ladrones. Frank Hibben, a professor at the University of New Mexico during the 1950's and 1960's generated a concept that certain endangered big game animals could be advantageously fitted into certain vacant niches in our state. In late 1973, the Sevilleta Grant was designated as a National Wildlife Refuge, with the same (exotic) restrictions stipulated by Nature Conservancy. It was dubious that even a high cyclone fence could keep the ibex off the Refuge. In 1975, after several public hearings and much deliberation, the BLM decided against the ibex plantings. The Wilderness Study Committee position was against the planting for two main reasons: repetition of the overgrazing damage by a new species of goat and the probable need for several more trick-tanks "or wildlife-waters", and the attendant access damage.

Until October 21, 1976, the BLM operated without an Organic Act. Their purest land catagory was "Primitive Area" until that date. Thereafter, Public Law 94-579, "Federal Land Policy and Management Act of 1976" (FLPMA) serves as an Organic Act and also provides many additional features for the BLM and other public land agencies like the Forest Service. Some provisions for registration of mining claims and also for land disposal and other matters broaden the uniformity of management practices among the agencies. Section 603 establishes a wilderness study procedure similar to the Wilderness Act of 1964, but this specifies the BLM as the affected agency.

A Public Meeting was held by the BLM in Belen in early January, 1977, for input on the entire 241,000 acre Ladron Planning Unit. The agency presentation contains a recommendation R-31: "Designate approximately 18,000 acres of Ladron Mountain area as primitive area by FY 78." The agency map shows a boundary along whole section lines for convenience.

Our wilderness area boundaries differ from those of the primitive area because we did not enclose any roads. We are delighted with the primitive area designation as interim protection until the wilderness area designation is available. The first national wilderness area in the nation was the Gila National Wilderness Area in the southwestern part of New Mexico, and is under the Forest Service jurisdiction. We think it appropriate that the first BLM Wilderness Area should be the Ladron National Wilderness Area, based solidly upon complete compliance with the new Public Law 94-579.

Various events had a way of postponing or delaying our previous attempts at obtaining enactment of our proposed Sierra Ladrones Wilderness. The area is in that portion of New Mexico which was represented by Congressman Runnels in the U.S. House of Representatives. Despite the fact that he was long a member of the influential House Interior Affairs committee, he resisted all of our urgings to introduce wilderness legislation. Our other representative, Congressman Manuel Lujan was more than helpful but indicated that he preferred sponsoring bills relating only to his own district.

In 1975, the Wilderness Study Committee pulled together a New Mexico Omnibus Wilderness Bill in which we proposed our principal areas for legislation. The Sierra Ladrones Wilderness proposal was among the candidate areas. The three state areas included in The Endangered American Wilderness Act (Sandia, Manzano, and Chama River) were selected from that Omnibus list as being the most threatened. It was felt that the FLPMA legislation would provide a vehicle for enactment of the Sierra Ladrones Wilderness.

The BLM revised their study methods in response to the requirements of FLPMA, and each District started its new land review regimen. The fact that the Ladrones were protected under their Primitive Area regulations reduced the urgency to obtain enactment. It appeared that an area called El Malpais (the Grant's Lava Flow) must be processed first. That area proved to be a considerable deterrent to get action on other areas in their echelon. Several Indian claims and other legal impediments appear to have stalled progress on the El Malpais Wilderness.

The inventory of the BLM lands was progressing in each District. All of the earlier work that was done on the Ladrones such as the resource planning analysis and mineral reports had to be revised to fit the newer format of FLPMA. Our contention has been that all of the required analyses had been favorably completed prior to FLPMA and thus little was to be gained by further delay.

Consequently, when the El Malpais complications arose, we began to get the message from the BLM representatives that a piece of separate legislation on the Sierra Ladrones Wilderness would not meet with any blocking objections from the Agency.

Other events began to intervene. A Court Order was issued which required the BLM to do studies and issue and ES (Environmental Statement) on some BLM Grazing Districts. There were many complications which led to an Appeal which overturned the original Court Order. There were some parts of the various Grazing Districts (the Rio Puerco for instance) which was being overgrazed in the estimation of the BLM when the siltation of streams induced by grazing was considered. Senator Domenici held a hearing in Roswell and another in Las Cruces in the summer of 1979. Figures were quoted by the newspapers out of the testimony presented by the ranchers on the three Districts (Rio Puerco, Socorro, and East Roswell) a total 123,259 AUMs (Animal Unit Months) would be lost to the grazing permittees, a total monetary loss of $1.7 million, and 90 jobs would be given up. The conditions of the Court Order, if executed, would suspend range improvements for eight years. The corresponding costs of the permanent loss of range soils to siltation and wind erosion were not quoted or talked about by anyone at the meetings.

Elsewhere in the country, ranchers were vocal under the banner of The Sagebrush Rebellion to similar reductions in AUM allocations in their "home ranges." There is some rub-off, some concomitant resentment also against the Forest Service grazing permit administration. There always has been griping about the Fish and Wildlife Service, and especially the National Park Service which allows no grazing at all.

Consequently, it may be too late to introduce the first BLM wilderness area during such a blizzard of public consternation. Sooner or later a realization has to be made that the public lands do not belong only to the 90 people who will lose their jobs and are so vocal, but to the thousands of other taxpayers who use the same lands for other purposes.

We shall try to find a way to get our Sierra Ladrones Wilderness legislation introduced anyway. Happily for our little mountain, it is not very good grazing for cattle; there is no timber and few mining conflicts. If the facts are allowed to surface, we could get passage.

Subsequent events have further delayed legislative opportunity for Ladron. El Malpais enactment has been blocked by some Indian claims and other complications about split estate (different ownership of mineral rights by others than surface owners). In 1983 the Socorro District Wilderness Draft Environmental Assessment recommended a 25,724 acre wilderness instead of their earlier 39,308 acre area. The roaded area to the west of the mountain was deleted. No action was taken. The Socorro District Office was shut down in midsummer of 1983 and some of the staff moved to Albuquerque during Watt's regime. Representative Richardson and Senator Bingaman introduced a bill to enact three BLM wilderness areas in the San Juan Basin (Bisti, De-na-zin, and Ah-shi-siepa) on August 3, 1983. It is unlikely that our proposed Ladron item could get any attention until the Bisti areas are dealt with. Consequently, our 31,000 acre area has yet to be negotiated.

SIERRA LADRONES ACCESS ROUTES

There are no trails except a few game trails on the mountain. It is rough hiking but rewarding. To visit the mountain, take the graded, gravel road west of Bernardo. The road swings around the north side of the mountain onto the western foothills on the way to the old mining town named Riley. It is about 14 miles from Bernardo to the Monte Negro route jump-off and about 25 miles to the northwest and west sides. Leave only footprints!

The best route onto Monte Negro is from the northeast. If you park about 500 meters northeast of the Lazy C Bar J Ranch buildings in Section 3 at the end of the road, take the ridge generally southwest to the peak. Some block-hopping near the top can get exciting. If you get off the ridge to the south on the way back, it can get slippery in a snowstorm. Your dog can pull out a toenail on some of these rocks. (Cactus-spine tweezers come in handy.)

There are several routes, but no trails, onto Ladron Peak from the north and west. The shortest and most direct is from the Sais ranch road in Canyon del Norte southeast up the ridge to the peak. It is about six miles roundtrip from the car. Near the top it is a rock scramble and one narrow ridge-pole ledge is heart-stopping if it is dark, snowy, or windy.

An easier route is to contour from the saddle west of the peak around to the south side and climb up one of the several rock chutes. The route is almost due north to the ridge about a quarter mile east of the highest point. There is live water in the col drainage to the south of the peak. Some hikers like to come up the abandoned pipeline canyon on the west side.

The best season to hike the mountain is from the late fall until late spring. Summers are too hot until you somehow get above the 8,000 foot level. In midwinter a seemingly strange phenomenon can be witnessed. Melon-sized aggregations of ladybugs are found in exposed ledges along the uppermost outcroppings. These masses of comatose bugs appear to live successfully throughout the coldest weather.

The maps of the area show an old road generally up the Rio Salado. That trip was exciting in that one drove up the middle of the stream when it was running. There could be mudholes under the surface and you may be quite far from shore. It really was no easier than the route around the north side of the mountain. The point is moot, however, because the road is no longer open through the Sevilleta Grant. One can drive down the Salado as far as The Box from about a mile east of Riley but that is relatively pointless as is getting stuck.

One recent rumor has it that the U.S. Corps of Engineers is thinking of building sedimentation dams on the Rio Salado. There appear to be some qualms in the minds of the Nature Conservancy folks. Even if the dams were full of either water or sediment, they should have little impact on our adjacent wilderness area. Such dams, however, would probably block off any possibility of vehicle access up the affected stream beds even if the Grant management softens in its attitudes. The BLM has added an area south of the Box which would be affected by a dam if built. So, if you have any thoughts of trying ORV in that direction, it would be best to call the Manager of the Bosque del Apache Refuge to inquire about access rules.

LOS PIÑOS MOUNTAIN

At the other (east) end of the Sevilleta Grant is an extension of the Manzano Mountains named Los Piños Mountain. The Los Piños are a strange and miniature reproduction of the Manzano Mountains with many notable exceptions. They are that separated extension of the Manzano Mountain chain south of U.S. Highway 60.

The Los Piños have been private property as the eastern end of the Sevilleta Grant. After the tax laws in that part of the world changed enough over the passage of a couple of hundred years, the people who were born, raised, and died on the old Spanish Grant ultimately were affected. These seemingly external things finally deposed them. They kept running off the Socorro County tax collectors.

Eventually the Sheriff showed up. He may have even been their cousin. Whatever happened, the land was subjected to a sheriff's sale for non-payment of taxes. General Thomas B. Campbell put up the back taxes, obtained title, and generally let the people and their cattle remain. Many of these people died off, and so did the General. Hard times, over-grazing, and a reduced range because of diminishing water supplies permitted a consolidation of most of the land.

The Campbell Estate, through the Nature Conservancy, turned over the lands of most of the Grant, including the Los Piños Mountain to the administration of the U.S. Fish and Wildlife Service in the early 1970's. Early in 1977, many of the remaining people in the small community of Lajoya discovered some of their cattle dead on the "Wildlife Refuge." The conditions of the land transfer include a provision that only indigenous wildlife would be permitted. Elsewhere in the state, the newspapers reported the mysterious slaying of cattle both off and on private, federal, state, and land grant areas. There are even reports of flying saucers and helicopters in the night and guns with silencers, etc. There are dead cattle with organs removed. A book, "The Mute Strategy," by Dave DeWitt (Albuquerque: Sunbelt Press, 1979) covers it all.

So, the Los Piños at the eastern end of all of this intrigue is a mite overgrazed, but still a 15-mile-long mountain at that. Montosa Peak rises above all. Bootleg Canyon takes off to the west from the part of the mountain which is the break between the southern clump and the northern mass.

Four of us, including the U.S. Fish and Wildlife Service Ranger, started at the southern end of the mountain and walked the approximately 15 miles in two days during mid-March in 1975. We made camp overnight at the pass near the head of Bootleg Canyon. The wind was estimated to have risen to 75-80-mph speeds that night. It was accompanied by some snow. We had two tents and they were severly buffeted during the night. The tent poles of the packpack tents worked themselves into the frost-fluffed ground and loosened the tent tiedowns progressively. I had placed rocks as big as your hand under the two poles when my tent was set up. Those were shoved into the ground as well. During the night I had to put a boot under the head pole and the tent still reeled under the blasts. Another five mph and we might have been down the mountain with Phil's watch cap. We found it a quarter-mile away in the brush the next morning. He simply pulled his head inside his sleeping bag and weathered out the storm — without a tent to keep waking him up.

The next day we discovered that very little of the snow that went by had lodged in the brush or scrub timber. The sun came out and a snappy breeze accompanied us most of the way to the truck at the north end. We were treated to an acrobatic aerial display by several peregrine falcons on the lee side of the ridges. There was an updraft off the west side and the birds would tumble around in the ruffled air below the downwind ridge and then pop into the clean updraft in a great arcing climb, scarcely moving a wing.

Unfortunately, we had taken too little water on that trip. So, even though the temperatures were low, the wind apparently dehydrated us. Finally the beer at the Dripping Springs Bar at the northern tip of the Los Piños was like nectar.

Our passage up the length of the Los Piños was probably the first party on foot for years. A few hunters on horseback get up there every other year or so, according to Haas Tinnin, the custodian of the Sevilleta Grant area who lives in the stone house at the Lajoya Refuge turnoff from Highway I-25.

You can hike or ride horseback on the Los Piños and on the rest of the Wildlife Preserve with permission from the manager of the U.S. Fish and Wildlife Service at Bosque del Apache.

A mild warning: the little mountain can be a deathtrap on a bright summer's day since there is little shade or water. The Los Piños are an ipso facto wilderness, along its very backbone. Our New Mexico Wilderness Study Committee probably will not attempt to obtain wilderness enactment on the Los Piños. It is a part of the Campbell trust deeded land and subject to the agreements binding the Fish and Wildlife Service. Consequently, the management should be even more restrictive than if it were enacted wilderness.

Since there are only game and cattle trails and because the whole area provides wide open views in all directions, you are on your own. You might want to have a look at the Indian pictographs at the northern tip to the Sierra Montosa ridge not more than a mile from the highway. Were they made by Apache salt robbers waiting in ambush?

CHAPTER 11:
Guadalupe Escarpment National Wilderness

The Guadalupe Escarpment Wilderness is located on the pre-historic Capitan Reef on which the Carlsbad Caverns occur. The reef extends south westward of Carlsbad Caverns about 30 miles. It straddles the New Mexico-Texas border about 110 miles east of El Paso. Maps are available at the Park Ranger Stations.

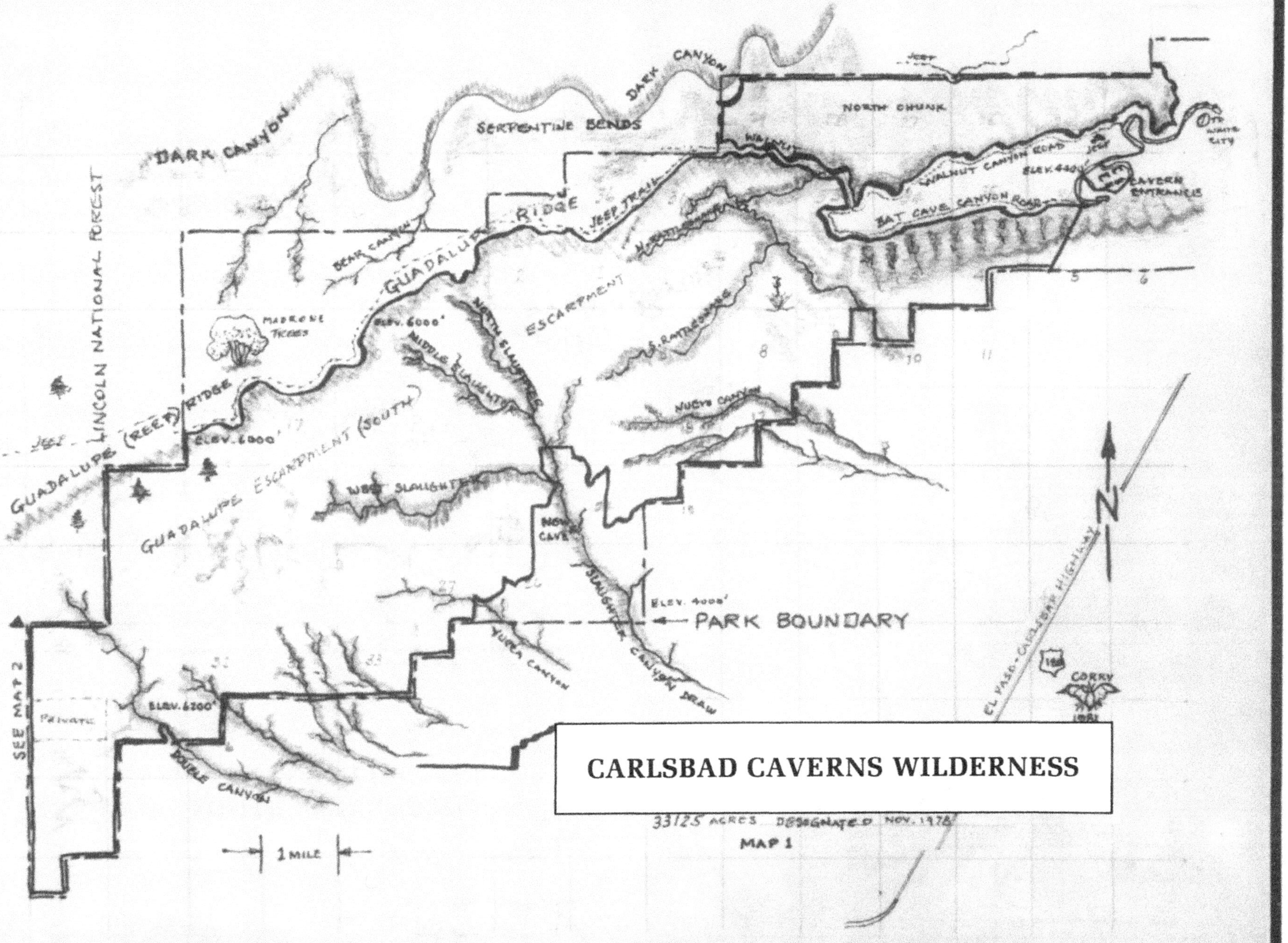

CARLSBAD CAVERNS WILDERNESS

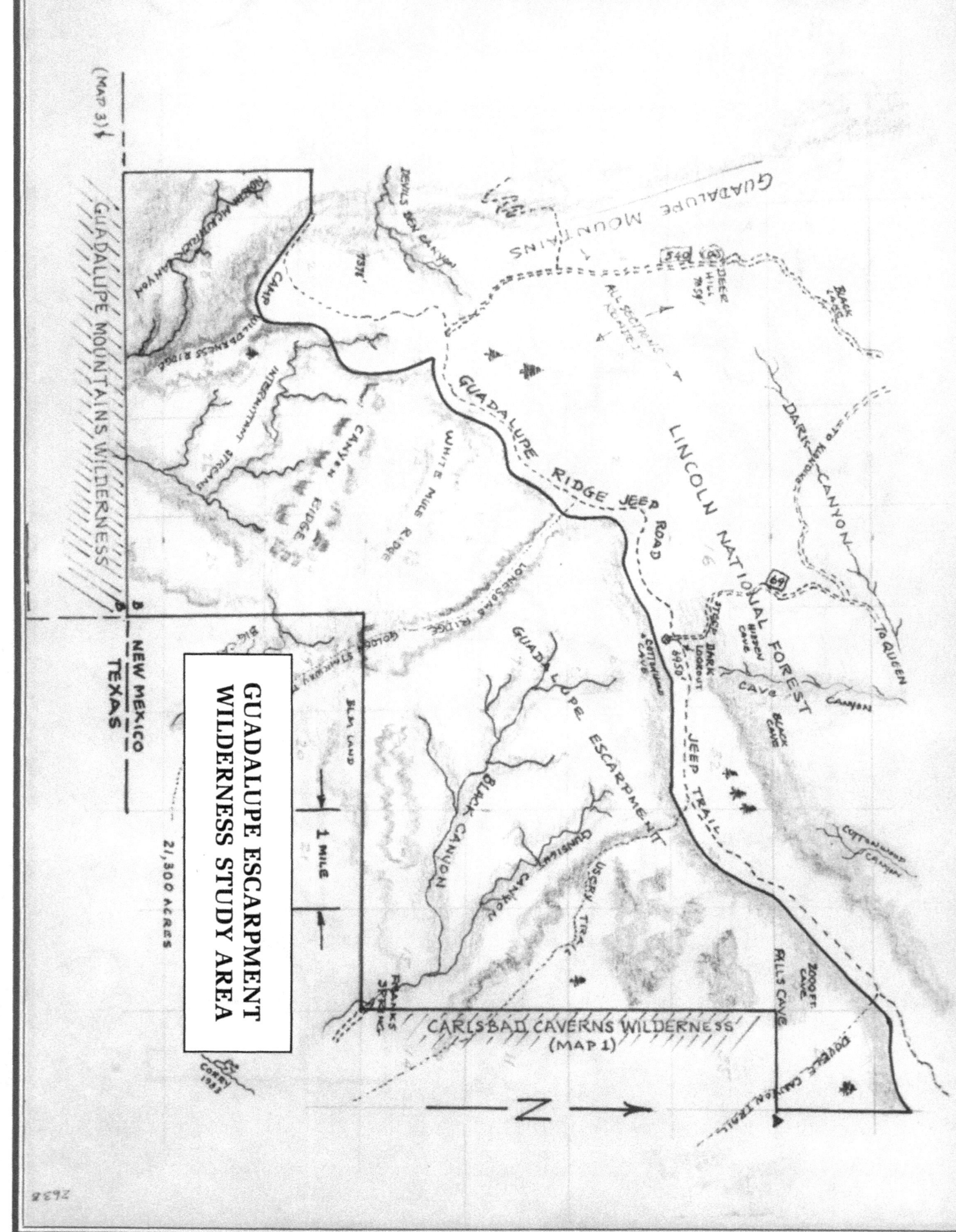

GUADALUPE MOUNTAINS WILDERNESS

A medicine man, fully steeped in the concept that all people emerged from the Sipapau, the underworld of all beginnings, made his way toward his mythical objective. His ancestors told him of the large opening to the underworld but its location was held as a secret known only to his line of religious forebearers. He felt — rather than knowing from experience — that he was close to the portal. Suddenly an unheard vibration in the air made the hair on the nape of his neck tingle and a chill sweep over him.

The madrone trees were so thick he could not tell what was in front of him for more than a few paces. The red madrone berries gleamed with an inner glow in the late afternoon sun. The magic magenta color cast its spell over the whole firmament in those last few minutes before the sun went down. He almost stepped over a precipice as he parted the branches in front of him. His lead foot dislodged some rock that struck ground far below. A wisp of black, sinuous smoke appeared to be coming out of a shadowy opening. He tossed another rock into the dark maw and it fell for a distance before resounding. This time he saw that the black smoke was bats emerging from the great opening. They were silhouetted against the sunset and he could almost hear a white-noise clicking sound that he had earlier only felt.

As he cautiously picked his way around the perimeter of the cave opening he found a small clearing free of brush and decided to spend the night there. His sparse meal of dried strips of meat were padded out with some agavé roots. The moon came up and bathed the white limestone with an eerie softness. He crushed a couple of mescal buttons which he carried in his medicine parfleche bag. As he chewed the buttons, he meditated on the various messages carried down to him through his shaman ancestors. His world flouresced in his mind's eye and he dimly saw twisting clouds of bats in the moonlight returning to the cave after their evening meal.

Many thousands of years later, his heavily decomposed skeleton was found under 50 feet of guano at the bottom of the chamber of Carlsbad Caverns known as the bat cave.[1] We can only guess he was exploring the shallower parts of the cave, slipped, and fell to his death. Perhaps he disturbed the bats and their rushing flight disoriented him and he lost his balance. Or did he hallucinate and stumble into the opening? The skeleton was only chalky remains when it was discovered in the early 1900's. One estimate has it that it required a hundred years to accumulate a foot of the bat droppings. That makes our medicine man 5,000 years our antecedent.

The anasazi who lived elsewhere in the region many centuries later identified their sipapu on the Little Colorado River where a spring discharges Glauber's salts (magnesium sulphate) onto a spectacular moundlike formation. Another group used a cave entrance in the Walnut Cave National Monument near Flagstaff, Arizona. That cave appears to inhale air strongly enough to pluck a tissue out of your hand — where the air comes from is not known.

Before that, long before man appeared, repeated invasions of Paleozoic seas spread lime muds, silts, and sands which now form extensive superimposed sheets of sedimentary rocks over the state. Near the close of this oldest era of fossil-bearing rocks, the ancestral Rocky Mountains began their rise in the northern part of the state; and quantities of red and gray mud, sand, and cobbles were washed away by streams from the rising highland and spread over lowland plains and margins of the sea.

In late Paleozoic time, the Permian sea prevailed in the southeastern part of the state. Among deposits in this sea was the huge limestone reef mass of the Capitan escarpment, the host rock from which Carlsbad Caverns were later to be dissolved by percolating ground waters. Within the basin partly enclosed by the reef, thousands of feet of salts including potash salts and other evaporites were laid down layer by layer in the closing stages of the era.[2]

The Capitan Reef was about 400 miles long, encircling the 10,000 square mile Delaware Basin. Capitan Reef was just below sea level until the later Permian when it was uplifted with the rest of New Mexico. The reef drained and took some of the limestone materials with it leaving extensive caves, many not yet discovered and explored.[3]

So, when man finally came onto the scene, even before our medicine man, the south end of the reef had lifted enough to expose 4,000 feet of Permian limestone to view. The elevation of Guadalupe Peak is 8,752 feet and the Pecos River at Carlsbad is 3,110 feet. New Mexico Institute geologist Frank Kottlowski said the Reef is "similar to Great Barrier Reef of Australia except that the Capitan and Goat Seep reefs surround an inland sea."[3] The part of the reef that is in our proposed Guadalupe Escarpment Wilderness is the southern part which extends from the Guadalupe Mountains National Park in northwestern Texas some 30 miles across the state line northeast to the eastern edge of the Carlsbad Caverns national park. In between the two National Parks, there is some Lincoln National Forest and some Bureau of Land Management fragments.

The Pecos River Basin and the Texas Gulf Basin make up the High Plains to the north and northeast of our Guadalupe Escarpment. The activities around the present day Clovis are recorded in the blackwater Draw where spearmen slayed mammoths in a boggy swamp along the west bank. Later, Folsom hunters felled and butchered large numbers of long horned bison. Still later, modern species such as short horned bison were ambushed by people of a culture period called Plano. All these kills and the articles lost or broken in the excitement of the hunt were sealed in sediment in perfect stratigraphic sequence: Clovis at the bottom, Folsom next, then Plano. The first seed-grinding mills were in the Plano period.[4]

A proposed Guadalupe Escarpment Wilderness document, issued in early 1979 by the Lincoln National Forest indicated that the general area had been occupied by Paleo-Indians since about 9,000 B.C. and by others in an Archaic period (7,000 B.C. to 400 A.D.). Then, beginning about 1400 A.D., for reasons which are poorly understood, the area was abandoned for at least 150 years until the Apaches used it seasonally. My guess is that locust plagues stripped the countryside bare. Coupled with that pestilence, the Little Ice Age drove man into Mexico.[5]

Some of the caves in the Guadalupe Escarpment have "paintings" or petroglyphs in them showing bison and other animals.[6] Despite millions of buffalo which originally populated the High Plains, they only lasted 10 years after the white man appeared.

The Comanches of the plains had made life tenuous for the nomadic inhabitants of the lands within the confines of the ancient reef. They had increased their mobility in the late 1600's and early 1700's by the acquisition of horses, and had even adopted a primitive navigation system to cross the Staked Plains (see the next chapter). When they saw the white man killing off the buffalo at wholesale slaughtering rates, they finished off the process in short order. Wagonloads of hides went past the Pecos crossings east of the reef on their way to west Texas and Mexico.

The hunters were not reluctant to use their same armament on their competition. The white hunters first discovered Sitting Bull Falls about 1845 when a posse chased a band of Indian horse thieves to the falls. The Indians escaped but the horses were recovered.[3]

Another Indian horsecapade happened in 1858 when they raided the ramuda at Fort Stanton, drove the herd 140 miles southeast to El Paso Gap and into Shattuck Valley near Devil's Den on the west end of our proposed Wilderness. The U.S. Cavalry borrowed enough horses to ride at night in pursuit and attacked the rancheria at dawn. They recaptured the horses and the Indians escaped onto the reef. The cavalry burned the Indian rancheria and supplies.[3]

The U.S. Postal Service opened bids to establish an overland mail contract from the Mississippi River to California in 1856. In 1857, John Butterfield and Associates signed the contract. The first stage made the trip in the fall of 1857. The route of the Butterfield Trail was from Tipton, Missouri to Big Spring, Texas, west to the 32nd parallel (at approximatley the New Mexico-Texas border) where it crossed the Pecos River. From there the trail swung southwest, up Guadalupe Canyon between the Guadalupe and Delaware Mountains; thence back into New Mexico to swing around the north side of the Cornudas Mountains. The trail again went southwest through the Hueco Mountains to Hueco Tanks, some natural limestone water basins storing 600,000 gallons (described by the Texans of the time).[7] The next leg of the Trail was westward to El Paso. The route then crossed over into Arizona where Interstate 10 now does near San Simon and on to San Francisco.

The trip cost $100 in gold in 1858 from St. Louis, used Concord Coaches, and took 24 days. The line ran semi-weekly, and hauled six passengers and the mail.[8] The first contract trip was in September, 1858. Dozens of Stations had been built and manned in that one year. Soldiers from Fort Bliss were kept busy trying to anticipate where the Indians would next raid one of the stations.

There was a Fort Phantom Hill just north of Abilene, Texas that was activated in 1851. Their scouts were issued rations of flour, coffee, sugar, and bacon. On his saddle each man carried a dutch oven with a folding handle to cook his own bread. The post was decommissioned in 1854 when one of the deserters set fire to it. However, it was five years after that when one of the guards riding shotgun on one of the stages shot at an Indian near Pine Springs because he was harassing their passage. The shot hit a dutch oven the Indian was carrying on his horse and must have stung his backside because he jumped off his mount and made appropriate clutching motions.[7]

A Post Office Order of August 1, 1859, changed the route of the Butterfield Trail to a more southerly location by way of Forts Stockton, Davis, and Quentin (all of Texas), abandoning the Guadalupe Mountain route because of the Indian menace. The Indians had learned where the most vulnerable spots were by that time.[9] In 1861, the line was discontinued due to loss of the mail contract.

The mail contract then went to the Pony Express which was run by the Butterfield Overland Dispatch, The Smoky Hill Route. It made the trip from Atchison, Kansas to Placerville, California, in 11 days and later from Sacramento to St. Joseph, Missouri in 8 to 10 days. It was routed through Forts Kearney and Bridger and Salt Lake City. The Express or Dispatch was operated and owned by D.A. Butterfield, no relation to the earlier John.

The stagecoach line on the Texas route operated sporadically on passenger fares for another year or so before it sputtered out with the onset of the Civil War. In 1866, the Pony Express was also closed down due to Indian raids and economic failure. Incidentally, a rider made it from Santa Fe to Kansas City in eight days on a bet during the early 1850's. In 1866, after the Civil War, a Stagecoach line from Santa Fe to Kansas City made the trip in 11 days. In 1867, Ben Holladay bought John Butterfield's Line via consolidation., In 1869, the Golden Spike was driven in the first transcontinental rail line and Ben Holladay sold out to Wells, Fargo, and Company. Civilization had come to the High Plains.[8]

Cotton gins and rail spurs showed up in the 1870's

in Texas and some of southern New Mexico. Sheep herds grazed much of the lower more rugged country around the inside foothills of the old Capitan Reef. The competition for the browse tended tp displace the deer from the lower hills and valley upward to the higher reef country. More and more meat hunters began to ride the ridge of the reef, along what we now know as the Guadalupe Mountains. The meat hunters found caves and overhangs containing extinct horse fossils, Taylor bison petrified remains, and four horned antelope evidence. Hermit cave (subsequently Carbon 14 dated) showed ancient human habitation evidences as 12,000 years old and there also was some 600 year old pottery.[9]

By 1880, cattlemen had begun to follow buffalo hunters into the Llano Estacado country and the scene was getting set for the Lincoln County Wars a bit farther north. By way of a tune-up, the Salt War of the 1860's and 1870's was a bloody dispute over the extensive surface salt deposits just south of the Guadalupe Mountains. It involved both Mexican and U.S. citizens, poitical parties, judges, and legislators, mob action, army troops, and Texas Rangers. Murder, assassination, and revenge killings took place on both sides.[9] The Rangers chased some of the murderers into our New Mexico mountains.

In the decade following the Civil War, the U.S. Army tried to shove the Indians onto various reservations. The Kiowa and Comanche Indians swept down from the Texas Panhandle and Indian Territory (Oklahoma) to raid the northern Texas settlements. During the summer of 1871, the Quahadi Comanches under Chief Quanah and some Kiowas under their own commands engaged soldiers from half a dozen forts throughout the Texas settlements.

Early in October of that year, General Mackenzie concentrated his army of about 600 men for the purpose of pursuing and closing with the marauders. The Army advanced onto the Llano Estacado, traveled as far as Blanco Canyon, and were harassed by hit-and-run Indian attacks. Severe weather, loss of horses, and outmaneuvering by the Quahadi forced the soldiers to return to their forts by early November. The next spring (1872), Mackenzie led another expedition against the Quahadi, pursuing them as far as Alamogordo, New Mexico, with no success.

The Indians were relatively quiet in 1872 and 1873 because of increased military activity in northern Texas and New Mexico. Some of the Indians found caves in the reef big enough to ride their horses into. A few raids in the vicinity kept things on edge. Some 65 deaths in the Texas Panhandle and southeastern New Mexico were Indian coups in 1874. This time Mackenzie got the jump on Chief Quanah at Palo Duro Canyon near Amarillo, captured and slaughtered more than 1,000 Indian horses. During 1875, the Indians straggled into the reservations to surrender.[10]

The large cattle drives from Texas to Montana, North and South Dakota, Wyoming, eastern Colorado, Dodge City, Kansas, and eastern New Mexico occupied the cattlemen. They managed to fill the void that the buffalo had left, except for the Indian. Those first generation reservation Indians gagged on Government beef.

A rancher named Charles B. Eddy managed a large cattle outfit in the southeastern part of the state in the 1880's. The cattle trailing activities generated a town near his headquarters. It was first called Eddy in 1889. However, in 1899, Eddy was changed to Carlsbad because the mineral springs on the Pecos River reminded somebody of Karlsbad, Germany.[1]

A young cowboy named Jim White (James Larkin White) worked for the Lucas 3-X Ranch. In 1901, while on a search for some missing cattle, he saw a cloud of bats emerging from a ridgetop and discovered Bat Cave (Carlsbad Caverns). He went into the cave several times that year, generally alone because no one would believe him. He worked up his equipment (ladders, packs, oil lamps) and spent several days on end in the caverns.

A character named Abijah Long showed up in 1903 and went out to the cave with Jim White. He was only interested in the bat guano which he knew he could sell in the date orchards of California for $90 per ton. Long put up the money and provided the mining engineering know-how and Jim worked with him off and on for 17 years. During that time some 100,000 tons of guano were removed from the one cavern, including our shaman's bones.[1] More and more people became interested in the caverns as time went on. Jim guided them in at every opportunity without fees for his services until he was joined by a fellow miner, Bert Wheeler, as a part time guide in 1909.

There was a Fergusson Act of 1898 in which the U.S. Congress granted the Territory of New Mexico the title to Sections 16 and 36 in each township. Carlsbad Caverns is in Section 36 of Township 24 South, Range 24 East, N.M.P.M. in Eddy county. Then Congress passed an Enabling Act on June 20, 1910, specifying how the state (territory) may dispose of its own lands.

The Government did not appear to be the least interested in the caverns as time went on. The Government made a preliminary study of a reservoir site to which they were going to pump Pecos River water. In the process they found the cave. So, in 1923, Carlsbad Caverns development finally started. Construction of stairways, lighting, observation platforms, road improvements, etc. went on apace.[11]

Cavers from all over the world started to show up. They not only took guided tours, but they rummaged around in the adjacent back country and found dozens of wild caves. Most of them were secretive about their discoveries.

In 1923, Mineral Examiner Robert A. Holley of the

General Land Office was detailed to make a survey and study of the cave and its environment. After a month's study (guided by Jim), Holley said:

> I enter upon this task with a feeling of temerity as I am wholly conscious of the feebleness of my efforts to convey in words the deep conflicting emotions, the feeling of inspired understanding of the Divine Creator's work which presents to the human eye such a complex aggregate of natural wonder in such a limited space.

The Master Plan for Carlsbad Caverns National Park, dated August, 1971, briefs the legislative history:

> On the strength of the report of Mineral Examiner Robert A. Holley of the General Land office in 1923, President Calvin Coolidge signed Proclamation No. 1679 on October 25, 1923, setting aside a 719.22-acre portion of the public domain as Carlsbad Cave National Monument, because "...it appears that the public interest would be promoted by reserving this natural wonder as a National Monument, together with as much land as may be needed for the protection, not only of the known entrance, but such other entrances as may be found."
>
> The area was designated as a public park "for the benefit and enjoyment of the people" under the name of Carlsbad Caverns National Park by congressional act on May 14, 1930 (46 Stat. 279). This act authorized enlargement of the park, within specified lands, by proclamation of the President.
>
> The park boundaries were adjusted in 1933 and 1939 under the authority of the 1930 act. An addition of 9240 acres in 1933 included the remaining known area of Carlsbad Caverns and adjacent lands. The primary purpose of the 39,4388 acres added in 1939 was for protection of caves, including New Cave and Painted Grotto in Slaughter Canyon.
>
> The act of 1963 (P.L. 88-249) provided that the Rattlesnake Springs tract, used as a water supply for the park, be included within the park as a detached section. Elsewhere, lands on the periphery of the park were added to facilitate the protection of scenic values and to improve administrative and protective activities. The act eliminated from the park those lands not required for park purposes, and also repealed section 4 of the 1930 act which allowed the boundaries of the park to be enlarged by Presidential proclamation.
>
> As a condition of 77 Stat. 818, the State of New Mexico has the right to construct a second road between park headquarters and U.S. Highway 62-180.

Frank Vesely, New Mexico State Land Commissioner in 1933, claimed that the state owned the Caverns on the basis of the Fergusson and Enabling Acts, and that the Congress disregarded its own two Acts in its proclamations. He proposed "the exchange of the state owned Section 36 for 3 million of the 16 million acres owned by the federal government in New Mexico."[11] There is no evidence that Congress even blinked at the charge.

Let's go back a short time and finish the Jim White story. The guano was mined out in 1919. Jim started to build trails in the cave and mapped them. After the 1923 Holley report, the Government asked him on what lands they ought to start condemnation proceedings. He pointed out that there were many more caves than the big one. Jim was given a permit to operate the cave from 1923 to 1926, at which year the Government took over management of the cave. Jim was hired as Chief Ranger and worked in that capacity for three years until 1929 when he was 47 years old and getting tired of the seven miles walking per day in the cave. He went on a month's vacation, but returned to discover that he no longer had a job. He had wanted to be called Chief Explorer, but the Government (National Park Service) said there was no such position. Jim put on a mail campaign over the next year but to no avail. (They said he was a boozer.)

Charles L. White (no relation to Jim) had come to New Mexico in 1914 and started White's City to sell souvenirs to the tourists on the El Paso-Carlsbad road near the fork to the Caverns. Jim White went to work for White City in 1929 and stayed there until about 1940. He and his wife moved into Carlsbad (the town) in 1941, and Jim died in 1946. He wrote a book that sold well enough to keep his family going but the Park Service thought that the cost of it was too high after his death. Jim did not fare too well with the bureaucratic Feds, according to his biographer.[1]

To this point, little has been said about the Guadalupe Mountains. Perhaps I hold some bias that they are not in New Mexico but are over the line in northwestern Texas. The Capitan Reef is vee-shaped and the point of the vee is aptly surmounted by the prow of El Capitan Peak that overlooks the Texan peneplain as its lord and master. Even the Delaware Mountains off toward the south are diminutive and inconsequential by comparison.

The big face of El Capitan has been described as a 2,000 foot sheer cliff, visible for 50 miles by Texans of an earlier vintage. Others, perhaps more meticulous, admit that the cliff might be 1,500 feet. Several advertising minds have thought about inscribing a lone star on its face. (There may be some deity who would strike such efforts down with a thunderbolt.) Off toward the northeast, the reef extends some 30 miles to Carlsbad Caverns. The west leg of the reef retreats to the north and northwest into the heart of New Mexico.

The dead of winter generates some tempestuous snow-storms along the southeast side of the big reef. However, within a few hours, the deeply incised canyons in the escarpment are bathed in sunlight again. South McKittrick Canyon has relics of past climatic conditons in its bigtooth maples, chinquapin oaks, and hop hornbeans. Summer temperatures in the shady spots and water seeps are preferential to some lush verdure in those dozens of canyons.

The mountains look barren and forbidding when they are seen in the noonday sun from the Guadalupe Canyon highway. They tend to come to life and even beckon as one tends to learn more about them. That same noonday sun beats down more fiercely on a summer's day some 50 miles southward. The Spanish and Mexican caballeros knew the Guadalupe Canyon route well because it was cooler. Indian transits on horseback used the age-old route around the tip of the mountains to follow their ancestor's route in avoidance of the Apache surveillance further north. There also was a salt deposit not far to the west of the stark El Capitan massif.

An old Spanish mine was located high up on the western side of Signal (now Guadalupe) Peak. The ore from that mine, and perhaps several others, was hauled to the flats below to be smelted as long as fuels for the process could be found in the early 1600's. During the Pueblo Revolt, the Indians covered the portal and made false trails to lead strangers astray of its location. Much later, during the Mexican regime, the mine was quietly and covertly worked by Indians. They had their ore processed by mediaries who took it to El Paso for smelting in the early 1800's.

The Indians had been waylaying Spanish bullion shipments for a couple of centuries during that period. The treasures were buried along much of the Guadalupe Canyon routes. The reasons were a combination of factors in whole or part. The early Spanish miners had tell-tale configurations to their expeditions that were easy for any observers to read. They prospected in parties of four to six men. All were mounted and they had three or four pack horses or, more usually, mules. The prospectors were heavily armed. Picks, shovels, windlass cranks, and crowbars were always tied on the outsides of the packs since they never have been easy to carry, whatever their vintage.

When the Spaniard was hauling ore, the configuration was four men accompanying mules laden with two ore sacks in crude panniers and they would travel fast. They often had one man at the lead position, one man at the rear, and one on each side of the string of pack mules. A lookout on their best horse would scout the route ahead. They would travel into the night as long as conditions of the transit would let them. They did not use fires at night but rather at midday and they tried to make as little smoke as possible. However, even fairly rich ores were seldom hijacked by Indians. But if the party looked too nervous and hurried, perhaps the ore sacks had some bullion secreted within and camouflaged with ore. The Indians liked bullion — it did not need smelting.

Bullion was carried in saddle bags and in green leather (not tanned) compartmented panniers on pack horses and mules with camp gear on top in an attempt to disguise the load. The pack animals' gait usually gave it away. The attackers tried to wound the pack animals first.

All told, gold and silver shipments were hard to transport. If the hijackers were successful, they would generally bury the booty after splitting up what they could escape with on their own mounts. They always planned on returning to their cache when the heat was off.

The Guadalupe Canyon route was rugged and transits could be made without being seen for great distances. There were many natural ambush locations along the way. Even during the Mexican reign, despite the fact that the miner's armament was better, the Indian success rates increased because they finally had good horses. The Indians used as slaves in the larger mines were either killed or abandoned when the mines were worked out. For these various reasons, there are many grave sites along the road.

In 1849, U.S. Army Captain Marcy found the gap south of El Capitan Peak and the Delaware Mountains. The fact that the route had been used for centuries had nothing to do with his wonderful "discovery." His breakthrough came just in time for the California and Nevada goldrushes. The tooling up of the mining operations was served by shipments around the Horn by all kinds of seagoing freighters that could make the rough four month trip. Many of those boats could not make the journey back to the eastern U.S.[8] Wagon trains through Guad Gap only took six weeks.

The Butterfield Stage followed a track made by some of the U.S. Army caissons and supply wagons through the Guadalupe Canyon. Although the usual Army supply route went through the lower route in Texas by way of their string of Forts (such as Fort Stockton) during the hot summer months, some of the gun and powder shipments went on forced march through Guadalupe Gap.[8]

So the Butterfield Stages carried not only people and mail to California, but high value items which could be sold in San Francisco for much of the newly mined gold. The stagecoach trip took only 24 days, as well. The bullion shipments back to the "States" made it on the return trip. The Army had a number of detachments stationed along the route at vulnerable spots. They even rode along with the stages during the most active period.[12]

Probably the Pinery Station, in the shadow of Guadalupe Peak (variously called Signal Peak by the soldiers) was one of the hottest spots. The horses were changed there and it was usually late in the day or early in the morning that the robberies took place.

Mexican miners had discovered what the Indians had known for centuries. Guadalupe turquoise was found in copper-bearing outcroppings on the mountain above the 6,000 foot elevation in vertical veins in widths from one to 12 inches. Sometimes the vein tipped over to as low as 60° from the vertical.[13] The quality was extraordinary in that much of it was shot through with gold, silver, and copper. It brought high prices in the Far East. Consequently, some of the turquoise found its way into the buried treasures in the vicinity.

The stages had been held up so many times by the fall of 1859 that the Post Office changed the Butterfield route to the southern route through Fort Stockton and the string of forts some 75 miles to the southward of Guadalupe Canyon route.[14] There were still some irregular freight hauls and some nervous wagon trains that went through the Guad Gap in the winters of the 1860's even after the Smoky Hill Route through Colorado was opened up.

The Civil War years saw much military traffic flowing through the Guad Gap. There were some limited engagements of the Union and Confederate troups but they paled in comparison to the disturbances caused by and attendant to the Salt War of the same period.

Many of the Californian and Alaskan gold miners came back disappointed but some of them spread out through the warmer mountains in their continued quest for the big strike. The Old Spanish Gold Mine was bought and sold several times. Many murders were caused by that and other mining operations in the vicinity. The Texas Rangers spent an inordinate amount of time in the vicinity since the area seemed to attract more than its share of renegades armed with the new Civil War guns and ammunition. The gunfighters were almost as virulent there as in the Lincoln County War (see Chapter 12).

Now for a somewhat incredulous tale. Ben Wattson was 17 years old in 1880. He was a wanderer in a disturbed world. As a child he had run away from home, become a sailor, and at sixteen returned with the intention of going to school. He was too grown up for the establishment of that time so he kissed his mother goodbye once again.

He surfaced in Lamesa, Texas, at the southern edge of the Staked Plains, walking. He was striking out westward when he took up with some horsemen heading the same way. They were pleasant fellow travelers until they reached the Guadalupe Mountains when he discovered too late that they were outlaws. It was three years before he could get away from them. They used him as general flunky, cooking, caring for the horses, and other camp chores. He refused their offer of a share of the loot and took tips only for actual services. He saved this money and waited for a chance to escape.[15]

In the interim, during his three years under their heel, he saw them hide and bury much loot. He finally got away from them by climbing over the crest of the Guadaulpe Mountains at night. Ben went to sea again but came back to the Guads several times over the next 50 years. He was a jack of all trades but unfortunately, as a plumber, he lost his left hand at the wrist. He made a prosthetic hook with an opposable digit unique enough to be reproduced in the Smithsonian collection. He could even pick up a pin with it.

Now known as Uncle Ben, he met and married his wife, Pauline, in the 1930's. She realized that the old wanderlust was catching up with him again in 1939 when he wanted to go back to the Guadalupes. Both Ben and Pauline were mystics and apparently on the same frequency. Ben believed that the many treasures of the Guadalupes carried a potent "karma" resulting from their having been involved in theft, murder, and violence of all kinds. However, there had been a heavy earthquake on August 16, 1931, which the town of Valentine, Texas reported. There it was estimated by the USGS to be rated as 8.0 on the Modified Mercalli Scale (5.5 to 6.0 Richter Scale) based on the damage in the town. It was probably stronger in the Guads, 60 miles to the north because whole chunks of the mountain slid down. One major slide covered up the Old Spanish Mine. Tio Ben had been at the mine before it was covered up and had seen a very rich ore lead. He found later that, although obscured by the slide, he could still crawl into the outer tunnel. He and a partner tried to reopen the mine in 1941 but the ground was too treacherous and they finally lost their lease.

Uncle Ben and Pauline worked at many of the ranches and gas stations throughout the Guadalupe Canyon area even before the blacktopped road was put in. There had been many small caves in that vicinity which were caved in or covered up by various storms and the big quake. Through his mystic subconscious directions, Tio Ben had been told to make a dowsing instrument. His wife Pauline learned to use it even better than he could.[15]

Pauline's book, "Hidden Gold of the Guadalupes," is must reading if you intend to set foot in that locality. Incidentally, Ben died in 1963, only three months short of 100 years. Pauline is 85 and lives in Albuquerque and is still vivacious and projecting a dynamic vitality. And when I picked up the dowsing instrument, it almost hit me on the jaw. Pauline said it was attracted to the gold or silver in my teeth. (Maybe it did not like mechanical engineers.)

Pauline's book ends with the following statement in its epilogue:

Tio Ben believed that the bandits and outlaws of the early days were inspired to bring their loot to the Guadalupe Mountains to bury it. He believed also that none of it could be recovered at this time, that it was being guarded for the future....for discovery by unselfish souls who only seek treasure that might expand their activity in helping people....for the enlightened souls of the great Golden Age so close at hand.

And I am compelled to leave this written record for their assistance.

Up to this point, you have heard about many of the events and people that surrounded the Guadalupe Escarpment. Originally, I had intended to only deal with the current aspects relating to our proposed Wilderness enactment because so much has happened in the last 10 to 15 years. Perhaps I was "directed" to tell more of the whole story of the fascination of the Reef. The remainder will be covered as briefly as I can and still do it justice. To this point, also, it has been hearsay, history, and at least second hand information. The balance is more first hand information and my own experience.

My first trip to Carlsbad Caverns was in 1940 when I worked as an automotive engineer for Packard Motor in Detroit. We had a fleet of cars touring the hot country in the summer time with newly invented air conditioners. We put up in Carlsbad (the town) for about a week to make some changes in some of the cars before driving into south Texas for our testing runs. The road to the Cave had been graveled and blacktopped several years earlier but that year it was broken up quite badly and full of potholes. It was a rainy and rough trip.

The elevator to the lunchroom had been running for a couple of years but that day I walked in and out twice, coming out the last time when the bats were emerging. I can still almost taste that sweet smell that accompanied their passage. On the way back to town we stopped at White's City, bought a piece of polished stalagmite, and met Jim White. We talked about his counterpart who had discovered and explored Morrison Cave in Jefferson County, Montana. They had similar experience and disappointments. He told me that, "The damned elevator was pumpin' the air out of the cave and the formations are losin' color."

Later, after World War II, my first trip to the Guads was up on the Blue Ridge in 1948. there was a new blacktopped highway from El Paso to Signal Peak that made the trip from Albuquerque fairly easy. It was still about 285 miles to El Paso and another 110 miles to Signal Peak. When we drove up to Guadalupe Spring, and parked the car, it seemed we had it made. But when we boondocked it up to the saddle between El Capitan and Guadalupe (Signal) Peak, we realized we had only begun. We took our sleeping bags and our canteens and climbed up onto the El Captian summit and spent the night. My notes say that there was one hands-on rock spine where we had to climb.

The next day we did Guadalupe Peak, Shumand and Bartlett Peaks, and turned back after topping out on Bush Mountain.[18] Some reference made claim that there are 36 summits higher than 8,000 feet in the even had timber in it!) by way of a good trail east from Bush Mountain. Some reference made claim that there are 36 summits higher than 8,000 feet in the Guads.[17] You can see them all from the Blue Ridge.

After spending the night in the bowl (much lightning, rain, and hail), we climbed back up onto the summit of Pine Top. There we had lunch and dropped down the trail into Pine Spring Canyon to the road. At Pine Springs we caught a ride in a pickup truck through Guadalupe Pass and hiked up to our car at Guad Springs from the Blacktop (U.S. 62 Highway). In 1968 when I tried to drive up to the Springs, the road was closed; so inquire at Pine Springs for the latest access infromation.

Frank Ewing and I had a birdseye look into south McKittrick Canyon from the bowl and decided we ought to get into it sometime. Frank was quite a fisherman and had heard there was good fishing in North McKittrick Canyon. I do not have any trip notes on it, but three of us tried to get into the canyon in the mid-1950's and found it gated and posted against entry. We talked to a caretaker at the Pratt place near the mouth of the canyon. He said that we had to get permission from either the Hunter or Pratt Lodge owners to go into the canyon and that the fishing was not much good anyway. We gave up and drove over into Slaughter Canyon. There were so many private roads and locked gates that we concluded that the access to the public lands was practically blocked off.

Since that time, happily, much has happened. Senator Yarbrough of Texas introduced a National Park Bill on April 15, 1966. The resulting Public Law 89-667 (H.R. 698) was enacted on October 15, 1966, by the 89th U.S. Congress. It had provisions for variously obtaining the several inholdings. Earlier, in 1961, the Federal Government had received from Wallace Pratt a donation of 5,632 acres in North McKittrick Canyon. Most of it was in Texas but some was in New Mexico. In 1965, some 70,000 acres owned by J.C. Hunter, Jr. of Abilene, Texas, was transferred to the National Park Service. The ranch had been used for raising angora goats for mohair.[13] Parts of it had been picked clean when the Park Service obtained title. The Park Bill in 1966 closed the area to mineral leasing but provided first mineral rights to the former owners if and when "an Act of Congress provides that the national welfare or an emergency requires the development and production of the minerals underlying the lands within the boundaries...." The public lands north of the Texas border in New Mexico were placed under the charge of the U.S. Forest Service.

Again in 1969 when I was in the vicinity, I asked in Pine Springs if McKittrick was open and found that it was open to foot traffic. During the summer a cloud burst had washed out the road in the canyon. It was an interesting day. A Park Ranger was at Pratt Lodge giving a brief historical summary of the previous use of the Lodge. He did not seem to know anything about the Grisham lodge in South McKittrick Canyon or the Hunter Lodge either. On that occasion I recall hiking to the head of North (McKittrick) Canyon and getting back to the car at the canyon mouth just after dusk. Those two big canyons do not seem to be any part of a Texas mountain-desert landform. They are green, have running streams, many varieties of birds, and thriving cool-country wildlife. The Canyon climbs through four climatic zones, Chihuahuan desert to Canadian. I saw deer within a mile of the Lodge. Elk and turkey signs were further up the canyon. We saw

Bighorn tracks up on Pine Top years before. The elk were imported from other Texas ranches in 1925 and 1926. The turkeys were reintroduced in 1954. A few years before, Wallace E. Pratt had turned loose five Bighorn sheep in North McKittrick Canyon.

It was sometime in 1953 or 1954 that Pratt had formulated an idea that his place ought to somehow become a National Park. He was a petroleum geologist on the staff of Standard Oil of New Jersey. It was only after having many government officials as guests in his Lodge that he was able to start proceedings in 1959 to donate his 5,632 acres to the federal government for use as a National Park. In 1961, agreement and transfer was completed.

As far back as 1920, the J.C. Hunter, Jr. family had tried to stir interest in a Park and would sell their 77,000 acres for such a purpose.[17] The problems of obtaining Carlsbad Caverns was almost more than the National Park Service could handle. The 1966 enactment managed to pull these two neighbors and the National Park Service into an accord. The Park Bill stipulated "a maximum of $10,362,000 is appropriated for the development of the Guadalupe Mountains National Park." It was not clear that the appropriation was directly for the purchase of the Hunter lands. About 5,000 acres of the original 77,000 acres had been sold in the interim since 1920. So, the total came to about 72,000 acres. Was that the same five thousand acres which Pratt donated?

The formal opening of the Park was in 1971. There were announcements relative to the withdrawal of mineral rights, a reconfirmation of the denial of grazing, and a new proclamation against hunting in the Carlsbad Caverns and Guadalupe Mountains National Park.

The Lincoln National Forest between the two Parks and the reef extension to the north has the largest herd of mule deer in the state of New Mexico. This could be the result of the two adjacent wildlife refuges that feed the herd along the entire reef. The Guadalupe Mountains browse appears to have recovered from its overbrowsed conditions of the 1950 period. In the mid-1960's, the madrone trees in the west side of the Carlsbad Caverns National Park were badly stripped by an over-abundance of deer. They did not seem to want to move out into the adjacent ranges. Park officials decided they had to take action to limit the overbrowsing damage. A research program was started.

My understanding of what happened is that some 50 deer were selected and killed to sample their stomach contents and to assess their condition. The intent was to attempt to determine their recent behavioral vagaries. (There probably are reports of their findings if I were that interested.) I became more aware when I heard that the State of New Mexico was claiming in court that the Park Service did not have custody of the deer, but that they belonged to the state. Consequently, the government was accused of conducting an illegal research study. The Federal Court concluded that the state was right and did own the game. This became a landmark decision. The deer must have agreed because they haven't stripped the madrone trees of bark since that time. They still eat the berries, however.

The Forest Service had been obtaining the land parcels between the two Parks since the 1920's. This area subsequently has been open for hunting, grazing, and mineral exploration in a multiple use mode of Management. Early on, the south side of the escarpment was a State Game Refuge and only open for hunting periodically. After the herd was rebuilt, an annual hunt was permitted in season. By 1970, it was one of the largest herds of deer in the southwest. It took a lot of hunting to keep it trimmed to a size that could be maintained by its range which by that time extended onto the BLM lands to the north of the National Forest and the Parks.

Another multiple use became frequent enough to attract attention. Cavers began to get into the wild caves of the region. By 1960, the reputation of the Reef Caves had become nationally well known. By 1970, they had become renowned internationally. One of the larger caves on the National Forest part is called Cottonwood Cave. Its mouth is located at the top edge of the reef near the Dark Canyon Forest Service Lookout (a fire lookout tower).

A rudimentary road climbs the north side of the escarpment to the tower and was extended along the ridgetop by adventurous souls all the way to Putman Tank on the west end of the Carlsbad Caverns National Park. I have not been much further on that road than a couple of miles northeast of Dark Lookout, but I understand that a Jeep can make it all of the way through into the park, A large metal water tank was somehow hauled up onto the ridge to provide water for cattle. Pumps were located below it in a canyon on the north side. When I saw it in 1968 or 1969, it was not being used. We simply remarked that if we could get Wilderness enactment, the tank would either be classified as non-conforming or removed.

That same road (or two-track-trail) has provided access for a strange breed of human beings that I call cave vandals. I have never seen one but only his horrible signature. Some use paint spray cans with awful effect. Most of the others remove cave formations including stalagmites and stalactites with hammers and pinch bars, probably for sale as souvenirs. The Forest Service and the Bureau of Land Management have attempted to arrest such wanton damage by placing gratings, grillwork, or gates, set in concrete, to block entrances to the more vulnerable caves.

The vandals variously gain access by blowing up the metal grating with dynamite and/or somehow using tow chains or cables probably attached to trucks. Some of the caves bear evidences of long cables chaf-

Guadalupe Mountains National Park Wilderness — South McKittrick Canyon.

ing the passages possibly during the act of removal of large chunks of formation. I spent a night in my sleeping bag on the reef top and was awakened by a four-wheel drive truck with a spotlight playing on my camp. They may have been jack-light hunters, a Forest Service patrol, or cave vandals. I was not prepared to find out which. I have heard the organized cavers say that the damage appears to be most pronounced near the roads in the area. I have been in only a few of the hundred or more caves, but that made me angry enough to curse and spit sulfur.

In season, deer hunters use that ridge trail to drive to and from their camps, to road hunt, and to haul their kills out if they are successful. Consequently, the local hunters were upset by the New Mexico Wilderness Study Committee's proposed Unified Guadalupe Escarpment Wilderness in 1970. Our proposal provided for a corridor for the road to Dark Lookout and Black River Well, but closure of the Jeep trail northeast of Dark Lookout. Most of the hunters know that driving on that ridge trail spooked the deer off the ridge but they preferred to (illegally) hunt from their trucks than to walk. The guides and outfitters admitted that if they had a camping or parking area near Dark Lookout on top of the reef, they could pack out of that trailhead. The hunters also feared that, if the whole Unified Escarpment proposal went through, the Park Service would be given the entire Wilderness to manage. That would mean that hunting would be closed on the whole reef. Hunting of the National Forest and BLM parts have become a yearly ritual with thousands of hunters. Despite these fears, our Wilderness proposal does not include any such changes in the administrative agencies.

Floods into Dark Canyon aperiodically result in some damage to the town of Carlsbad. One of the reasons proffered by the Forest Service against our Study Committee's north boundary is that flood control structures could not be built in Dark Canyon. To the date of this writing, the Forest Service has not constructed any such structures in the canyon and we have not heard of any funds being budgeted for that purpose. We have suggested that they proceed to lay out their check dams and that it would be seen that our north boundaries would little interfere.

The Forest Service recommended that their RARE

II Area Number 03077, being 21,300 acres, would extend from the ridge Jeep trail southward to include all of the roadless areas of the southern escarpment face. Our area would block off the ridge road at Dark Lookout and extend into the Dark Canyon bottom on the north. Our boundaries had many corridors for continued access to wells, drilling pads, tanks, and other nonconforming structures. We could understand the continuing pressures exerted upon the Forest Ranger in the area to make the Wilderness Area as small as possible. Our sympathy does not go as far as agreement.

Our New Mexico Wilderness Study Committee, in conjunction with the National Speleological Society, made the proposal of a 156,000 acre composite National Wilderness, in 1970.[16] It dwelled upon the fact that the area was one geological entity despite the considerable division of the administration of the reef, and the unique aspect of its being an above and below ground wilderness. The enactment obviously had to be considered in parts because of the divided agency jurisdictions. The two National Park Wildernesses, first introduced at our request as S.602 on January 29, 1973, was finally enacted in October, 1978. The areas were 46,840 acres in Guadalupe Mountains National Park and 33,125 acres in Carlsbad Caverns National Park. The Park Service had only rudimentary maps as late as April, 1980, of both of these areas. The Superintendent's Office indicated that they would again pulse their Denver Office for completion of the maps and the legal boundary description.

I will not bore you with how many meetings and hearings there were in those ten years. Some of our folks tended to wear down and accept the smaller Forest Service-BLM proposed area recommended by the Agencies in RARE II, just to get the process completed. Others of us pushed on the Unified proposal for 12 years and do not think that the RARE II proposed area is adequate. The New Mexico Ominbus Wilderness Bill of 1980 which contains our Senators' and Representatives' compromised decisions between our conservationists proposals and the RARE II (Forest Service) recommendations was released for comment in April, 1980.

At least a couple of events during that decade are worth covering briefly. A tramway up to The Bowl had been proposed by the Park Service as a part of an earlier Master Plan. I am not sure how long it took, how many hearings, and how many letters, but the Park Service listened and finally responded to the public pressure to delete the tramway from the plans. It had been called many euphemistic names by the Park Service instead of a tramway, but the ploy did not work. One must work hard to hike or ride up to see that surprising mountain microcosm. Be sure to carry your own water and tread ever so gently.

The other threatening vector arose suddenly in February, 1977, in the form of a proposal to the Forest Service's Guadalupe Ranger District and the BLM by the Freewheeler Motorcycle Club of Carlsbad. They wanted to hold a One-Day Enduro Motorcycle Event. By that time, the Ridge Jeep Trail had been labeled Forest Road 201. The Enduro route proposed would have traversed the trail from Big Canyon Ridge northeastward to the intersection with road 527, some 13 miles. Allan L. Hinds, the dedicated and capable District Ranger, held a public hearing to listen to all sides. Most of the conservation organizations recommended against allowing the fragile, unconstructed road to be used for the race. The Guadalupe Cycle riders added their clamor to the proposal. They said they had been getting the runaround by the Forest Service for a couple of years. The enduro event is not a race in the traditional sense, in that it is not a speed race. It is rather a competition whereby participants aim for accuracy in completing each phase of the circuit, with top speeds reaching about 20 miles per hour. Official refusal was slow in coming, but it finally was expressed. The Agency people made a very thorough analysis before making the decision.

Jim White's admonition about the elevators pumping moisture out of Carlsbad Caverns was recently rectified by appropriate air locks and other corrective measures. The final assessment was made by John McLean, a very capable Cave Research Foundation representative. John is a hydrologist with the U.S. Geological Survey, a spelunker, and a progenitor of the above and below ground wilderness concept as it applies to our Captian Reef. John and William P. (Bill) Bishop, former Director of the Cave Research Foundation, have had a long and abiding love affair with the 300 or more caves in the reef.[16] They were leaders of the speleological groups that helped put together the first Wilderness proposal.

TRAILS AND ROUTES ON THE GUADS

Once on top the Reef, you don't need a trail. There are many trails marked on the Park Service maps and most are easy to follow. The 15 Minute Quad Series of maps is quite old (1935-1945) and they show many trails that were fairly good pack trails at that time. All of the Agencies have been doing some work on many of the trails but there are many that have not been maintained at all. As a result, some of those neglected trails are perhaps the least used and the most interesting. A few of the canyons on the southeastern escarpment have duck rocks marking erstwhile routes possibly laid out as a survival exercise. If that is what you are into, the 7-$\frac{1}{2}$ Minute Series is a better choice of map. However, take plenty of water because the blue thread you see in some of the canyons may have been someone's illusion, or it was right after a cloudburst. The springs and waterholes can be variable from year to year. It may seem strange that all the really good sources are on private land. Water treatment pills should be used on all wild water. (See the

Wheeler Peak Chapter about leptospirosis.)

Trailhead locations are not the easiest things to find. There are a few general rules that have held solid since I first set wheel to the area. The road from White's City to Carlsbad Caverns is one of the few paved roads. It would be well to stop by the Park Service Office in Carlsbad (the town) to get their latest road information about your area of interest. For example, there has been considerable roadwork on the Slaughter Canyon road to a parking lot at the trailhead to New Cave, Ogle Cave, Goat Cave, and Painted Grotto. The road recipe is much easier than it used to be. But most of the other trailheads are just like they used to be, at the end of a rocky road.

There are now many more roads than the old Quad maps show. That is one reason it is so confusing, particularly on the Southeast Escarpment side, but one can usually see the mountain off to the northwest of U.S. Highway 62-180. It is usually a good six to 10 miles from the highway to the trailheads and the signs are not all that clear. Many of the roads have at least a dozen forks so you will need a map.

During the summer months, wet weather can give rise to complications such as water coming in the bottoms of doors of small sedans. Some of the roads go up dry washes that flush occasionally. The first good gullywasher of year may bring a saucy clatter of beer cans down with it and can also move a few boulders onto the crossings.

The north side access is best by State Road 137 to Forest Road 68 and up to the old town of Queen. If you use the Forest Service Hunter's Map (Lincoln National Forest), you will find a multiple junction about three miles southwest of Queen. The fork going south leads to Forest Road 69A to Dark Lookout. Road Number 307 is a better one to Devil's Den vicinity and a lookout down into North McKittrick Canyon. From that same fork, one may follow the signs to El Paso Gap. The road to the south of the Gap opens the way to the west side of the mountains and a number of trailheads. One can drive to the Williams Ranch access road from the southwest corner of the Guadalupe National Park if you have a Jeep or a four-wheel drive. The Park Master Plan says they are going to improve the access to the west side, sometime.[17]

So now to a few of the trails and routes, if you can solve the ways of their respective trailheads.

TRAILS AND ROUTES IN THE GUADALUPE ESCARPMENT

Big Canyon trailhead puts you onto Forest Trail Number 56, the Golden Stairway Trail. You start at about 5,000 feet and climb to 7,000 feet as you top out on Lonesome Ridge. It is about four miles to the ridge road from where you started. Black Canyon Spring has been equipped with a gasoline driven pump and can be heard a half-mile to the northeast of your ridge trail junction. The spring runs sometimes when the pump has not been running (off season). It is about two miles more northeast on the ridge to Dark Lookout and Cottonwood Cave.

You may want to return to your car by retracing your steps. Because I found the Big Canyon trailhead late in the morning, I sacked out for the night on top and decided to go down the Ussery Trail. The Ussery Trail intersects the Ridge Trail (Forest Road 201) about a half-mile east of Dark Lookout. The trail goes southeast for about three miles on the timbered top before plunging off the escarpment to the east. By the time the (Ussery) trail intersects the first road at the "bottom," you are then a good five miles northeast of your car in the mouth of Big Canyon.

Another time you may want to drop down Black Canyon from Cottonwood Cave. Use your 7-1/2 Minute Map and strike off straight south down into the bottom of the ravine. There was no trail but enough cavers have been up and down the canyon walls to augment the game trails. We were able to pick our way down to the mouth of the canyon by staying in the bottoms of the draws. When you emerge from the canyon and run into a road, you will be about three miles northeast from your car in Big Canyon trailhead, an easy fence hopping trip back. A flock of turkeys flushed out in front of us as we came the last couple of miles down Black Canyon.

Another trip is to go up the Ussery Trail to the Ridge Road and return down the Double Trail (Forest Trail Number 203). Double Trail leaves the Ridge Road (201) about three miles east. Be sure to take the left hand trail that skirts along the rim of Double Canyon. It soon switches-back and down into the canyon and bumps into the old Thurman road. At the canyon mouth, this time you are only about a mile and a half from your car to the Ussery Trail Junction.

There is a trail of sorts up the west branch of Double Canyon that goes to the foot of the escarpment below the mouth of Two Thousand Foot Cave. My enthusiasm for climbing up to the entrance was dampened by a rainstorm. I might have persisted had I been a real caver. We could make out through our binoculars a yellow jacket hanging near the entrance. My friends went into the cave on a subsequent trip and only reported that they had to rappel and that it was probably easier to get to from the rim above.

There are trails all throughout the three branches of Slaughter Canyon. These trails are great for dayhiking with a light pack because you can be fairly sure of reaching your car by dark. There are enough interesting caves and features to keep you from topping out of the canyons even if all you do is surface exploration. The Park Service likes you to get a permit and to know your intended route and destination. Get the permit either in town or at the Caverns. New Cave is an escorted trip.

For the Walnut Canyon-Putman Tank Trip, park your car at the Carlsbad Caverns parking lot and take

Carlsbad Park National Wilderness — West Slaughter Canyon.

your overnight pack. Walk back down to the Walnut Canyon road junction and turn west onto the Walnut Canyon road. Walk about 11 miles on the road in a west, southwest direction. Appreciate why the Park Rangers generally prefer to ride horseback on that road instead of drive. You are still two or three miles from Putnam Tank, but watch for the North Slaughter Canyon Trail sign. Sack out somewhere in the vicinity for the night, hopefully about where you told the Park (Wilderness) Permit Ranger you would stay.

You have the option of hiking on the road another couple of miles to the Middle Slaughter Canyon Trail. In either event, you can follow the Slaughter Trails about six or seven miles down to the New Cave roadhead and parking area. If you do not have a second car there awaiting you, you can easily beg or buy a ride back up to the Caverns to your (first) car. This is a wonderful winter trip and quite safe alone, as long as you stay on the trails for which you registered.

Bowhunting for deer is good along the whole north slope of the Guadalupe Ridge from the Park boundary on west. If you get one, you can drag it downhill (NW) a couple of miles to the Dark Canyon road.

Deer hunters (generally rifle hunters) go through the park to the northwest on the Putnam Tank road and drive their four-wheel drives and other off-road vehicles across the BLM lands in the Serpentine Bends vicinity. There is a Jeep trail that ascends the Serpentine Bends canyon floor to the vicinity of Mudgetts Cave, but there was no way (in 1980) to drive a four-wheeled vehicle in or out of the Bends floor from the south (Park) side. Trail bikes have chopped up an old horsetrail just west of Mudgetts Cave. The 7-1/2 Minute Series USGS Map shows the old trail in the wrong location. There are four or five trails on the west side that climb the steep Blue Ridge escarpment, but I am familiar with only two of them.

The Devil's Den Canyon Trail starts about three miles south of El Paso Gap on the main road. The trail had fallen out on some of the switchbacks but it showed heavy prior usage and must have been a main route at one time. One can look down into the head of North McKittrick Canyon from the rimrocks.

I rode up the Bone Canyon Trail in the fall of 1972 or 1973 but cannot find a record in my notes. About all I can recall is that I was so saddle sore that I had to lead the horse down most of the way. My memory is short on remembering trips that were more work than they were worth. We started at the old Williams Ranch, where we had to get the key to a gate and a map at Pine Springs first, so it was late at the start. There was not water for the horses until we got up to Goat Springs near Shumard Peak. We did not see any deer until about dark down near the horse trailers at the ranch just as we finished the trip.

All told, I have only touched the surface. There is a whole underground wilderness to which someone must ultimately attest. There are some who think that someday we will learn of an entire city under the Guadalupe Escarpment, much deeper than the 1300 foot level chambers of the Carlsbad Caverns. Others think it will be found under the Magic Mountains of Our Lady of Guadalupe when men's hearts are pure; and that much gold will be there.

CHAPTER 12:
Capitan Mountain National Wilderness

Capitan Mountain is about seven or eight miles to the northeast of the village of Capitan on U.S. 80; Capitan is about 20 miles east of Carrizozo in the south central part of the state. Capitan Mountain is about 50 airline miles west of Roswell, or about 70 miles by road. The Wilderness Area encompasses most of the mountain except for a road corridor up the west end to an electronic site on top of the ridge. Get a map at the USFS Ranger Station in Capitan.

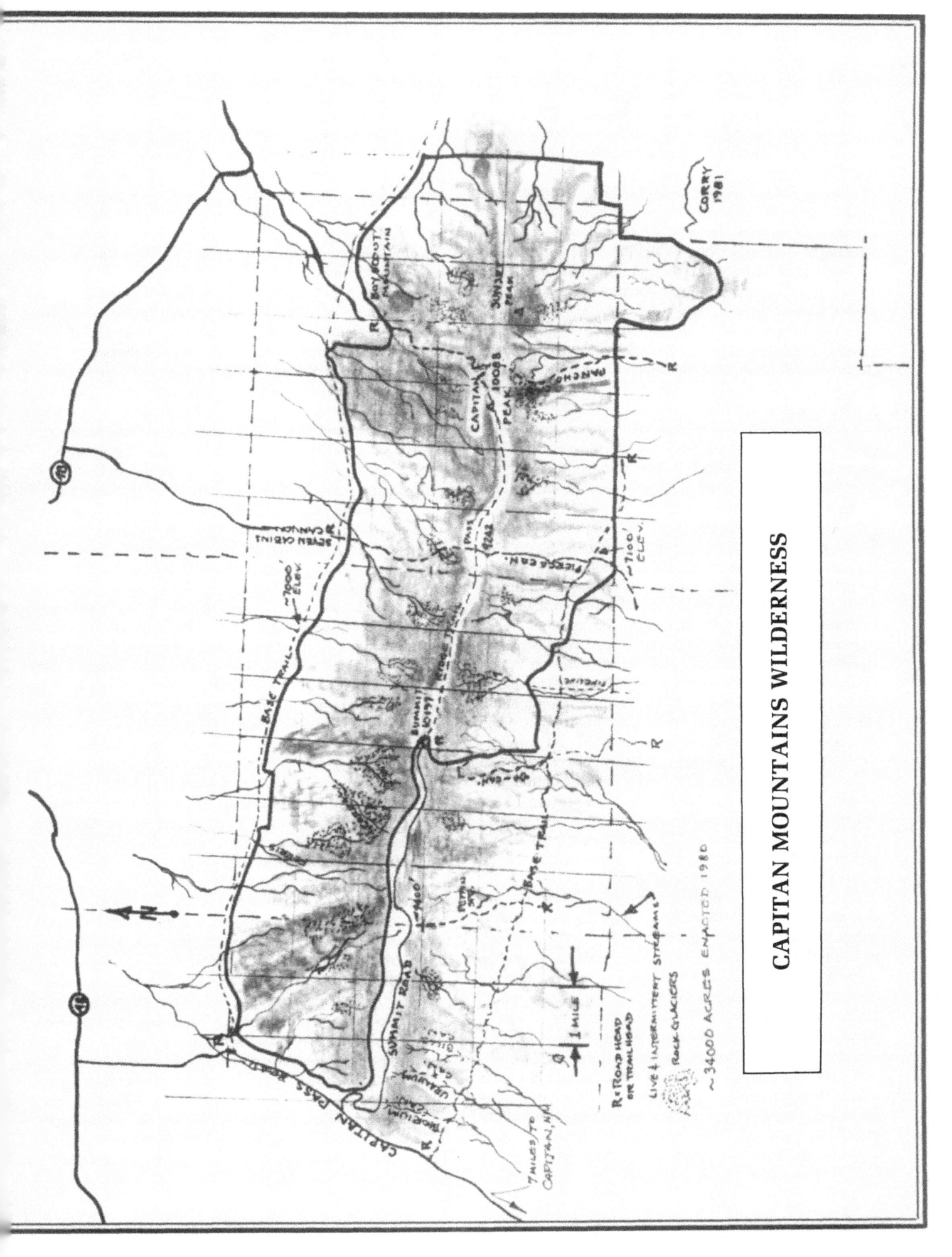

The inland Permian seas of 200 or 300 million years ago contained a high concentration of calcium carbonate. Consequently, a thick layer of San Andres limestone was deposited in what is now the Delaware Basin in southeastern New Mexico as these seas receded. The thickness of this limestone layer is approximately four hundred feet.

Red shale and the red Santa Rosa sandstone were deposited in the Triassic seas over much of the area in subsequent geologic time. Finally, the late Cretaceous seas, which were the last extensive marine bodies to cover western North America, engulfed New Mexico and coal deposits accumulated in swamps along the margins of these seas.

The molten interior of the earth was cooking not so quietly all of this time. As the changes took place on the primordial surface down through the eons of geologic time, the expansions and contractions of the earth's mantle generated fault zones. These were weak cracks in the solidified crust which could leak some of the hot magma from the interior. Most of the mountain-building faults in New Mexico are north-south trending like those in the rest of the Rocky Mountain region.

It was probably during the Cretaceous period that a big magna intrusion occurred under what is now the Capitan Mountains. This time the huge pressures found relief along an east-west fault. The magma lifted the San Andres limestone and the younger formations above at least 3000 feet. The geologists are not certain of the exact mode of formation but it appears that a large magma stock pushed up chimney-like until it encountered the San Andres limestone and started to spread out along the bedding planes of the limestone in a lenticular (lens shaped) mass of igneous rock about 20 miles long and four miles wide. The whole mass of cooled igneous rock is called a laccolith. It may have a number of feeder stocks under it, or only one. Anyway, it did not blow its top like a volcano. In subsequent time, sediments were eroded away and left the present Capitan Mountains standing some 3000 feet above the surrounding countryside at an elevation of about 10,000 feet.

The north and south slopes of this ridge are dissected by many deep and rugged canyons and tributary gullies. Numerous springs issue from the base of the talus slopes in the canyons and gullies, thereby providing good habitat for wildlife including deer, bear, and mountain lion.

The upper reaches of the mountain are in many ways unique. The east-west ridge is relatively sharp as one follows the ridge trail. The Permian sandstone remnants on the crest are now little more than caps where they remain along the ridge. The caps that have fallen on the flanks can almost be reassembled in the mind's eye with those remaining on the crest.

A unique feature of the Capitan Mountains is the numerous rock glaciers which occur on both the north and south sides of the ridge. John Blagbrough, a geologist in our New Mexico Study Committee ranks, describes these features as periglacial which means they developed under near-glacial conditions. The rock glaciers have average elevations of 8,300 feet on the north and 8,500 feet on the south flank of the range. Three major types of rock glaciers are recognized on the mountain. Lobate rock glaciers are as broad or broader than they are long and have average lengths and widths of 200 feet. They are along the base of steep, talus-covered canyon walls in the major drainages.

Tongue-shaped rock glaciers with lengths greater than breadths are the most common, having lengths of 200 to 1000 feet, and average widths of about 200 feet. They are at the base of steep talus slopes on the floors of tributary streams and in the major drainages.

The third type comprises elongate rock glaciers with lengths of more than 1,000 feet and average widths of about 300 feet. They are on the floors of canyons which constitute the major drainages. My first impression of these rock glaciers was that they just seemed like endless rockslides and I crossed or climbed them gingerly. Subsequently, when I began to understand the mechanism that caused their movement, it became apparent that these formations are now stable, being at their angle of repose.

The mechanism of flow is similar to the movement of glacial ice and took place in the late Pleistocene and possibly Neoglacial time. The average or mean temperature was below freezing at those elevations in protected localities. The talus fragments forming the rock glaciers were cemented by interstitial ice which developed when water in the spaces between the rock fragments froze. The rock fragments are slabs of microgranite in the form of angular blocks with average lengths of about two feet. Since these rocks were on an incline usually greater than five degrees, the weight of the mass of rock and ice flowed downhill. When the climate changed on the Capitan range, the ice melted and left our rock glaciers. This explains why the rock fields are stable — without the ice they cannot flow downhill.

The lower ends of these glaciers are steep frontal faces up to 200 feet high having a slope of about 30 degrees. Perhaps if the slope were 45 or 50 degrees, we would have a rockslide, since the two foot blocks probably would have an angle of repose in that order. In any event, the rock is stable and you can climb them like stairs while enjoying the lichen displays and listening for marmots which I have only heard but never seen on the Capitan rock glaciers.

Rock glaciers also exist in some of the other wilderness areas.[1] There are at least seven in the Apache Kid Wilderness Area, but they are not as spectacular (to me) as those in the El Capitan Wilderness. The ones in the Apache Kid are steeper and are composed of rhyolite instead of granite. The rhyolite blocks seem to have more colorful lichen on them in the northern, shaded slopes of the Apache Kid rock fields.

The climates associated with past geologic ages caused changes in altitude in the orthographic snowline. Above the orthgraphic snowline, snow remains the year around. The orthogrpahic snowline generally is at a lower elevation on the steep north slopes where the sun's strength is reduced by shading. This effect is more noticeable in the northern latitudes than it is in New Mexico where the sun is almost directly in the zenith overhead at midday in summer. Due to the orthographic effect, the rock glaciers on the northern slopes of the Capitan Mountains are better developed and more numerous than on the southern flank. But let's lift our eyes and look out at the churning panorama long before man was privileged to see it.

The mud flats which remained after the Permian sea had retreated from southeastern New Mexico did not quickly convert to grass lands.[2] The remnant lakes became ponds or salt lake sinks. Extensive potash deposits are evidence of the millions of years of transition. The immense Delaware Basin with its deposits of oil-bearing sand was sealed by the thick marine deposits over them. Those marine sediments solidified into strata above the platform of bedded salts and earlier deposits.

As the continent arose from its earlier sealevel elevations to its present 3,000 feet above our present sealevel, the area tipped slightly from north to south.[2]

Now imagine that you were watching the Rocky Mountains eroding. Compress the many millions of years into minutes and spread the sand and gravels onto a great plain above the marine strata. Then cement these alluvial sediments with calcium carbonate which was carried by ground water moving eastward from the mountains. Finally, because of that gentle tipping from north to south, the Pecos River cut down through the cemented sediments and drained off the eastward percolating ground water. This left our present Llano Estacado, the gravel capped plain that extends eastward beyond our state border.[3]

Let's now bring time back to a normal pace and realize that it took thousands of years to develop the soils and the grasses on the Llano Estacado and the Great Plains. Wildlife thrived under the influences of rainwater and prairie grassland conditions. Grass fires, kindled by lightning strikes, swept the plains.

Evidences of early man have been discovered at Folsom and elsewhere in the area.[4] The plains Indians followed the buffalo up onto the high plains and found other Indians living there. War parties toured the area looking for victims. The mountain-based tribes hunted the lands and occasionally met the plains peoples in conflict. Although hunting bands could travel 40 or 50 miles per day on foot when pressed, the battles were actually little more than scrimmages. They seldom were hand-to-hand conflicts, but limited to arrow and lance exercises. Whatever the circumstances, there were no villages or houses made of much more than brush. Some caves in the area, including those at Tinnie, had some evidences of long term occupation. Clovis spear points are indigenous to the area.[4] A couple of fluted ridges made them unique.

A dominating characteristic of the area is its lack of geographic diversity. On overcast days, every direction looks the same. Some wise man decided that he did not want to get lost each time he crossed those wide open spaces. Consequently, he erected a line of posts which could be seen, one from the other to mark the route. Many of those posts, or stakes, were planted at least 100 hundred miles from the nearest timber stands and had to be carried or dragged the whole distance. When the Spaniards discovered those route markers, they named the area Llano Estacado, or Staked Plains. The stakes were later replaced with taller posts farther apart because mounted men could see farther. A few more route branches were added by the Spanish in the fifteenth and sixteenth centuries. There is some question about the origin of the name Llano Estacado. Some say it was the name used to describe the stockaded appearance of the eastern boundary cliffs of the vast plain.[5]

When the United States troops rounded up the Indians and placed them on reservations in Indian Territory (now a part of Oklahoma) in the early 1800's, the days of the buffalo and antelope were numbered. (As mentioned previously, it took only 10 years to kill off the buffalo.[6]) In the 1870's, settlers poured into East Texas from the States and displaced those ranchers into the Texas Panhandle and New Mexico.[8]

The East Texans soon found the grassy high plains ideal for their cattle. The short grass (black grama) and allied species of grasses had not been damaged by the buffalo seasonal use. Thirty years of cattle grazing and drives converted the lands away from the main watercourses to brush, mesquite, creosotebush, cacti, and adventive weeds. Gullying and erosion took place.[7] And the grassy plains changed character.

Lincoln County was enacted in 1869 by the Legislature of the Territory of New Mexico, using the words: "embracing all that territory between the 34th parallel on the north, the Texas boundary line on the south, the 104° of longitude, or Pecos River on the east, and the eastern slope of the San Andres Mountains on the west." Lincoln County thus encompasses our El Capitan Wilderness within its fastness.

Potter County, Texas, as late as 1879, was thought to extend westward "to the Pecos," not only by Texans but by some New Mexicans. The facts of the law, however, were different. In 1849, by a $10 million payment to Texas, New Mexico established its official boundary between the two states. Communication didn't adequately acquaint all parties with that fact, it appears.

The small town of Placitas, just south of the Capitan Mountains, became the county seat and was subsequently called "Lincoln." The deputy sheriff of Placitas, probably in 1872, shot and killed Ben Harrold, a Texan with a belligerent attitude. His four brothers, fresh from a bloody feud with the Higgins family in Texas, settled down in the vicinity of Ruidoso and tried to get revenge. They terrorized the whole vicinity and essentially started "the Lincoln County War." Then Governor Giddings asked General Granger to bring in federal troops to quell the disturbance. The Harrold brothers and their cohorts disappeared into Texas in February, 1874, and things thereafter were not the same. Gunplay and liquor became the continuing recreation. The Civil War hand guns with their fixed ammunition changed the attitudes of a couple of generations. Violence in Lincoln County appeared to transcend itself.[8]

Fort Stanton was built before the Civil War about 11 miles southeast from Placitas (Lincoln) to hold the Mescalero and Jicarilla Apaches in check on their reservation near there. The Indians had little means of supporting themselves on a mountain reservation since they could neither hunt, as they had for centuries, nor could they raid other Indian settlements for necessities. And they could not farm to any extent on their hillsides, not only because of the location, but because it was never their character to be vegetable growers. The Army had trouble buying enough beef, let alone the other staples, for the troopers and the Indians — everyone was hungry. To add to this, smallpox was a principal vitiating enemy of the Mescaleros on the reservations.

A homesteader named Gray settled on Salado Flat and put up a small store and post office in 1894. When the railroad put in a line to the coal mine in 1900, the town of Gray was renamed Capitan after the dominating mountain close by. The store prospered but did not help the grinding hunger of the Indians.

Ranchers tried many ways to defend themselves and their cattle, even including hiring lawyers and calling in the troopers. There is no brief way to tell about the dozens of altercations in the Lincoln County wars. If you are interested, Keleher's "Violence in Lincoln County" covers it in 370 pages. It includes a chapter on Billy the Kid and how he attempted to plea-bargain with Governor Wallace after shooting five or six citizens. The famous escape and the comeuppance are also covered. There was some conjecture that the Kid's escape route was through Capitan Pass on his way to the vicinity of Fort Sumner. Since it led to the open country to the north of the Capitan Mountains where few people lived, it was probably a good choice for his purposes. The Lincoln County Sheriff Pat Garrett deduced the escape route and shot the Kid one night at a ranch near Fort Sumner.

There were not many cattle in that whole blank sector north of the mountains because there was not much water throughout the year. Some of the draws had been dammed by cattle ranchers through the use of mules and dragline scrapers. They extended the time that the summer rains and the winter snows were available for watering the cattle. The cattle would forage for grass not more than two or three miles from the water sources.

The miners from White Oaks were an intense and hungry lot. They ate antelope, deer, beef, and anything else that gave them energy to dig for gold and silver. While they were mining, at least a dozen young men ranged the countryside for anything they could shoot and sell to the local butchers in White Oaks. There was no refrigeration and the limited streams in the vicinity had no fish in them in the 1880 era. The siltation caused by the mining clogged the fish gills. That either suffocated them or drove them up the small side streams where there was not enough food for more than fingerlings. That process essentially decimated the native fish even before the cyanide milling process came along shortly thereafter.

The mines at Galena (later Nogal) a few miles west of Capitan town took care of the stream in that canyon. The American and the Helen Rae mines there possibly made the loss of the potable stream worthwhile, but the main mining action was at White Oaks.

Supplies for the shaft mining at White Oaks presented a formidable and continuing job for the teamsters. They had to haul powder, drilling steel, steel rails, mine cars, pipe, wood, mining timbers, and coal all of the 90 miles from San Antonio on the new railroad along the Rio Grande. Coal was discovered at Carthage, 10 miles from the big river. Later it was found and mined only about a couple of miles east of White Oaks. It sold in town at $1.35 per ton. Firewood, at first was $2.00 per cord in the early 1880's. Later, after Baxter Mountain and the Carrizo Mountains were stripped bare, wood at $4.00 per cord in 1890 came from the Capitan Mountain canyons and foothills. Miners made $3.00 per day for most of the two decades at such mines as the South Homestake, North Homestake, Old Abe, and Lady Godiva. The total production of the White Oaks mines up to 1900 was approximately $4.5 million.[9]

Bear hunting on Capitan Mountain was one of the few recreations available outside of the small towns of the area. The meat and hides sold immediately in Lincoln, Capitan, and Fort Stanton. Some eastern sportsmen came in and shot dozens of bear, if their pictures are to be believed. They brought a photographer with them. He had one of those new fangled cameras that used glass plates. He stayed around afterward to try to get some pictures of Billy the Kid but he failed.

The Jicarilla Reservation was immediatlely north of the Mescalero Reservation. And the unnamed photographer apparently made some startling pictures of Jicarilla Apaches. Those pictures, or copies of them, appeared at the 1904 Louisiana Purchase Exposition in St. Louis causing a wave of consternation. "Harpers" had some articles as a result, with "Lo, the poor Indian" as the theme. It did play upon our national guilt complex.

Morris B. Parker was a boy and young man in White Oaks.[9] He went to school at Rolla, Missouri, and studied mining engineering as did his brother James at Golden, Colorado. The newest innovation at that time was the cyanide process for treating gold mill tailings and recapturing values lost in earlier milling processes. Parker built and operated the first plant in New Mexico, one of the first in America in 1893. The gasoline engine and pump was used for the first time in White Oaks in an industrial process.

Morris Parker married Genevieve (Genny) McCourt. Her mother was Frances McCourt, who had been married to T.B. McCourt until he died. Frances subsequently married Wm. C. McDonald, the Carrizozo Ranch owner who later became the first Governor of the State of New Mexico in 1912.

In the Apache Kid Chapter you were left hanging with the tale of my father arriving at Carrizozo with his cousin in the summer of 1895, having ridden across the Malpais on horseback some 80 or 90 miles. Dad's cousin was John McCourt, one year older than he, at 16. The bedraggled boys were directed to the McDonald ranch not far northwest of town. Dad was probably dehydrated and drank too much milk. His aunt (Frances) had given him a dipper and told him to go down to the spring house and dip into the pans of milk that were cooling on the water sill. He was allergic to milk the rest of his life. He recalled that an old Mexican woman gave him an emetic and took care of him.

Dad remembered that when he woke up his clothes had been washed and pressed, his shoes shined, and he was "paraded" with his cousin "all over White Oaks and Carrizozo." His uncle would not hear of his going to work in the mines. "No shirt-tail relative of mine will ever work in the mines if I can help it," or some such sentiment was his reason. My dad not only had to pay for his train fare but had to send some money to his mother in Montana, since the country was in a deep depression. He found his stay at the McDonald home on Willow Street in White Oaks pleasant but he still wanted to get into the mines. He recalled being given a tour in the Henry Clay and Little Mac mines north of town. Later, he stayed for a couple of days at Analla (later Tinnie) on his way to Roswell and a job in a potash mine. He did not like it (wages too low) and went next to Green Cananea, Mexico, to work as a mule-skinner in the copper mines. Mules then pulled the ore cars in the mines.

Ere we leave Morris Parker, I remember that he had mining interests in Mexico inland in the Sierra Madres from Mazatlan and also in Nuka Bay north of Seward, Alaska. He spent his declining years at Hermosa Beach, California, where I visited him in the 1940's. He, of course, remembered more about Wm. C. than he did my father, although dad had met him as an adult some time around 1910 in San Francisco.

Morris' wife, Genny, reminded me a great deal of my grandmother who also was one of the McCourt girls. Her name was Mary Eliza (Lill). Those ladies were all very much grande dames of their day. (Recall that dad's mother was taking care of half-a-dozen children with dad's small wage-earning help.) Being more of a couturier than a plain dressmaker, and living in a fairly cosmopolitan town (people from all over the world came to Butte, Montana, to work and gamble), grandmother succeeded wonderfully. Genny Parker talked about Lill so much I could not get in one edgewise work. But she also told me about Ancho.

Ancho was a short siding on the branch line railroad spur a dozen or more miles north of White Oaks. I do no know when the tracks were laid, but it was in time for the prodigious task of shipping the bricks to San Francisco for its rebuilding after the big earthquake. Not only was the right kind of clay available, but the fuel, the skilled workforce, the equipment, and the management were ready for the task. The quality and uniformity of the bricks were unsurpassed. When struck, "they rang like bone china," Genny told me. It is a sad commentary that we have to get our bricks from out of state to obtain comparable high-fired ones.

In the interim from 1900 to the present, a number of events took place which changed the use pattern of the Capitan range to some degree. The towns of Capitan, Lincoln, White Oaks, and Nogal diminished in population. Fort Stanton became an Army Hospital. Carrizozo grew in population, being on the railroad, and serving as a railhead for the ranching community. Ancho became little more than a siding.

The McDonald Ranch Headquarters burned down a couple of times, probably because of faulty electrical wiring. Before the REA (Rural Electrical Administration), rural line voltages were not well regulated. Line surges caused by lightning would often set houses and barns afire.

Truman Spencer married the Governor's daughter, also named Frances. The Governor died shortly after his second term in about 1918. Truman's son showed me the Governor's safe and study when I stopped off at the Ranch in the early 1950's. There were photographs on the wall which I should go back to see one of these days when I am on the way back from El Capitan Wilderness.

When I first went into the Capitan range, I heard all kinds of stories from the natives thereabouts. Few people, other than bear and deer hunters, seem to go up on the mountain. "There is no water up there," they say. "It must be cold up there." "My son went up to the Electronic Site with his motorcycle." "You cannot drive up in that." "The man at the service station can tell you where you can rent a Jeep." "The Forest Service is afraid you will start a forest fire up there and discourage driving." "You can rent a horse in Lincoln and go up the eastside." "Why don't you drive around to the north side of the mountain and ask one of those ranchers to guide you?" "You might get struck by lightning up there on one of those peaks." All kinds of things can be heard if you ask a few questions in Capitan.

The hunters say to me: "Be sure you have a gun. There are bears up there." "I wouldn't shoot a buck up there. No way to get him down." "I shot a buck up on the ridge and he ran down a side canyon." "You will never get a deer up there with a bow." "Go up there with snowshoes? You're out of your skull!" "My horse went lame on me in Pierce Canyon and I thought I'd never get out." "There is an outfit in Roswell that will pack you in." "I see a couple of turkeys in Mitt and Bar Canyon every year or two but never get one." "I saw a fella on a motorcycle on the summit trail and almost took an shot at him." "It always rains or hails on me when I try to hunt up there." "I lost two good huntin' dogs up there a few years ago." What they are talking about is hunting in real wilderness. Most of them do not get more than a mile away from their trucks.

Springtime came early in 1950 in the Capitan Mountains. Heavy winds in March brought dust from the Pecos plains which hastened the melting of the remaining snow in the high country. Flowers flashed only briefly into their brilliant displays high in the canyons on the south side of the mountains.

There was an air of uneasiness in the Capitan Ranger Station during that last week of April. The smell of balsam was heavy in the air and the humidity was very low and the sun's heat generated massive thermals in the plains. Summer rains were not expected until mid-June. Winds slowly brought a fire threat in the forests.

This set the scene for the famous story of Smokey the Bear. The Forest Service's story appears on their 1967 Lincoln National Forest Recreational Map:

Time: May 1950. The beginning of the Southwest's late-spring fire season.

Place: A pass in the Capitan Mountains of the Lincoln National Forest. It is dry and dusty, a strong wind blowing. Somebody flips a cigarette or burning match along the Capitan Gap road. In the next several days 17,000 acres of timberland rage into flaming ruin. Hundreds of firefighters labor to control the blaze, including many of the townsfolk of nearby Capitan. Then, clinging to a charred tree, a small bear cub is found by a state Game man and a crew of firefighters. The mother-less little bear is badly burned and hungry and is taken to the home of a local rancher where he is doctored and fed. He is then flown by the Game Warden to Santa Fe for veterinarian care and later flown the the National Zoo in Washington, D.C. There the cub is heralded as the living example of Smokey, the forest fire preventin' poster bear of the U.S. Forest Service and State Foresters.

Smokey, whose story has been carried to the ends of the earth by the public service efforts of The Advertising Council and many others, is now an international symbol of forest fire prevention. But to the folks on the Lincoln he is also a very real part of their forest. They can still see the scars of the terrible fire in which the poster bear came to life — and so many animals and trees perished. They can feel the loss to the local logging and sawmill industry. They remember other bad fires in recent years — the Allen Canyon blaze of 1951, 16,000 acres of destruction wrought by a lightning strike which wasn't corraled quickly enough. And the Circle Cross fire of 1953, a 25,000-acre monster that went 14 miles in four hours before a 60-mile-an-hour gale. The Circle Cross started when a logging debris-burn got out of control.

The folks of Capitan have built a log museum to commemorate the birthplace of Smokey the Bear. And they hope you and every American will take to heart the lesson of what a moment of carelessness can do to your National Forests.

A subsequent News Release for the USFS in 1975 carried further details:

As the years went by, Smokey became one of the most popular animals in the world, as well as a very popular symbol. His slogans were printed on posters, he appeared in cartoons as well as television and radio commercials and received fan mail from everywhere. At the age of 25 he was showing signs of being tired, listless and in need of a rest, and was retired in a large ceremony at the National Zoo on May 2 of 1975. During the same ceremony, another bear was appointed to succeed the original Smokey Bear.

During his 25 year reign as the living symbol of fire prevention the original Smokey played host to millions of visitors at the National Zoo. During his retirement he had a relaxing life in seclusion, and was away from the daily hustle and bustle of photographers, TV cameras and people talking to him.

The new Smokey Bear had a similar background. He was also found in the Lincoln National Forest of New Mexico. Unlike the original Smokey, who suffered from burns, this young cub was found in 1971 abandoned and half starved. He was brought to the National Zoo and served as an understudy to the original Smokey Bear. When Little Smokey officially took over the post in 1975, he was well trained to carry on the fire prevention program.

Since its inception the forest fire prevention campaign under the leadership of the USDA Forest Service and the National Association of State Foresters has distributed more than 30,000,000 pieces of forest fire prevention materials annually to mass media outlets, forestry agencies, teachers, and the public at large. Dur-

ing a 1968 survey, Smokey was recognized by 90-percent of 1,800 persons interviewed as the forest fire prevention bear. In 1942 there were 201,511 man-caused fires in the United States, and by 1974 there were 145,868 fires; a significant drop considering the expansion and increased population in the country. The forest area burned annually dropped from 31,000,000 acres to less than 3,000,000 acres; a 90 percent reduction.

Through the efforts of the National Association of State Foresters and with saving the United States more than 16 million in timber that didn't burn, in recreation areas that were not destroyed and in watersheds that were not blackened.

As the symbolic head of the State, Federal and industry campaign against wildland fires, Smokey's image appears on $8 million worth of products bearing forest fire messages each year. Through the cooperative efforts of Foote, Cone and Belding/Honig, the volunteer advertising agency, and the Advertising Council, $45 million worth of air time and print space is donated annually by the mass media.

The Smokey Bear movement grew from that point. The Forest Service really militated against fire. My nephew, Ed Heilman, having graduated at the School of Forestry at the University of Montana at Missoula, was instrumental in the development of borated slurries delivered by fire bombers.

The slurry originally used was a borate solution. It was a good fire inhibitor. However, it had an environmental impact which was recognized as detrimental and so was replaced by a diammonium phosphate and sulfate solution. This combination is not only an effective fire inhibitor but is a fertilizer as well. Although I am interested in the way these slurries work, I suspect that it would not be as intersting to the reader. You might find the reference somewhat curious.[10]

Maybe I have mentioned the "Smokey the Bear Syndrome" previously, and if not, it is an acquired alertness. After you have seen a series of forest fires and the damage they do, you tend to get a bit alarmed about the possibility. So you tool up and snuff them out at every opportunity. You count the number of fires started by careless campers and you get indignant. You mull over how senseless is the waste. You put up posters and you patrol campgrounds. You show slides and try to educate the public. You do your job with the slurry bombers and firebreaks. You even call in the Apaches when you need them. (They have become a tough and effective team to combat bad fires.) You use smoke jumpers (with parachutes) to get to spot fires quickly. You watch the weather when it is hot and dry. You may close forest access when fire probabilities get too high. You try to get timber companies to clean up fire damaged timber. And you reseed the burned areas to try to hold down the violent cloudburst runoffs. The results: fewer fires. And the forests appear to flourish.

But then, when things seem controlled, there are scattered reports of pine beetle infestations. So you decide to take corrective measures to try to eradicate the pine beetles. Some of the measures may be to kill off the gooseberry bushes which are part of the blister rust cycle. Others may be to spray the infected timber patches with specific insecticides, preferably ones which will not also kill fish and birds. So now you have stopped the fires and the insect infestations. You have literally halted natural forest accession.

But what is forest accession? In my oversimplified terms, it is the succession of events in the natural life and death of the forest. It differs at various attitudes. For instance, at about 8,000 to 11,000 feet, fires open up the forest to upland parks which soon are naturally sought out by aspen seedlings. They apparently like the burned out forest land as a germination bed. Later, as they quickly grow, aspen trees provide shade in the summer for the slower growing pines. The aspen, being a deciduous tree, lose their leaves during the winter months and allow full sunlight to fall on the young conniferous trees on the forest floor, and then, when the sun is too strong for the young trees in the summer, the aspen leaves again shade them. At some time during the growing periods of these trees, deep snows will accummulate and even cover the small connifers. The sap in the pine trees is a sort of antifreeze being so constituted that it keeps the ice crystals in them small so that they do not extensively damage the pores and fibers of the wood. This reduces winter kill.

Ultimately, the aspen trees mature and die. They will have left not only their annual fall of leaves behind, but the twigs and branches and finally their trunks to decay and renourish the soil. By that time there will be young and healthy evergreen connifers now able to withstand the full summer sun and the winter winds without the protection of the aspen.

These pine trees annually lose some of their needles and they accummulate with the twigs and grasses, pine cones, leaves, brush droppings and other detritus to become "duff." This duff decays to renourish the forest soils and consequently the living plants in it. Rains assist the process to help break the duff down for its use as fertilizer. With the rains, lightning fires start. These fires during the rainy season tend to do the housekeeping of the forest floor, generally reducing the depth of combustible materials in the forest. These fires burn more briskly where insects have killed the connifers and tend to interrupt the insect hatching cycles. The pine trees, having earlier emerged above the brush, are equipped to survive these wet weather housekeeping fires. They have thick, green bark, and also a fluid within, their sap, which tends to make them fireproof. A few of their lower dead branches burn and tidy up the trunks of some species. But the tops do not burn.

In places where timber is diseased, old, and/or insect ridden, possibly blown down, or overrun by brush, the fire may become hot enough to burn that area of the forest completely. These areas open up and become mountain parks, covered with grass.

And now man enters the scene. He starts fires, sometimes at the wrong time when the forest is not fireproof. The rains have stopped and the timber has dried out. The housekeeping fires may have cleaned up enough to keep the forest duff from spreading the man-made fire, but maybe not. The fire can quickly become a crown fire and generate its own wind. Such fires can turn into holocausts and become hot enough to burn trees to death, hot enough to kill living timber.

But there are many hazards left to endanger our lands. The forest duff and brush accummulate into deep fuel beds. The insect cycles flourish. Man sprays insects. This pesticide kills the bugs. The birds eat the bugs and die; rain washes the insecticides into the streams and kills the fish and/or the stream biota on which they feed. The resulting hot fires, fed by the deep fuel beds, increase the incidence of gullying and erosion and cause siltation of the streams. Such siltation can be persistent enough to kill the stream's living community. Man seems to have brought this problem.

Another man-managed phase is to thin the trees out so the remaining ones will grow faster and make better timber. Spray and fertilize the trees, use prescribed burning to keep the forest duff cleaned up. Practice silvaculture. Grow timber for the market. Harvest it in time. The New Mexico mountain deserts grow timber under such management in some areas of our National Forest to maturity in 75 to 100 years. Climax condition is the time when the timber is ready to be harvested. The trees have essentially stopped growing rapidly, and the forest floor is so shaded that it grows little grass, weeds, forbs, or, for that matter, wildlife.

However, the wilderness condition, in which no tree cutting is practiced, permits the natural forest accession to take place. Man may interfere, despite regulations, by cutting down trees which appear on the meadow and park margins to prevent invasion of these areas where cattle can graze. Man may destroy beaver dams and interfere with aspects of the forest accession. Many variations of the natural processes occur at various elevations and climates.

Our New Mexican forests tend to produce knotty, dry, and brittle lumber. The growth is slow, about 150 to 200 years. Many factors cause that slow growth: the elevation, the small amount of annual precipitation, the heat, the winds, and the rocky thin soils. Consequently, the timber industry has learned to harvest only a limited amount of timber from those ares. For many of the above reasons, we do not grow pulpwood. But firewood harvesting is a time honored use of our forests.

It has become more and more apparent that our management of forest fires has not produced the expected results. There was a consequent revision of the Smokey the Bear policies to permit naturally caused (lightning) fires to burn in season, and to do prescribed burning to accomplish the same housekeeping functions. Meanwhile, the promulgation of a continuing campaign of attempting to reduce inadvertant (campfire) carelessness throughout the multiple use public forests was followed.

Our New Mexico Wilderness Study Committee was one of the pioneers in the thinking that led the Forest Service to change its policy to one that is more in tune with the original ecological system, but which accommodates the perturbations introduced by man, namely controlling those man-made fires out of season. So you can expect to see naturally caused fires permitted in Wilderness Areas during the rainy season, and occasionally even some prescribed burning will be evident in one of your favorite areas if it is needed.[11]

One other consequence of wildfire may be beneficial. Do a little pseudo-scientific dreaming with me. I have had a conjectural theory about the possible connection of forest fires and the incidence of rainfall. (If you are a professional meteorologist, go to the next chapter, please.) So, first are a few postulates. Assume that a forest fire or a grass fire generates heat. Then as the fire burns, several kinds of particles are also generated. Assume that the smoke is comprised of carbon bits and ash particles. Assume that the burning generates some gasses which you cannot see, but can smell.

So, the scene is set. The heat of the fire lifts the combustion by-products skyward. The heavier particles fall to the ground and are probably carried some distance by the wind. Some of the particles are carried into the upper atmosphere to drift along with it as the earth turns below. Sit near the cairn on Capitan Peak and try to guess the elevations of the cloud levels knowing that you are just over 10,000 feet above sea level and that the valley down below is at about 5,000 feet. Some of those clouds have to be as high as 25,000 to 30,000 feet. Admit that you can see the clouds because they have water vapor in them. So how does the forest fire make it rain or even enter into the process?

The water vapor in the clouds came from some body of water, probably the ocean. The sun heated the water, it evaporated, and the air above it absorbed the water vapor. The air and clouds, not being very dense, just hung there and the earth turned under the upper atmosphere. The lower atmosphere is partially pulled along by the turning earth and tends to mix with the adjacent layers above it.

But remember that the upper air had some smoke particles in it and some fire gasses. The clouds have some water vapor in them. The water vapor needs to somehow coalesce or condense into droplets to make raindrops. I think the carbon particulates provide the condensation nuclei for the water molecules. The mixing turbulence brings more particles and water

Capitan Wilderness. Ripples are old rock glaciers.

vapor together and some of the droplets collide and run together. Now a little wild guessing on my part. Recall that when a pine tree burns it has a pungent smell; I think it is the smell of aromatic olefins. Those very volatile gas molecules possibly act as a catalyst to make or assist the droplets run together and get heavy enough to start falling. Maybe it freezes on the way down, turns to snow, frost, or hail.

There may be other particles than carbon that will act as condensation nuclei such as fly ash from power plants and industrial processes. However, it rained long before man and his processes came on this earth. You may have read that there were some unusual winters for several years after the Krakatoa volcano eruption shot volcanic ash into the upper atmosphere. It reduced the mean temperatures probably because the sun did not reach the earth surfaces with full force. New weather records were made in 1883 and for several years afterward. Tree rings of some old tree stumps on Capitan slopes recorded the event by not growing much for those several years.

I think man's actions have succeeded in causing the rain and precipitation patterns to be modified without plan or intention. Meanwhile, our National Wilderness Areas help capture whatever precipitation falls on the watershed it contains. Hopefully, the weather research being carried out at the Langmuir Lab atop South Baldy (see Withington Chapter) will provide the crucial facts of the precipitation process.

As for deforestation, even the Bible tells about the giant cedars of Lebanon being used for the masts of the sailing ships of those times. And firewood was used almost exclusively for cooking fires as well as heat during the winters. By the time of the Crusades, the entire eastern Mediterranean landscape was deforested. However, it took us a lot less time to deforest our midwestern hardwood forests during the 1800's. Now the insidious clearing of tropical forest is taking place.[12] And destruction of the watershed goes hand in hand with the deforestation.

We appear to be bent on this same course by introducing chain or cable clearing. It is usually done with two bulldozers with a cable or chain attached to both of them, marching through the piñon-juniper mesas. Trees and brush are cleared to allow more grass to grow for better cattle grazing. Sometimes it works, but often it only reduces the absorbency of the watershed.

Fortunately there has not been extensive cabling in the Capitan Mountain surrounds. The fact that there was good coal for home heating and running the mills at White Oaks and Nogal reduced the need for stove wood. The result is a survival of piñon-juniper in the foothills, some good timber in the canyons and a reasonably intact watershed. Early on, however, the Spaniards named the stream through Capitan, Saladas Creek. In dry years it hardly trickles. The overgrazing during the late 1800's put it underground practically every year. Its flow seems to be improving now. Perhaps we are entering another wet cycle.[9]

TRAILS AND ROUTES

The ridge trail is the prime experience for the ridge runner. The first time I tried it, three of us went up in a wheezy old Jeep wagon only to discover that a good sedan could have made it to the Summit Electronic Site. We drove in from the north into Capitan Pass on what is now marked Forest Route 616 and 56. Starting at about lunchtime from the car, we hiked over to Capitan Peak and back. It was dark when we made it to the car in the moonlight. The road was spooky coming down because the Jeep did not have good compression and the lights were poor. The roundtrip is about 14 miles at about 10,000 feet elevation and we should not have tried to go as far. We did not have enough water and even though it was late in June in 1953, we had no wind shells or any rain protection.

The next time, two of us went, and took my sedan. The road was in terrible shape, so we hiked to the Summit from Capitan Pass road. My notes say that, although we had our backpacks and could have stayed overnight, it started to rain and sleet (Memorial Day) so we went down the Mitt and Bar Canyon trail (60), went west on trail 59, and walked back to our car on Forest Road 338. Both Uranium Canyon and Thorium Canyon were running muddy water over the road at that time.

The second and last time I hiked the whole ridge was in August of 1961. We parked one car on the Boy Scout Mountain road (130) just inside the Forest Boundary about a mile west of the main road (48) on the northeast corner of the range. We drove the other car, a pickup truck, around (west) on 48 to the Pass road 616 only fo find a gate locked on the private property portion of 616 going to the National Forest. We went back to Capitan, complained to the girl at the Ranger Station, and took the Pass road (56) two miles east of town on U.S. 380 highway.

We parked the truck near the Summit road turnoff and started hiking up the road. It was in bad shape from the summer gully-washers. A couple of kids came along in a Jeep and took our packs up the hill for us. At that point it was about five miles to the top and it was dinner time when we caught up with our packs. We vowed not to be separated from our packs again.

The next day we hiked over to Sunset Peak and stayed overnight. It is a boondock climb back up to Capitan Peak without a trail. My notes say, "tight scrub oakbrush." We dawdled over some of the rock glaciers west of Capitan Peak and dropped down trail 64 to my car below Boy Scout Mountain.

A trail goes up Pancho Canyon from Forest Road 57. The road (57) we took (Bill Stevens and I) went west from the State 368 main road (blacktopped) just west of South Arabella Peak on the east foothills of the range. A stream comes down Pancho from the rock glacier field southeast of Capitan Peak. The trail follows an old mine road up to about the 9,000 feet elevation. The trail above the road end was then recently reworked (1973) and more rock and tree removal was done than was necessary.

There was a family of eagles that patrolled the canyon. I was quietly making my way up the stream, bow in hand, early one morning on October 11, 1975, deerhunting. The creek was only a couple of feet wide then, but it flowed down a 10 foot wide rock stream bed which was much like pavement in many places. One of the eagles was touring the streambottom looking for breakfast as he (or she) came around the turn not more than four or five paces in front of me. What I saw first was two relaxed fist-sized yellow tallons in front of my face. He simply banked one wing over my head, scarcely blinked an eye, and proceeded unperturbed downstream. He had about a six-foot wingspan and did not look like a mature bird.

I picked up four or five pinon feathers from a couple of places near the stream where an eagle lost them making a kill. Since it is illegal to own eagle feathers unless one is an Indian, I gave them to an Indian friend from Santo Domingo Pueblo.

There is a base trail around much of the mountains. The trail is virtually our wilderness boundary. One can drive in to it from the north on Forest road 256 from the blacktopped Number 48 Road. It goes south about five miles to Seven Cabins Canyon and had some rough spots. There are no seven cabins, but the trailhead there goes east or west on the base trail Number 65, or Number 66 on up to the top of the ridge at Pierce Canyon Pass. The trailhead has a tank and trough for cattle. There is a small stream going down the canyon. Treat it before you drink.

There used to be Fox and Fur Lodge in Section 31 that was defunct. It was completely removed before 1978. (The Forest Service can really make things go away when they want to destroy old evidences.)

There are only two main trails on the north side of the ridge. I have mentioned both of them. On the south side, west of Pancho Canyon there is trail Number 61 up Pierce Canyon to the pass. There is a trick tank and a small metal cabin about a mile west of the ridge trail junction. Besides the Mitt and Bar Canyon trail, there is one going up to Padilla Peak in upper Peppin Canyon. There is another trick tank near Padilla, and one at Bear, a mile to the northeast. The logging done in that vicintiy was particularly messy and a lot of needless bulldozing has been done. The side canyons are still wilderness, however, even though the 1950 fire damage is still evident.

In winters of heavy snowfall, the road to the summit makes wonderful snowshoeing and climbing with skins (on skis). Maybe crosscountry (skinny) skis would work, but the road is fun to ski down with a pair of downhill skis, particularly if you have an overnight pack like I did in the 1978-79 winter. The breeze turned to a gale that night and blew yesterday's tracks completely over.

Bill Stevens and I hunted Tucson Mountain to the west of Capitan Mountain during the mid 1970's, but unsuccessfully. We spent the night in my pickup truck inside a fiberglass shell while it rained two inches. The roads were greasy slick. So, take your poncho, even if you go into Pancho Canyon. You may need it. Hint: it did not get that green without moisture.

Oh, yes! You probably should not cook bacon unless you want a bear rummaging around your camp that night. If you do, hoist your pack up at least 10 feet in the clear.

CHAPTER 13:
Polvadera Peak Defacto Wilderness

Polvadera Peak is about 20 miles airline west northwest of Espanola and about 10 miles airline south of Abiquiu. It is the northern-most peak in the Jemez Mountain chain and can be reached from the Clara Road, there being a trail head about 27.5 miles out of Espanola. See trail and route details at the end of this chapter. Get a good contour map in Santa Fe at the USFS District Office.

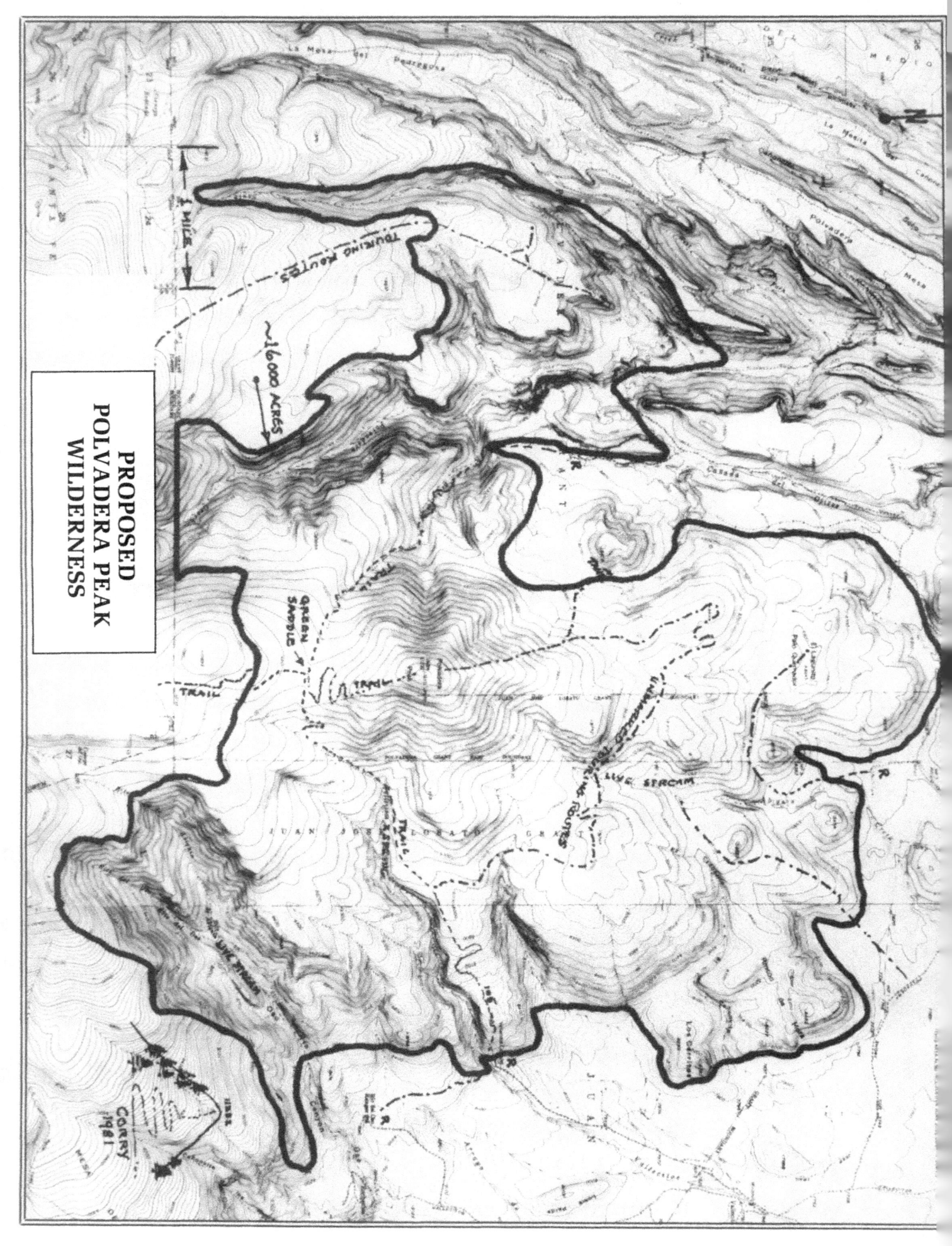

A clearing in a saddle at the 10,400 foot elevation immediately south of Polvadera peak is covered with bright green grass. A few granite outcrop fragments protrude through the surface. Only a few small trees have been able to invade the clearing over time. Perhaps some kind of defense mechanism operates to keep it free from timber and brush encroachment.

Fog spilled through the saddle from the eastern basin and filtered through the timber with the just-emerging sun. The light intensity cranked up and down as wisps of fog were stripped off the cloud bank and wafted through the saddle. A great bull elk cautiously stepped into the clearing, nostrils emitting steam into the nearly freezing air which was suddenly electrified by a blasting bugle call from the creature. The bugling quavers through a rising register in three distinct steps, followed by grunting snorts of the challenging bull. This call was answered by the charging rush of a compact young bull that had fought herd bulls for several days running.

Horns crashed only a few times when half a dozen arrows found their marks. Hunters from Puyé, the nearest Indian settlement a dozen miles to the southeast, had climbed up the canyon from the west (El Rechuelos) during the night in anticipation of the dawn battle of the bulls. This had happened many times before that eerie morning.

Sometimes the bulls had to be lured to territorial battle with an elk whistle. But this time the hunters had been able to kill the bulls without making a sound. Now, in an elated celebration, the two callers cut loose with crescendos and glissades on their calls. They field dressed the animals and hung them in trees to cool. They argued about whose man-smell blanket would be draped on the hanging carcasses to hold off coyotes and mountain lions.

Now, someone had to return to the pueblo to tell the women where the kill was. They played a game of odd man out to decide. These men were the best hunters in their group and they must kill as many elk as possible during the two weeks of the rut when the bulls were not wary. The others in the pueblo had to get the meat and hides to their drying racks to be converted to jerky and winter robes. They traded some of the elk robes and hides for buffalo robes from their neighbors to the east, and it had to happen before the snows came. It took 14 or more women to carry out the meat and hides of the two bulls before they spoiled. The hunters expected to make two or three more kills that same day.

This scenario must have taken place in the second or third century A.D. Puyé was occupied for several hundred years until the deep droughts of the eighth or ninth centuries made it necessary to abandon the site.[2] Some of the people probably went to the Frijoles Canyon sites at Bandelier, and a few were able to survive in the upper reaches of the Santa Clara canyon.

When the first Spanish soldiers rode up Santa Clara Canyon from the vicinity of present day Espanola, they were looking for the Seven Cities of Cibola. They only found a canyon village with clusters of houses along the canyon walls for more than a mile. There were smoking fireplaces, but the people had disappeared. It probably was either Alvarado or Cárdenas and a few other soldiers who were the advance men on that foray. They reported little about what they found since they arrived back at Tiguex (near Bernalillo) during a battle at their winter headquarters. Soon they were off on a wildgoose chase toward the present day Kansas when the fighting stopped.[3]

Later, the Indians acquired a few horses to haul their elk and deer meat home during the hunting seasons. Their hunting territories expanded and limited cavalry engagements took place over contested areas. Their neighbors to the west of them, the Jicarilla Apaches, would not agree on boundaries. The Jicarillas had a few small horse herds in their more open home lands and the Tewa speaking people (San Juans and Santa Claras) had larger elk herds in their traditional lands. Thus the situation was far from stable for the years from 1540 to 1600 A.D.

The next major event that occurred which probably had some influence on the mountains in the vicinity was in 1598 A.D. when a large party of Spanish colonists under Don Juan De Oñate came up the Rio with horses, cattle, sheep, goats, and dogs. The Indians stole most of the Spanish horses and when the Spaniards furiously appeared at the Santa Clara settlements, the Indians claimed that it must have been the Jicarillas that took the horses. And so it went.

The first winter was hard on the new Spanish settlers and they had to trade some of their sheep for food. The Santa Claras refused to be indentured by the Spaniards and Governor Oñate's early reports mentioned several times that his capital was called San Juan de Los Caballeros.[7] It is not clear whether the settlement was named before or after the horses were stolen. (What is a Caballero without a horse?)

The next year the settlement expanded across the river to the west into the somewhat newer but abandoned pueblo site of Yunque-Yunques and it thus became the more permanent capital until 1610 when the seat of government was moved down to an old pueblo site which had been abandoned for centuries, la villa Real de Santa Fé, along the Rio Santa Fé.

It was during the time before the move to Santa Fé that some of the younger Spaniards, perhaps out of curiosity, went up to Chicoma Mountain during one of the Santa Clara's secret religious ceremonial periods. They were brought back to San Gabriel (the capital on the west side of the Rio Grande) firmly bound and gagged. The word-of-mouth history of the Santa Claras indicates that the Governor applied for a land grant from the King of Spain for the Santa Claras in return for the errant and nosey young men. The parchment document on which the grant deed was written no longer existed in 1856 when a trial was being held in Espanola pertinent to some contested land ownership in the mouth of the Santa Clara Canyon. The verdict was in favor of the Indians, although it was held in abeyance for two years pending the consultation of old Spanish records in Seville.[2]

After the colonists moved out of San Gabriel to Santa Fé in 1610, a dozen or so families remained in the vicinity on small ranches they had developed. The cattle that had come up the river with the original party stocked these ranches. The Indians objected to the settlers at first because they killed the elk and wildlife on the Indian hunting territories. The settlers believed that the big game competed with their cattle for the sparse forage.

A Dulce Apache told me that he remembered hearing a story about how some of the ranchers traded sheep for Apache horses. The horses kept going back to the Apache herds, so the ranchers wanted their sheep back. The Indians told the ranchers that wolves and lions had killed the sheep. The ranchers thought they were getting cheated and started a big fire that burned the timber around a favorite spring used by the Indians. That spring may be the one at Dulce. The Indians retaliated by stealing horses and cattle from the ranchers.

One of the most heavily raided ranches was at Hernandez, not far from the old capital at San Gabriel. The Santa Clara and San Juan Indians were blamed for much that the Apaches did when they came down from their Jicarillla country. The Indians and the ranchers went to church together on Sundays and accused each other on Mondays. The foment went on for 70 years until the Pueblo Rebellion in 1680. The Indians vandalized the ranches they did not move onto.

It was during the 1680's that the Utes and Jicarilla Apaches became real capitalists in the Indian world.[9] They gathered up all of the horses left in New Mexico after the Spanish exodus and traded them a few at a time to the plains and northern Indians. The Navajos were particularly wary of horse stealing and probably advised the Commanches where to trade for Ute horses. The plains Indians did not have enough horses for warfare until 1740 to 1750.[4]

It was not until about 1695 that most of the ranchers came back. The Spanish Governor De Vargas named Santa Cruz the second Villa in New Mexico, Santa Fé being the first in 1610. A new rancher, Bartolome Lobato by name, came with the new crowd and soon had some old ranches gathered up from some of the previous families that did not return to their lands. One of his sons was to be the owner of the Juan Jose Lobato Grant.

Others managed to obtain Grants from the King of Spain over the next 50 years. To name most of them, there were the Bartolome Sanchez Grant, the Black Mesa Grant, the Plaza Blanca Grant, the Piedra Lumbre Grant, the Juan Bautista Valez Grant, the Plaza Colorada Grant, the Ojo Caliente Grant, Antonio De Abeyta Grant, and the Abiquiu Grant.

The Mission of Santo Tomás Apostol was built in 1740 on the site of the future village of Abiquiu. The clerics were unhappy when they learned about a favor granted by then Governor Diego de Vargas. In 1747, the Abiquiu Grant was given to Antonio Montoya, a captain under Governor de Vargas. The Montoyas only ran cattle on the land but did not settle on it, and were deposed of the title by a later Governor (Cachupin). In 1754 that same Governor entitled the Indians and some Spanish mixed bloods with the Abiquiu Grant. The Abiquiu Grant extended south of the town for about eight miles, only four or five miles from Polvadera Peak. It included practically all of the live water in the Abiquiu Creek and its branch Vallecitos Creek. As the cattle grazing and sheep pasturage was permitted to become excessive, and the firewood harvesting proceeded to strip the watershed, erosion increased dramatically. The same thing happened in the Lobato Grant to the east. Franciscan Friar Silvestre Velez de Escalante recorded that the water in Abiquiu in July, 1776, tasted of cattle dung and smelled badly.

The people of Abiquiu told Friars Dominquez and Escalante that they could not herd their cattle properly because of the Jicarilla Apache, Ute, and Commanche raids down the Chama and Rio Grande rivers. Governor de Anza pulled together some troops and chased the Commanches into Kansas and wiped out Chief Cuerno Verde and most of his braves.[3] the raids had been over for about two years so Escalante doubted the excuses.

The Frenchmen, supposedly in retaliation for Spanish incursion into Louisiana Territory, sold as many as 100 guns to the Santa Clara Indians in 1759. These guns were traded among the Indian dissidents but did not appear in any concerted attacks, even during the disturbed 1760's. There may have been a problem with adequate ammunition. The Commanches that raided in the 1770's had much better French and English guns and apparently better ammunition. Armed insurgence was always a threat from the Jicarilla Apaches but they seemed calm after the de Anza caper to Kansas. They probably buried their guns when the Governor's Caballeros were making one of their inspection tours.

The Friars Dominguez and Escalante were brave. They wandered through Jicarilla territory without knowing about the smoldering resentment that it generated. Their robes probably saved them. Those two luminaries appeared to have more stamina than direction. Their probable route looks like that of lost explorers. Theirs was a full eight months, however, and Escalante's account of a fanciful way to get to California from Santa Fé is well worth reading.

By 1790, the Abiquiu and Vallecitos Creeks had

recovered from their cattle tramping and supplied beaver dams from the sources on down to the town. The years from 1790 to 1830 were well watered times[4,6] and the mountain men cleaned out the beaver most efficiently. Abiquiu prospered accordingly, as did all the Land Grants sitting on water sources.

With prosperity came some of the agonies of the world. To counteract them the religious souls of the communities had constantly been at work. As far back as 1744, the settlers had installed Santa Rosa de Lima as their patroness in a little riverside chapel near the confluence of the Chama River and Abiquiu Creek.[1] However, in about 1754, after some flooding, they moved up to the hilltop plaza where the mission of Santo Tomás Apostol had been established. Subsequently, the gentle Franciscan Friars allowed Santa Rosa to outcompete Santo Tomás for the allegiance of the village-folk.

Abiquiu had 1363 people in 1793, being third to the 1650 inhabitants of Santa Cruz and to the 2419 people in Santa Fé that same year.[1] Most of the buildings were adobe and stone obtained in the immediate neighborhood. About ten percent of the population were genizaros, previously liberated Indian captives. They comprised much of the labor force. They scoured the foothills for vigas to make roof supports for the houses and they gathered firewood for all of the fireplaces, kilns, and hornos. By 1800, they were getting firewood 15 to 20 miles from town. Beaver dams up toward Polvadera Peak on the headwaters of Abiquiu Creek prevented the removal of timber of any size. They cleaned out the Cañones Creek watershed to the west and obtained their best vigas from the foothills of La Mesa de los Cañones. It was rumored that the genizaros either escaped their freedom (their back-breaking existence) or were recaptured by the marauding Indians to the northwest. Those that remained with their toils were sometimes accused of apostasy or witchcraft.

By then, the penitente brotherhood was quietly growing and several branching groups such as the Cofradias also conducted Lenten processions with flagellation. The Penitentes were believed to be a Third Order of the Franciscan ranks. They built moradas or chapels into which only the initiated could enter.

One part of the lenten service was to burn a wooden cross of appreciable size. There were at least two occasions in the mid 1800's when fiery crosses were observed by countryfolk up on the peaks in the vicinity. Such a cross was also observed on Chicoma Mountain by the Indians of Santa Clara, and another one or more on the Polvadera Peak. In my lifetime I have heard of the Penitentes' fiery crosses being observed in remote areas of much lower altitude but I have not seen one, nor its site.

Following the Spanish Colonial period, the Mexican Governors at Santa Fé changed events in the Polvadera Mountain area very little. However, the churches became more secularized and the people became less Spanish and more Mexican. Language became less stilted and the middle class city and town dwellers became less evident. The mestizos appeared and sounds of the outside world began to be heard in our land.

Occupation of New Mexico in 1846 by United States troops tended to solidify traditional Hispano life throughout the territory and a small detachment rented quarters in Abiquiu to protect the surrounding countryside from Navajos, Utes, and Jicarilla Apaches. The Navajos, particularly, went on the warpath from 1847 to 1859 because they sensed that young Anglos might not have the support of the Hispanos.[6]

At least around Abiquiu, the Indian raids let up and a trading post for Utes was set up in 1853. These passing phases little perturbed the Hispano way of life. The Old Spanish Trail through Abiquiu brought transient traffic into and out of the area, including gold seekers. Some tore up the beaver dams on all of the streams in their insatialble search for placer gold.

A well-worn trail developed up Cañones Creek, on up Polvadera Creek, and up one of its branches (El Rechuelos Creek) to our green (Polvadera) saddle and on down Vallecitos Creek to its junction with Abiquiu Creek. It was a beautiful tour even if it invaded a number of the Land Grants. Many prospectors were encouraged to hurry on by gunfire.

When the Indian Trading Post was moved to the Tierra Amarilla vicinity in 1872,[6] Abiquiu was abandoned. By about 1890, the population had dropped from over 3000 to fewer than 800. Anglos started to move in. As a result, many Hispanos at Abiquiu withdrew into the penitente organization which promised to preserve and even intensify their traditional way of life and beliefs. These attitudes were materialized in the building of more penitente moradas to dam out the alien Anglo influences.[1]

Fires, perhaps signal fires or flaming crosses, began to appear on Cerro Pedernal, the nearby 10,000 foot volcanic plug that climbs skyward just east of Coyote. The fires were not always during Lent. That gave rise to conjecturing that it was the Jicarillas or a wandering party of Utes reminiscing about their old stamping grounds, or even a hunting party of unpredictable Anglos. In more nearly current times, it may have been Penitente cermonies at other times of the year. It is known that the Penitentes of Truchas (east of Espanola) make pilgrimages to Cerro Pedernal at regular times. Early in the century, the Anglos in the area thought that the lights or fires might even be set by the new Forest Service that was busy buying up timber lands.

Late in the 1800's, the narrow gauge railroad (The Denver and Rio Grande Western Railroad) was built and operated through the wild lands on both sides of the New Mexico-Colorado border. The Cumbres and Toltec Line was also put in during that period. There were some very dry years following the start-up of the railroads and they possibly started some of the forest fires. It was suspected by the young Forest Service that several fires were started by ranchers to open up more grazing. In any event, great areas of prime timber burned. The ranchers said that Indians were trying to burn up the railroads. Almost every able bodied man from the Espanola area and the other settlements in the Chama River Basin was fighting fires for several years running. And many lost their lives.

The timber on the northern end of the Jemez Mountains was spared, however. Only a few fires were started south of the Chama River and they were controlled or burned out without much damage. The area around Abiquiu was so picked over for several centuries that it was fairly fireproof. Consequently, the timber on Polvadera Peak itself was not burned off and is now in the climax stage. Clara Road was built in 1970 to accommodate a Forest Service timber sale in the areas immediately south of our proposed wilderness boundary. The Clara Road makes a lot of beautiful backcountry accessible for day hikes where it took three days previously. It also opened it up to poaching. The road's vivid scar across the south face of Clara Peak woke up a number of people who took our beautiful landscapes for granted.

Mountain desert streams characteristically fluctuate in flow rate throughout the year and over the centuries and the Chama and Puerco streams are no exceptions. In October, 1911, the Chama River flooded for two days to levels higher than man could remember. Damage was widespread even well down the Rio Grande past Albuquerque. The Chama at Abiquiu flodded in July, 1952, to its highest record elevation actually measured, but perhaps not as high as in the 1911 flood.

The flow of the Puerco upstream from Abiquiu has its own wild history but its watershed is not as large as that of the upper Chama. It was often possible to walk across both streams in November and December without getting wet. In all, the Chama was a very interesting stream to live near for centuries.

El Vado Reservoir was put into operation in 1935. It was designed for irrigation control and has moderated the runoff. The Bureau of Reclamation also added another dam called Heron Reservoir to stand in the way of Willow Creek floods and to store water diverted from the Colorado River Basin through some tunnels penetrating the Continental Divide.

The Rio Grande compact is a multi-state agreement on the water budgets of each state along the course. It apparently was not possible to control the water throughout the Rio Grande complex with the dams in place in the 1950 period. Abiquiu Dam was started in 1958 and placed into operation in 1963. It is only some eight miles upstream from Abiquiu. The 325 foot elevation of the earth filled dam brow makes it one of the highest such dams in the United States. The dam is 1,540 feet long and hopefully is capable of holding 1,215,000 acre feet of water at its maximum capacity. Like so many of the dams in our southwest, it must have a finite sediment storage capacity. Many of us wonder what happens after that time. We have seen the upstream mess at the headwaters of Lake Mead and watched high banks of silt cave in as the water receded.

The impact of the high dam on the Chama River at Abiquiu has been largely favorable. After its water level filled and stabilized the stream flow has been moderate and it does not dry up anymore. The water is generally clear unless Frijoles Arroyo is running mud for a day or so. Fishing is good some of the time.

The input pulse of spring snow melt in 1979 tested the Abiquiu Dam at higher levels than normal. When the runoff was at its peak, in early June, 1979, several of us floated the Chama from Cooper's Ranch below El Vado Dam to the takeout point about six miles below the Christ in the Desert Monastery. The standing waves were some six feet high just before the low concrete foot bridge. The oar lock struck the underside of the bridge as we ducked beneath it. At that time, the gates of El Vado were not throttling the steamflow. Later they were closed to fill the lake to accommodate its role as an irrigation reservoir.

Over the last 60 years or so the Hispanic lifestyles have been changing. The pickup truck has replaced the horse. Migration from the ranches to the cities took many of the young ones. Schooling was improved. Taxes were levied by the counties. The Land Grants were subdivided or broken up in many ways. The menfolk went off the several wars and some did not come back. Wives and heirs had to sell out in some instances. Taxes went unpaid and Sheriff's Sales were too frequent. Unscrupulous real estate operators roamed the lands and county records.

Belatedly, a champion appeared. A well-educated Chicano named Reyes Tijerina attempted to represent the deposed Hispano in his various miseries. The passage of events is too complicated to fairly represent them here. But briefly, a confrontation was staged at Echo Amphitheater in which the deposed Chicanos seized the area. The Carson National Forest, under the custody of the U.S. Forest Service had been buying, trading, and otherwise obtaining title to the forest lands. The Amphitheater was a small campground among some echoing red rock formations a dozen miles west of Abiquiu. Shots were fired, tempers flared, Federal charges were leveled, and the grievances were aired.

Two other events also happened in the 1960 decade impelled by the same injustices. The Rio Arriba County Courthouse officials were attacked in a shootout, several were killed, and the Champion Tijerina was sent to a Federal Penitentiary. The County

Tax/Sheriff's Sale process was somewhere at the root of the troubles. Divided allegiances also played a part.

The town of Coyote as long ago as 1830, was known to be a bandit hideout. It is probably no more than 20 miles west of Abiquiu. The resentment flared anew to the extent that the National Guard was called out, replete with tanks and armored vehicles to roust the brotherhood out of the Canjilon Lake Campgrounds during a wintery storm.

The Alianza De Pueblos Libres has had a stormy existence but is determined to bring its case, based on the Guadalupe-Hidalgo Treaty to a fair and equable conclusion. They have claims against the Episcopal Church over some Ghost Ranch lands, and against the Federal Government for Abiquiu Dam land titles. The champion, Reyes Tijerina, has served his sentence and is back in the fray in various capacities known only to himself.

The Hispano culture still resides in deep pockets of Rio Arriba County and had been detrimental to the economic development of the area. Since the children cannot find employment on the ranches to suit them, most move away. Various attempts have been made to alleviate the situation but without much success.

A proposal was made to the State government to sponsor "Bed and Breakfast" or Pension (vacation-lodging) accomodations. It was intended to provide a stable income for the working ranches wherein reservations could be made through the State Tourist Bureau to entertain visitors at all seasons. Provisions for the housing, the training of local help to maintain and service the operation, transportation and even emergency medical help were all in the bill. But Lieutenant Governor Ferguson was stonewalled by people in the northern counties. They let it be known they did not want interferences with their lives.

Various other interferences have also been rebuffed by Los Viejos. There were reports of below-standard housing when the census was taken. The government built a few houses but the folks did not want them. Under their breaths they called them "los plasticos," their kids broke windows, and a few were burned.

Down through the centuries the Indian hogan underwent notable changes. The brush covered wickiup was modified into pit houses and then to pueblo apartments. In turn, the Spanish and the Mexican evolved their adobe houses, and on into the larger and more spacious Spanish colonial structures. Northern New Mexico did not embrace the colonial architecture since stone and adobe homes with viga roofs were better suited to the climate and economic conditions. Consequently, the onsets of the house trailer and prefabricated houses were not accepted. However, with fewer young people to help build the labor intensive adobe dwellings they have accepted los plasticos, but begrudgingly.

The most recent adaptation is evident in the Abiquiu Sundwellings. The Sundwelling Demonstration Center at Ghost Ranch was constructed to compare different types of solar heating systems in conjunction with low cost construction practices indigenous to the locality. (See February 1980, "New Mexico Magazine".) Passive systems are being evaluated by engineers from Los Alamos. Peter Van Dresser, for years a pioneer in the study and use of alternate energy systems, was coordinator of the Sundwellings Technical Committee — an advisory group of nine architects and engineers, all leaders in New Mexico's solar energy field. (Will the Hispanos warm up to this kind of innovation?)

So the milieu is set for you to enjoy the Polvadera Wilderness around which all of these events have taken place. How has the mountain area survived all of these peripheral activities of man without losing its naturalness, its agelessness, its freshness? I am almost afraid to tell you how to get into the area because your use, loving as it may be, might debilitate the qualities we want to retain forever. But I'm sure you will help protect the area from continuing threats that it will always attract.

The Roadless Area Review and Evaluation (RARE II) process concluded from the public input (92 percent pro wilderness out of 150 letters) that the area should be classified as "Further Planning" instead of "wilderness." That rating resulted from the timber industry interest in the area's tempting timber, and the dictum that the Santa Fé National Forest has a quota of millions of board feet which must be satisfied. It might have made a difference if 500 people had written their recommendations, but then it might not.

The easy timber has already been high graded or creamed off. It looks as if there were some adjacent blowdowns after some of the timber sale areas were opened up. The clear cutting allowed the wind to topple over the newly exposed trees. The timber that remains is on the steep sides of Polvadera Peak. The logs could not survive if they had to be snaked down the mountain to the roads in the foothills; they are too brittle. However, if someone wants to finance a tower on the peak for a cable attachment and a peripheral road and staging area around the base, the logs could be lifted down to trucks by the cable-logging technique. Because the road would cost more than the Clara Road (the route is much more rugged) and the operating costs would be high, even the Duke City Lumber Company has not tried this method on low grade timber. Such unrequited possibiliites may bar the eventual enactment into Wilderness.

The difficult access to the area and its unremarkable appearance from afar (along the highway) has prevented many people from going into the area. It's almost the same story at Glen Canyon where Lake Powell now covers it because there were not enough supporters. When I tried to find out where the Clara Road turned off the main highway north of Espanola, the service station men and townspeople did not know where it was, or how to get up in the mountians. Several of them told me to go to Abiquiu and ask. The road junction is a mile north of the city limits of Espanola off U.S. 84.

So, maybe if enough of us find out how wild and happy that last peak in the Jemez Mountains is in its natural state, we may be able to save it. Do not wait too long. The roadless area to the east of it is aptly named "Erosion." Is the same fate due our Polvadera (dusty) Mountain wilderness?

TRAILS AND ROUTES

The easiest access to Polvadera Peak itself is via the Clara Road which turns west of U.S. 84, one mile north of Espanola city limits. Note your odometer reading. Drive 27.5 miles and park. The ridge due north of Chicoma Peak above you to the south has a pack trail on it. Find the trail and follow it on a bearing approximately 17 degrees west of north. The trail will traverse a clearcut area and skirt a blowdown area of tangled timber. The trail swings around on a contour to the east of the unnamed round hill about two miles north of your starting point. The round hill is at an elevation of 10,900 feet. Some maps show the trail going around the west side of that peak, but that is erroneous. You will be able to see Polvadera Peak off to the north another mile and one-half from the round peak.

One word to the wise. When crossing timber-cut clearings, note well where the trail emerges from the forest into the clearing. Then also note where the trail reenters the trees on the opposite side. In thick timber you can be ten paces away from the trail and not know it. You might be tired on the way back and lose the trail. If you do, the car can be much further away than you hope. The trail will bring you onto the green saddle where those Puyé Indians shot the two bull elk those many centuries ago.

If you see any game in the area, it may well be in that saddle-meadow, so be quiet and look carefully before you step into the open. If you decide to set up camp there, you may want to go into the woods just on the northern edge of the clearing so as not to inhibit passages of various creatures of the night.

There is no water near the saddle. However, if you really need some, there is a spring along the trail to the east down Vallecitos Creek at about the 9,200 foot level. (That is only 2000 feet below Polvadera Peak.)

You may want to set your alarm to quietly awaken you just before first light so you can observe any wildlife in the mountain meadow. I have seen elk and deer there; hawks and peregrines; a fox and a bobcat; rabbits and squirrels as well. A coyote cut loose one dark night not 100 feet from the sleeping bag. (I stepped in some fresh bear sign one early morn on the margin of the green on the east end of the meadow.) Once in midsummer a herd of cattle had taken over the meadow and the flies were terrible. Conversely, I

Polvadera Peak — Green Saddle Meadow.

have lain in wait there during deer hunting season with my bow and did not see a hair.

If you carefully calculate your trip to be at the meadow and unobtrusively camped on the edge with a full moon coming up at about 9 at night, you could be in for a treat. By all means do not have a fire going. Cover up anything that might reflect the moonlight. Get in your sleeping bag and be as still as possible. One such night, the bull bats (night hawks) were feeding by moonlight overhead. A couple of owls made several captures in the meadow. It may have been mice or chipmunks providing them dinner. Some rabbits spent 20 minutes cavorting until something I could not see frightened them away. My backpack binoculars were not optimum for such nocturnal use. Two or three deer headed west into El Rechuelos Canyon without making a sound. Shortly afterward I was awakened by several running deer being chased by a small mountain lion. It may have been the same deer that passed earlier, so wraithlike.

My notes say that at about 3 in the morning, it rained for 15 minutes, there was one thunder bolt and a strike somewhere to the westward. My pancho blew off just as the rain stopped. Occasionally, I do not take a tent during the rainy season, gambling on the pattern of the afternoon showers leaving a cloudfree night. When I stood up to stretch as I was getting up at dawn, two fawns pointed their noses and craned their necks at me in my yellow nylon sleepers.

The trail up onto Polvadera Peak can be found emerging from the saddle-meadow on its northeast edge. The trail then contours to the west as it climbs. One can take a compass bearing and climb almost directly to the summit without staying on the trail. The several times that I have been on the peak there was no cairn or sign-in log. Some survey scaffolding has long been blown down or knocked over. There are enough flat spots up there to sleep a dozen if you want to. Be sure you clean up every last bit of trash, no matter who left it.

If you get your map and compass out you will find a ridge dropping down to the northwest. There is no trail but you can use Cerro Pedernal for a route sighting monitor. If you head just to the north flank of the Cerro, you will emerge into a clearing at the head of Cañada del Ojitos just outside our Wilderness boundaries. There is a spring marked on the map which is the remains of some metal water troughs with a delapidated fence around the source. It was entirely dried up when I saw it.

To get back up onto the saddle south of Polvadera, one can follow the road from the spring to the southeast. When the road ends, go straight south about a half mile to get into El Rechuelos Canyon (it has water in it). If you follow the cattle trail due east at that point, it leads you up a dry canyon almost directly back onto Polvadera peak and over a series of boulder fields on the way up. The trail up El Rechuelos is more nearly southeast. The last time I went up it, the lower part had been recently maintained and the upper part was unused and essentially only a game trail. The route is generally south of the canyon bottom, perhaps 100 yards uphill. I found a knocked-down trail sign, Number 127 alongside the trail.

Another route of considerable interest starts on the summit of Polvadera Peak and drops down straight north for the first mile without any surprises. If you get off the ridge, the timber is too thick to make out much below for route alignment, but the deer hunting is great. Staying on the ridge which bears off 10 to 12 degrees to the west of true north (our declination is about 13 degrees east of north), in about four miles you will run into the Polvadera Short Cut road in Section 29. If no one is there to pick you up, you can walk south on the Short cut up Cañada del Ojito and find El Rechuelos canyon trail back to the saddle. It is probably too long a trip for most ridge runners to do in one day. Incidentally, when you stepped onto Short Cut, you were on the north end of our Wilderness boundary. My trip notes say that, in mid-June, 1977, Scott Simmons and I saw hundreds of acres of timber in the Cañada infested with tent caterpillars. There were at least a dozen per square foot dead on the ground. We did not think they had been sprayed with insecticide.

You can boondock due northeast of the Peak and be at the headwaters of Abiquiu Creek in about a mile. follow the stream down (the east side is clearer walking) to the timbered flat at the 8,500 foot level at the junction of Sections 3 and 35. Continue on the ridge to the northeast (in back of the Cone Peak, elevation 8923 feet in Section 35). Cut into the Short Cut Road in Section 26 and walk east and south for a couple of miles to the old townsite of Vallecitos. follow the water pipeline from there up Vallecitos Creek Canyon on trail Number 105 to the saddle-meadow. This is a two-day trip.

If you're looking for bear, and if you park where the Clara Road crosses into Section 38 from 27, you will find an old pack trail 144 headed downhill and east into the Cienega del Oso. The west branch of the Rio del Oso is called the Rito de Abiquiu. It plunges down a steep canyon which looks as choked up as its branch to the east. I made the mistake of being a couple of hundred yards below the fork of the two little freshets in the willows when I kicked out a bear and her cub. I was not even hunting. I was looking for a good place for our east boundary.

You should probably get permission from the Santa Clara Governor if you plan to go up onto the summit of Chicoma Mountain, even from the north. Then stay away if you cannot get it. White man sometimes wears out his welcome. Technically, the forest boundary goes right to the top but the Indians do not completely agree. The old maps have it as Tschicoma or Santa Clara Peak. It is the highest peak at 11,561 feet in the Jemez Mountains and is a mile south of our Wilderness boundary.

Cerro Pedernal is not in our Polvadera Wilderness Area, but you may want to give it a try some day. Drive five miles south of Youngsville on the Encino Lookout Road. Pedernal is about three miles to the east, northeast. Climb up through the notch on the northwest corner of the escarpment and you cut into a switchback trail to the top. You are not supposed to pick up the chert, agate, and chalcedony, not because it is controlled by the Antiquities Act, but because it was a principal source for primitive weapon and cutting tool materials. Also, unless you are a Penitente, the Easter Season may not be the best time for you to climb the plug.

The Clara Road was designed as an all-weather road and it may well be. It could be plowed in a few stretches where the drifts tend to form. One weekend in February of 1976, a couple of us made it as far as the north slopes of Chicoma Mountain in Section 29 before the snow was too deep. We skied along the drifted road to the place where it crosses the ridge north of Chicoma and starts down to the west. We returned to the cars when a blizzard swept down on us from Chicoma. Maybe I should not have done my snow dance?

CHAPTER 14:

The Legal Process

Organizing people either as individuals or as members of outdoor clubs toward using the legal process to obtain congressional enactments of wilderness areas is the only way to preserve and protect our lands.

The story of New Mexican wilderness may never end and possibly we should supplicate: "may our wilderness never end." Many a wilderness can die of overlove, of attracting too many people. Already we have trodden the same path of thousands before us who have worn footpaths into the very sandstone of their own prehistoric stamping-grounds. And those people did not have cleated boots or joggers to accelerate the process as we presently can. To retain the impression that one is setting foot on one spot on this earth that not one single human has ever trodden may be forever beyond our capabilities even if we revert to bare feet.

Our aim in the New Mexico Wilderness Study Committee has been to do what we can to obtain enactment of those remaining areas of our state which still qualify as National Wilderness before rapid development and increasing population overtake them and disqualify them forever. Those same pressures threaten our existing National Wilderness Areas and force us to admit that we must ascribe to the new adage, "the solution to polution is dilution." The enactment of our remaining qualified areas into National Wilderness status should entice some of the people away from some of our more abused areas like the Pecos, San Pedro Parks, and Gila National Wilderness areas and hopefully reduce the impacts of such loving use.

It has been with some reluctance that I have told you of some of my own secret places. Some of the areas I have not included have had too much written about them already. You can readily find information on the Gila, the Pecos, and the White Mountain Wildernesses. I did not leave them out because they are unknown to me but rather because they evoke in me not only a possessiveness but a fear of impending doom of a vital pristine quality which can never be recaptured.

When I started this book several years ago, I had hoped to include chapters on the Pecos additions in both the Santa Fe and Carson National Forests. Both the Gila and the White Mountain Additions have some captivating tales attached to them. The San Pedro Parks National Wilderness was to have been the vehicle for telling you about the conflicts waging there among the cattle grazing interests, the elk range, and the seasonal recreational uses.

Extensive files and trip notes beckon on other areas like our proposed Osier Mesa-Cruces Basin, the proposed Canjilon Mountain-El Rito Meadows, including the valiant appeals of Milo Conrad and George Grossman to have them included in the Forest Service's RARE II wilderness recommendations. The controversies which have churned the resilient waters of the San Francisco Box would fill a book by themselves. The Hooker Dam battle which we have waged for years begs to be told. The pleas of the proposed Sierra Negra Wilderness northeast of Abiquiu, of the Caballo area northwest of Los Alamos, and of the Sacramento Escarpment so rich in history, all staunchly defending their own wilderness integrities against virulent threats — these are stories that must be told, but at another time and place.

Through all of these years, we have tried to follow and rely on the legal process despite the desires of some hotheads who felt moved to action in methods which might have paled those in Ed Abbey's *Monkey Wrench Gang*. It seems fitting that the events of 1980 should culminate this particular book. A large spectrum of events have made it a watershed year in our efforts. Since it is real life, the happy ending for all may be only a dream. I have recorded it for obvious reasons from my observations for all to see and perhaps to be infuriated or inspired to continued action.

The legal process for which this chapter is named involved a large number of private citizens wanting a given enactment so much that they are willing to work toward it as a group for as many as 10 years. Then, after they have communicated their preferences clearly to the public land agency and to their Congressmen as well as the House Interior and Insular Affairs Committee, enactment might follow.

Our New Mexican Wilderness Study committee managed to induce legislation on a dozen areas which were enacted in 1980. The 1980 enactment of the twelve areas, added to our existing National Wildernesses, comes to 20 separate Wildernesses in New Mexico. Five of the areas were additions to previously enacted Wildernesses. The total acreage in 1980 came to 1,468,946 acres of National Wilderness in New Mexico, 1.9% of the area of our state.

1.	Aldo Leopold	211,300 acres
2.	Gila Additions	140,000
3.	Blue Range	30,000
4.	Pecos Additions	55,000
5.	Wheeler Peak Additions	14,700
6.	Latir	20,000
7.	Apache Kid	45,000
8.	Withington	19,000
9.	Capitan	34,000
10.	White Mountain Additions	16,860
11.	Dome (Bandelier Additions)	5,200
12.	Cruces Basin	18,000
		609,060 acres

The act included six areas for Further Study until January 1, 1986. They are Lower San Francisco Wilderness Study Area, Guadalupe Escarpment WSA, Bunk Robinson WSA, Columbine-Hondo WSA, Hell Hole WSA, and Whitmire Canyon WSA.

To wrap-up the earlier and later enactments, the areas are given here. These are all National Wildernesses; the abbreviated names are used.

Gila	438,626
Pecos	165,000

Wheeler Peak	4,963
White Mountain	28,230
San Pedro Parks	41,132
Salt Creek	8,500
Bosque del Apache	30,850
Manzano Mountain	37,000
Sandia Mountain	37,375
Chama River	50,300
Carlsbad	33,125
Bandelier	23,267
Total (acres)	898,368

Representative Richardson obtained two enactments in 1984. They were the Bisti (3,968) and the De-na-zin (23,872), making a total of 27,840. Thus we have a total area of enacted Wilderness at year end of 1,535,268 acres, or 1.98% of the area of our state.

The roadless area review process of the Bureau of Land management territories has just begun. Could it be that the successes and battles described in this book would encourage you to greater accomplishments? But take heed: It is lonely work in the wilderness! May you develop the heart and eyes for it. Those of you inclined to look and not act, it is suggested that you visit the de facto wilderness areas not yet enacted. Organizing outdoor clubs and people toward using the legal process to obtain congressional enactments of our National Wildernesses is the only way I know to protect our lands. Maybe you will be a part of this in the future.

A map, "Wilderness Status Map 1985" is available free at any BLM Office.

REFERENCES

INTRODUCTION
1. Frome, Michael. *Battle for the Wilderness*, New York and Washington: Praeger, 1974
2. Virost, Milton. *Outsider in the Senate, Senator Clinton P. Anderson's Memoirs*. New York World Publishing Co., 1970.
3. Hoard, Dorothy. *A Hiker's Guide to Bandelier National Monument*. Albuquerque: Adobe Press, 1977.

CHAPTER ONE
1. U.S. Department of the Interior, Bureau of Reclamation, and the State of New Mexico. *New Mexico Water Resources*. Washington, D.C.: Bureau of Reclamation, November, 1976.
2. Lloyd, W.L. *Final Environmental Statement, Sandia Mountain Land Use Plan*. Albuquerque: Cibola National Forest Plan, U.S. Department of Agriculture Forest Service, 1975.
3. Gray, James R., George D. Fisk, and Marie Matthews. *Environmental Costs of Recreation in the Sandia Mountains*. Institute for Social Research and Development, The University of New Mexico. New Mexico Business, October, 1974.
4. Hornocker, Maurice. "Cougars Up Close." Vienna, Virginia: National Wildlife Federation. *National Wildlife*, October-November, 1976.
5. Pursley, Dan. "Minus X, The Poaching Factor." *New Mexico Wildlife Magazine*, March-April, 1977.
6. Fergusson, Erna. *Dancing Gods*. Albuquerque: The University of New Mexico Press, 1957.
7. Horgan, Paul. *Great River*. Minerva Press, Funk & Wagnalls, Div. of Reader's Digest Books, Inc., 1968.
8. Northrup, Stuart A. *Minerals of New Mexico*. Albuquerque: The University of New Mexico Press, 1959.
9. Jones, F.A. *New Mexico Mines and Minerals*. Santa Fe: New Mexican Printing Co., 1904.
10. Frome, Michael. *Battle for the Wilderness*. New York and Washington: Praeger, 1974.
11. Quintana, Lucille. "Look It's a Bird." *New Mexico Magazine*, March, 1977.
12. Hill, Mike. *Hikers and Climbers Guide to the Sandia Mountains*. Albuquerque: Adobe Press, 1977. Albuquerque: The University of New Mexico Press, 1983.

CHAPTER TWO
1. Oswalt, Wendell H. *This Land Was Theirs*. New York: John Wiley & Sons, Inc., 1966.
2. Pearce, T.M. *New Mexico Place Names*. Albuquerque: The University of New Mexico Press, 1965.
3. Taylor, Norma. "Vista New Mexico, Manzano Foothills, Locale of Rich, Tragic History. Albuquerque: *Sandia Lab News*, March, 1977.

CHAPTER THREE
1. Winkless, Nels III, and Iben Browning. *Climate and the Affairs of Men*. New York: Harper's Magazine Press, 1975.
2. Oswalt, Wendell H. *This Land Was Theirs*. New York: John Wiley & Sons, Inc., 1966.
3. Calvin, Ross. *Sky Determines*. Albuquerque: The University of New Mexico Press, 1965.
4. Bandelier, Adolf F. *The Delight Makers*. New York: Dodd, Mead & Co., 1949.
5. Moore, Joan W. *Mexican Americans*. Englewood Cliffs, New Jersey: Prentice-Hall, Inc., 1970.
6. Lange, Charles H., and Carroll L. Riley. *The Southwest Journals of Adolf F. Bandelier, 1880-1882*. Albuquerque: The University of New Mexico Press, 1966.
7. Northrop, Stuart A. *Minerals of New Mexico*. Albuquerque: The University of New Mexico Press, 1959.
8. Waters, Frank. *Masked Gods*. Denver: Sage Books, 1950.
9. Harrington, Eldred. *An Engineer Writes About People and Places and Projects*. Albuquerque: Calvin Horn Publisher, Inc., 1967.
10. Jones, F.A. *New Mexico Mines and Minerals*. Santa Fe: New Mexican Printing Co., 1904
11. Hunter, John D. *Alternatives for Managing the Feral Burro Population Within Bandelier National Monument*. Santa Fe: National Park Service, 1977.
12. Hibben, Frank C. *Hunting American Bears*. Ch. 5 Albuquerque: The University of New Mexico Press, 1950.
13. Hoard, Dorothy. *A Hiker's Guide to Bandelier National Monument*. Albuquerque: Adobe Press, 1977.
14. Niklaus, Phil, and Staff Writers. "Restoration of La Mesa Fire Area May Take Centuries." *The Albuquerque Journal*, June 21 through June 26, 1977.

CHAPTER FOUR
1. Leopold, Aldo. *A Sand County Almanac*. New York: Oxford University Press, 1949.
2. Giammattei, Victor M., and Nanci G. Reichert. *Art of a Vanished Race*. Woodland, California: Dillon-Tyler, 1975.
3. Horgan, Paul. *Great River*. Minerva Press, Funk & Wagnalls, Div. of Reader's Digest Books, Inc., 1968.
4. Nesbitt, Paul H. *The Ancient Mimbreños*. Beloit, Wisconsin: Beloit College Press, 1931.

5. Ungnade, Herbert E. *Guide to the New Mexico Mountains.* Albuquerque: The University of New Mexico Press, 1973.
6. Twitchell, Ralph Emerson. *The Spanish Archives of New Mexico,* 2 Vol. Cedar Rapids, Iowa: The Torch Press, 1914.
7. Thomas, Alfred. *The Plains Indians and New Mexico.* Albuquerque: The University of New Mexico Press, 1940.
8. Jones, F.A. *New Mexico Mines and Minerals.* Santa Fe: New Mexican Printing Co., 1904.
9. Dobie, J. Frank. *The Ben Lilly Legend.* Boston: Little, Brown & Co., 1950.
10. Watson, Dorothy. *Pinos-Altos.* Silver City, New Mexico, A Silver City-Grant County Chamber of Commerce Pamphlet, 1973.
11. Frome, Michael. *Battle for the Wilderness.* New York and Washington: Praeger, 1974.
12. Viorst, Milton. *Outsider in the Senate, Senator Clinton P. Anderson's Memoirs.* New York: The World Publishing Co., 1970.

CHAPTER FIVE
1. Oswalt, Wendell H. *This Land Was Theirs.* New York: John Wiley & Sons, Inc., 1966.
2. Waters, Frank. *Masked Gods.* Denver: Sage Books, 1950.
3. Jones, F.A. *New Mexico Mines and Minerals.* Santa Fe: New Mexican Printing Co., 1904.
4. Northrop, Stuart A. *Minerals of New Mexico.* Albuquerque: The University of New Mexico Press, 1959.

CHAPTER SIX
1. Fergusson, Erna. *Dancing Gods.* Albuquerque: The University of New Mexico Press, 1957.
2. Pearce, T.M. *New Mexico Place Names.* Albuquerque: The University of New Mexico Press, 1965.
3. Harrington, Eldred. *An Engineer Writes About People and Places and Projects.* Albuquerque: Calvin Horn Publisher, Inc., 1967.
4. Jones, F.A. *New Mexico Mines and Minerals.* Santa Fe: New Mexican Printing Co., 1904.
5. Horgan, Paul. *Great River.* Minerva Press, Funk & Wagnalls, Div. of Reader's Digest Books, Inc., 1968.
6. Blacker, Irwin R. *Taos.* Cleveland and New York: The World Publishing Co., 1959.
7. Jiron, Governor Teresino. *Statement of Taos Pueblo on the Proposed Management Plan for Wheeler Peak Wilderness Area.* Albuquerque: Rodey, Dickason, Sloan, Akin, & Robb, P.A., Counsellors and Attorneys at Law, December 27, 1973.
8. Ungnade, Herbert E. *Guide to the New Mexico Mountains.* Albuquerque: The University of New Mexico Press, 1973.
9. Viorst, Milton. *Outsider in the Senate, Senator Clinton P. Anderson's Memoirs.* New York: The World Publishing Co., 1970.
10. Foreman, Dave. *Designating Wilderness — Asking for Destruction?* Lander, Wyoming: High Country Press, June 4, 1976.

CHAPTER SEVEN
1. Northrop, Stuart A. *Minerals of New Mexico.* Albuquerque: The University of New Mexico Press, 1959.
2. Hibben, Frank C. *Hunting American Bears.* Ch. 5 Albuquerque: The University of New Mexico Press, 1950.
3. Hibben, Frank C. *Hunting American Lions.* Albuquerque: The University of New Mexico Press, 1973.

CHAPTER EIGHT
1. Bolton, Herbert Eugene. *Coronado.* Albuquerque: The University of New Mexico Press, 1964.
2. Horgan, Paul. *Great River.* Minerva Press, Funk & Wagnalls, Div. of Reader's Digest Books, Inc., 1968.
3. Grinstead, Marion C. *Life and Death of a Frontier Fort: Fort Craig, New Mexico.* Socorro: The Socorro County Historical Society, 1973.
4. Myers, Lee. *New Mexico Military Installations.* Globe, Arizona: Southwest Parks and Monuments Association, 1967.
5. Giese, Dale F. *Echoes of the Bugle.* Silver City: Western New Mexico University Booklet, 1967.
6. Jones, F.A. *New Mexico Mines and Minerals.* Santa Fe: New Mexican Printing Co., 1904.

CHAPTER TEN
1. Fergusson, Erna. *New Mexico.* New York: Alfred A. Knopf, 1951.
2. Horgan, Paul. *Great River.* Minerva Press, Funk & Wagnalls, Div. of Reader's Digest Books, Inc., 1968.
3. Calvin, Ross. *Sky Determines.* Albuquerque: The University of New Mexico Press, 1965.
4. Woods, Betty. "101 Trips in the Land of Enchantment." *New Mexico Magazine,* 1959.
5. Pearce, T.M. *New Mexico Place Names.* Albuquerque: The University of New Mexico Press, 1965.
6. Pearsall, J.R. "Wells Fargo Bounty Hunters." *The Saturday Evening Post,* February, 1937.

CHAPTER ELEVEN
1. Caiar, Ruth, with Jim White, Jr. *One Man's Dream — The Story of Jim White Discoverer and Explorer of the Carlsbad Caverns.* New York: Pageant Press, Inc., 1957.
2. U.S. Department of the Interior, Bureau of Reclamation and The State of New Mexico. *New*

Mexico Water Resources. Washington, D.C.: Bureau of Reclamation, November, 1976.
3. Kline, Doyle. "Great Hollow Reef." Santa Fe: *New Mexico Magazine,* March/April, 1973, Vol. 51. pp. 23 - 29.
4. Billard, Jules B. *The World of the American Indian.* Washington, D.C.: National Geographic Book Service, 1974, p. 39.
5. Winkless, Nels III, and Iben Browning. *Climate and the Affairs of Men.* New York: Harper's Magazine Press, 1975.
6. Renner, Frederic G. *Charles M. Russell.* New York: Harry N. Abrams, Inc., 1976.
7. Webb, Walter Prescott. *The Handbook of Texas.* Austin: The Texas State Historical Association, 1952.
8. Root, Frank A. *The Overland Stage to California.* Topeka, Kansas, 1901. Reprint, Columbus, Ohio: Long's College Book Co., 1950.
9. Judd, Ira B. "The Overland Mail." Tucson, *Arizona Highways,* October, 1958.
10. Travis, Charles D., Executive Director. *Facilities Directory.* Austin: Texas: Parks and Wildlife Department, 1946.
11. Vesely, Frank (Commissioner of State Lands). "Who Owns Carlsbad Caverns?" Santa Fe: *New Mexico Magazine,* December, 1933, p. 17.
12. Hansen, Harry. *Texas — A Guide to the Lone Star State.* New York, Hastings House, 1969.
13. Tilden, Freeman. *The National Parks.* New York: Alfred A. Knopf, 1968. pp. 206-208
14. Wilson, Gladys Marie. "Saga of Butterfield's Overland Mail." *American History Illustrated,* January, 1967, p. 14.
15. Wattson, Mrs. Ben (Pauline). *Hidden Gold of the Guadalupes.* El Paso: Tumbleweed Press, 1968.
16. Stitt, Robert R., and William P. Bishop. "Underground Wilderness in the Guadalupe Escarpment." Huntsville, Alabama: *The National Speleological Society Bulletin,* 1972, 34(3):77-88.
17. Chapman, John, Area Manager of Guadalupe Mountains National Park. *The Top of Texas.* Austin: Texas Parks and Wildlife Department, May, 1974.
18. Kurtz, Don and William D. Goran. *Trails of the Guadalupes.* Champaign, Ill., Environmental Association, 1982.

CHAPTER TWELVE
1. Blagbrough, John W., and Steven E. Farkas. *Rock Glaciers in the San Mateo Mountains, South-Central New Mexico.* New Haven: Yale University, American Journal of Science, Vol. 266, November, 1968, pp. 812-823.
2. U.S. Department of the Interior, Bureau of Reclamation, and the State of New Mexico. *New Mexico Water Resources.* Washington, D.C.: Bureau of Reclamation, November, 1976.
3. Kelley, Vincent C. *Geology of the Pecos Country, Southeastern New Mexico, Memoir 24.* Socorro: State Bureau of Mines and Mineral Resources, New Mexico Institute of Mining and Technology, 1971.
4. Oswalt, Wendell H. *This Land Was Theirs.* New York: John Wiley & Sons, Inc., 1966.
5. Bolton, Herbert Eugene. *Coronado.* Albuquerque: The University of New Mexico Press, 1964.
6. Renner, Frederic G. *Charles M. Russell.* New York: Harry N. Abrams, Inc., 1976.
7. U.S. Department of Interior, U.S. Fish and Wildlife Service. *Unique Wildlife Ecosystems of New Mexico-Region Two.* 1979.
8. Keleher, William A. *Violence in Lincoln County.* Albuquerque: The University of New Mexico Press, 2nd Printing, 1957.
9. Parker, Morris B. *White Oaks, Life in a New Mexico Gold Camp, 1880-1900.* Tucson: The University of Arizona Press, 1971.
10. Hardy, Charles, E. *Chemicals for Forest Fire Fighting,* 3rd edition. Boston: National Fire Protection Association, 1977.
11. Kilgore, Bruce M. *From Fire Control to Fire Management: An Ecological Basis for Policies.* U.S. National Park Service, in National Wildlife Federation Conservation News.
12. Keenan, Bill. "Tropical Deforestation: Getting the Green Out." Washington, D.C.: *National Wildlife Federation Conservation News,* Vol. 44, No. 23, December, 1979.

CHAPTER THIRTEEN
1. Ahlborn, Richard E. *The Penitente Moradas of Abiquiu.* Washington, D.C.: Smithsonian Institution Press, Paper 63, 1968.
2. Pearce, T.M. *New Mexico Place Names.* Albuquerque: The University of New Mexico Press, 1965.
3. Horgan, Paul. *Great River.* Minerva Press, Funk & Wagnalls, Div. of Reader's Digest Books, Inc., 1968.
4. Oswalt, Wendell H. *This Land Was Theirs* New York: John Wiley & Sons, Inc., 1966.
5. U.S. Department of the Interior, Bureau of Reclamation, and The State of New Mexico. *New Mexico Water Resources.* Washington, D.C.: Bureau of Reclamation, November, 1976.
6. Twitchell, Ralph Emerson. *The Spanish Archives of New Mexico.* 2 Vol. Cedar Rapids, Iowa: The Torch Press, 1914.
7. Dutton, Bertha P. *Indians of the American Southwest.* Englewood Cliffs, New Jersey: Prentice-Hall, Inc., 1975.
8. Winkless, Nels III, and Iben Browning. *Climate and the Affairs of Men.* New York: Harper's Magazine Press, 1975.

9. Thomas, Alfred. *The Plains Indians and New Mexico*. Albuquerque: The University of New Mexico Press, 1940.

MISCELLANEOUS BIBLIOGRAPHY

PECOS NATIONAL WILDERNESS AREA

BARKER, ELLIOT S. *Beatty's Cabin*. Albuquerque, New Mexico: The University of New Mexico Press, 1953.

EVANS, HARRY. *50 Hikes in New Mexico*. Pico Rivera, California: Gem Guide Book Co., 1984.

MONTGOMERY, ARTHUR and SUTHERLAND, PATRICK K. *Trail Guide to the Upper Pecos*. Albuquerque, New Mexico: The University of New Mexico Printing Plant, 1972.

OVERHAGE, CARL. *6 1 Day Walks in the Pecos*. Santa Fe, New Mexico: Sunstone Press, 1984.

SANTA FE GROUP — SIERRA CLUB. *Day Hikes in the Santa Fe Area*. Santa Fe, New Mexico: National Education Association Press, 1981.

GILA NATIONAL WILDERNESS AREA

GILES, JAMES S. *Mogillon — The Town That Refuses to Die*. Anthony, New Mexico: Valley News, 1970.

IRVING, BLANCHE M. *Five Deer on Loco Mountain Road*. Santa Fe, New Mexico: Sunstone Press, 1982.

McFARLAND, ELIZABETH. *Wilderness of the Gila*. Albuquerque, New Mexico: Publications Office, University of New Mexico, 1974.

SAN PEDRO PARKS NATIONAL WILDERNESS

PETTITT, ROLAND A. *Exploring the Jemez Country*. Los Alamos, New Mexico: Pajarito Publications, 1975.

INDEX

Albuquerque Game Preservation Association
    SEE Albuquerque Wildlife and Conservation Association
Albuquerque Wildlife and Conservation Association: 12, 31, 52-53
Aldo Leopold National Wilderness: 32-43, 80, 127
Apache Kid National Wilderness: 69-77, 108-109, 127
Apache Kid, The: 75-76
Armendariz Land Grant: 72-74
Atlantic Richfield Co. (ARCO): 41, 68, 81-82

Baca, Jesus (Chewy): 23, 25
Banco Breaks Defacto Wilderness: 44-48
Bandelier, Adolph: 29
Bandelier National Monument and Wilderness: 8, 26-34, 127-128
Barton, Bart: 31
Beatty's Cabin: 13
Billy the Kid: 110
Bishop, William P. (Bill): 103
Bishop, John: 103
Bisti National Wilderness: 128
Black Mesa: 46, 48
Black Range: 37-43
Blagbrough, John: 108
Blake, Ernie: 52, 54, 56
Blue Lake: 51-53, 58
Blue Range: 37, 39, 127
Bosque del Apache National Wilderness: 6, 75, 128
Bosque del Apache Wildlife Refuge: 8, 74, 86, 88
Bosque Peak: 21-24
Bowman, Carl: 33
Brunner, Bud: 77
Burros: 8, 30, 32, 34
Bursum, Holm: 74

Campbell, Don: 33
Campbell, Gen. Thomas B.: 88
Capitan Mountain National Wilderness: 106-116, 127
Carlito Springs: 13, 18
Carlsbad Caverns: 94, 96-97, 100-101, 104-105, 128
Carlsbad Caverns National Park
    SEE Carlsbad Caverns
Carleton, Kent: 43
Cebolleta Mountains: 46
Chakerian, Armen: 64
Chavez, Ignacio Grant: 46
Church Rock: 47
Cibola National Forest: 46
Cochiti Canyon: 29-30
Cloud seeding: 40-41, 80
Cochiti de Cañada Grant: 29-30, 33

Collins, C.K.: 41
Conrad, Milo: 13, 18, 30-31, 33, 43
Culbert, Jim: 77

De-Na-Zin National Wilderness: 128
Diluzio, Frank: 32
Domenici, Sen. Pete: 33, 41, 87
Dresser, Peter Van: 123
Drum, Heister: 31, 33-34

Eddy, Charles B.: 96
El Malpais Wilderness: 86-87
Endangered American Wilderness Act: 15, 23, 86
Environmental Policy Act of 1969: 12
Ewing, Frank: 100

Federal Land Policy and Management Act of 1976 (FLPMA): 8, 86
Ferguson, Fred E., Jr.: 41
Fergusson Act of 1898: 96-97
Finch, Kathryn: 31
Fires: 12, 34, 41, 60, 112-114, 122
Fisher, Dr. A.K.: 39
Foreman, Dave: 34
Fort Craig: 71-74, 76
Frijoles Canyon: 29-30

Gallegos, Elena Grant: 12
Garrett, Pat: 110
Ghost Ranch Sundwellings Demonstration Center: 123
Gila National Wilderness: 6, 37-42, 86, 127
Goodman, Gerry: 31
Green, Tom: 23
Grocke, Bill: 31
Grossman, George: 33
Guadalupe Canyon: 98-99
Guadalupe Escarpment National Wilderness: 90-105
Guadalupe Mountains National Park: 101, 103-104

Hawk, Alfred D.: 52
Hawk, Walton: 52
Heart Lake: 64-65
Heilman, Ed: 113
Heiser, Laine: 34
Hernandez, Lou: 31
Hibben, Frank: 29, 65, 86
Hinds, Allan L.: 103
Hinsdale, Jim: 29-30
Hoard, Dorothy: 33-34
Holley, Robert A.: 96-97
Hondo Canyon: 51-52, 54
Hunter, J.C., Jr.: 100-101
Hunting: 12-14, 22, 101-102, 105, 110, 112
Hurst, William D.: 13, 54

Indians: 11, 21, 28-30, 37-39, 46, 51-53, 63, 71-73, 75, 85, 94-96, 98, 109-111, 113, 116, 119-121

Ingram, Jeff: 31

Jones, Fayette A.: 73
Jornada del Muerto: 38, 71-73

Kayser Mill Canyon: 22, 24-25
Kingston: 39
Kottlowski, Frank: 94
Krehbiel, Paul: 86
Kutz, Jack: 31

Land Grants: 120-123
    SEE also names of individual grants
Land Use Plan (1975): 11
Latir Peak National Wilderness: 61-68, 127
Legal issues: 127-128
Leopold, Aldo: 6, 37, 40
Lilly, Ben: 39-40
Lincoln County: 109-110
Lincoln County War: 74, 96, 99, 110
Lincoln National Forest: 101, 104, 112
Llano Estacado: 95-96, 99, 109
Lloyd, Wally: 13
Logging: 11, 114, 116, 123
Long, Abijah: 96
Los Alamos Ranch School: 30
Los Alamos Scientific Laboratory: 30, 32
Lujan, Rep. Manuel: 32, 47, 68, 86

McCourt, Genevieve (Genny): 111
McCourt, John: 111
McDonald, Doug: 65
McDonald, Frances: 73
McDonald, Kent: 53, 57-58
McDonald Ranch: 74, 111
McDonald, William C.: 73-74, 111
McDowell, Jack: 65
Mackel, Lou: 30
McKinley, A.D.: 22
McKinley, Cora: 22
McKinley, Marvin: 22
McLean, John: 103
Manzano Land Use Plan: 23
Manzano Mountain National Wilderness: 19-25, 128
Martinez, Antonio Grant: 51, 55
Maxwell Land Grant: 51, 59
Maxwell, Lucien B.: 51
Metal, Andy: 33
Miller, Jack: 13
Mines and Mining: 14-15, 22, 29, 38-42, 46-47, 51-52,
    55-56, 60, 63-64, 66-68, 72-73, 76, 81, 85, 98-99,
    110-111
Molycorp: 56, 60, 64, 67
Moore, Charles: 80
Mosca Peak: 23-24
Mount Withington National Wilderness: 78-82, 127

National Park Bill: 100
National Speleological Society: 103
National Trails System Act: 12
National Wildlife Federation: 13
New Mexico Dept. of Game and Fish: 14, 40, 53,
    65-66, 86
N.M. Environmental Improvement Agency: 54
New Mexico Mountain Club: 12-13, 30-31
New Mexico Omnibus Wilderness: 86, 103
N.M. State Environmental Assessment Office: 47
N.M. State Park & Recreation Division: 53
New Mexico State Trails System Act: 12
New Mexico Trails Committee: 12
New Mexico Wilderness Study Commission: 8, 18
New Mexico Wilderness Study Committee: 7-8, 13,
    18, 30-32, 34, 37, 41, 47, 53, 55, 64, 67, 75, 81,
    85-87, 89, 101, 103, 108, 114, 127
New Mexico Wildlife Federation: 13, 31
Nicklaus, Phil: 64

Off-road Vehicles (ORV): 42-43

Pankey, Joe: 74-76
Pankey, Ruben: 76
Parker, Morris B.: 111
Peckumn, Jim: 14
Pecos Wilderness: 6, 12-13, 127
Perdreauville, Farrell: 54
Placitas: 12, 14, 18
Polvadera Peak Defacto Wilderness: 117-125
Pratt, Wallace: 100-101
Price, Al: 37

Ray, Dick: 23
Richter, Fred: 77
Rio Costilla Cooperative Livestock Association:
    65-67
Rito del Medio: 63-64
Roadless Areas Review and Evaluation (RARE):
    8, 15, 42, 47, 67-68, 75, 81, 102-103, 123, 127-128
Rock glaciers: 108-109, 116

Sagebrush Rebellion: 87
Salt Creek Wilderness 6, 128
Salt War, The: 96, 99
San Pedro Parks Wilderness: 6, 128
Sandia Mountain Land Use Plan: 13
Sandia Mountain National Wilderness: 7, 9-18, 128
Saylors, Dave: 65
Sevilleta Grant: 85-88
Sierra Club: 31
Sierra Ladrones Defacto Wilderness: 83-89
Silverstein, Richard: 46, 48
Simmons, Cindy: 59
Simmons, Joe: 59
Simmons, Scott: 34

Skiing: 12, 15-17, 52-53, 116
Smokey Bear: 41, 112-114
Snyder, Bill: 54
Socorro: 71-76, 85-88
Spencer, Truman: 74, 111
Staked Plains:
    SEE Llano Estacado
Stevens, Bill: 53-57, 59, 116
Stevens, Peggy: 56-57
Stevens, Richard: 56-57, 59
Stone Lions Shrine: 29, 32-33

Taos Ski area: 52, 54
Threadgill, Joe: 55
Tijeras Canyon: 12-13, 15, 21
Tijerina, Reyes: 122-123
Timber skiing:
    SEE Skiing
Tinnin, Haas: 85, 88
Tollefsrud, Phil: 14, 18, 23, 56-60, 75, 86, 88
Tollefsrud Trail: 14, 18
Trails: 12-14, 17-18, 21, 23-25, 43, 48, 55-60, 68,
    75-77, 82, 87, 103-105, 115-116, 124-125
Treaty of Guadalupe Hidalgo: 72, 123
Trinity Site: 74
Tunnel Springs: 14, 18
Twining: 52, 54
Twining Cooperative Water and Sewer Association:
    54-55
Tyler, Carol: 32

U.S. Bureau of Land Management: 7-8, 46-48, 57,
    85-88, 101-103, 128
U.S. Bureau of Mines: 41
U.S. Corps of Engineers: 88
U.S. Environmental Agency (EPA): 54
U.S. Fish and Wildlife Service: 7-8, 86-88
U.S. Forest Service: 7-8, 12, 33-34, 37, 40, 42, 47,
    52-55, 64, 66-68, 75, 77, 81, 85-86, 100-104,
    112-114, 116, 121-122
U.S Geological Survey: 41
U.S. National Park Service: 7-8, 30-34, 87, 100-101,
    103-104
U.S. Office of Management and Budget: 47
U.S. Sports Fisheries and Wildlife Administration: 74
University of New Mexico: 30, 33

Vandalism: 13-14, 33, 43, 101-102
Vermejo Park Ranch: 65, 67
Vesely, Frank: 97
Vonnegut, Bernard: 80
Walker, Woodville J.: 41
Walling, Harold: 57
Watt, Bob: 31, 55
Wattson, Ben: 99
Wattson, Pauline: 99
Wheeler, Bert: 96
Wheeler Peak National Wilderness: 6, 49-60, 127-128

White, Charles L.: 97
White, James (Jim) Larkin: 96-97, 100, 103
White Mountain Wilderness: 6, 127-128
White Oaks: 73-74, 110-111, 115
White's City: 97, 100, 104
Wildlife: 12-15, 22, 28-30, 34, 57-59, 65-66, 75-77, 82,
    86, 88, 100-102 109-110, 112, 116, 119-120,
    124-125
Wilderness Act of 1964: 6-7, 30, 40-41, 52, 74, 86
Wilderness Attribute Rating Score (WARS): 47
Williams Lake: 51-52, 55, 60
Wolfe, Tony: 75